KU-652-450

THE
JIGSAW
MURDERS

THE JIGSAW MURDERS

THE TRUE STORY OF THE RUXTON KILLINGS AND THE BIRTH OF MODERN FORENSICS

JEREMY CRADDOCK

The History Press

First published 2021

The History Press
97 St George's Place, Cheltenham,
Gloucestershire, GL50 3QB
www.thehistorypress.co.uk

© Jeremy Craddock, 2021

The right of Jeremy Craddock to be identified as the Author
of this work has been asserted in accordance with the
Copyright, Designs and Patents Act 1988.

All rights reserved. No part of this book may be reprinted
or reproduced or utilised in any form or by any electronic,
mechanical or other means, now known or hereafter invented,
including photocopying and recording, or in any information
storage or retrieval system, without the permission in writing
from the Publishers.

British Library Cataloguing in Publication Data.
A catalogue record for this book is available from the British Library.

ISBN 978 0 7509 9520 7

Typesetting and origination by The History Press
Printed and bound in Great Britain by TJ Books Limited, Padstow, Cornwall.

Trees for Life

For Louise, Emily and Matthew

'If he be Mr Hyde,' he had thought, 'I shall be Mr Seek.'
Robert Louis Stevenson

The most terrifying thing is to accept oneself completely.
Carl Jung

CONTENTS

PART FOUR: MURDER

PART FIVE: THE DEVIL'S PATHOLOGY

PART SIX: SEEK

PART SEVEN: TRIAL

PROLOGUE

THE DEVIL'S BEEF TUB

September 1935

The macabre irony of the name would not be lost on police and newspapermen who were soon to descend on the sleepy Scottish Borders, nor the ghoulish sightseers drawn by sensational headlines like scavengers to carrion.

The Devil's Beef Tub: a remote natural landmark, formed by four huddling hills, creating a spectacular contoured bowl. It took its name from the Border reivers, or raiders, who for hundreds of years stole cattle and hid them in the 500ft-deep chasm. The Johnstone clan, the reivers, were known to their enemies as 'devils'. Scottish freedom fighter William Wallace was said to have held covert meetings there to orchestrate his first attack on the English in 1297. The spot was notorious locally for a bloody seventeenth-century killing in which Covenanter John Hunter was shot by English soldiers as he clambered up the hillside, persecuted for his religious beliefs.

A tributary of the River Annan emanates from the Devil's Beef Tub. It courses through ragged-cut ravines, around rocky outcrops, steadily snaking 3 miles south to the small market town of Moffat. Keen walkers sought out the spot for its eerie solitude, often leaving the warm embrace of the town's hostelries for the bleak isolation.

But now a fresh, altogether more gruesome horror had been uncovered in the dying days of September 1935, a mile or so south of the Devil's Beef Tub. It was a discovery that would forever link the spot with murder in the public consciousness. A deep ravine between the Devil's Beef Tub and Moffat, called Gardenholme linn, through which the modest tributary of the Annan flows, would soon be notorious to readers of newspapers around the world.

✢

On the morning of Sunday, 29 September, a young woman, Susan Johnson, went walking with her mother. They were on holiday from Lanarkshire, north of the Borders area, staying at a hotel in Moffat. Susan's brother, Alfred, was also staying with them but he had chosen not to join them on their hike. The two women made their way north out of the town, striding through patches of woodland, gently climbing before emerging into the barren, rugged Borders countryside. There had been heavy rain in the days prior, but that morning was bright and cool, typical of autumn in that part of the country, which was generally colder than England, to the south. Susan and her mother, no doubt, were wrapped up warmly for their stroll.

They followed the old Moffat to Edinburgh road, the A701, and it is possible they were heading for the Devil's Beef Tub. But the morning's events ensured they never got there.

The road brought them to a simple, stone bridge, typical of those found on country roads in the Borders, too narrow for two-way traffic. As they walked across, Susan peered over the edge into the deep ravine of grass and rocks and the flowing stream. It was called Gardenholme linn – linn being a Scottish name for a waterfall or deep, narrow gorge. The drop was about 80ft. Susan could see a bundle lying on the banks of the stream. She screamed when she saw what it was.

Protruding from the bundle was a human arm.

Shaken, they rushed back to their hotel to tell Alfred, where he asked the landlord for whisky to help calm them after their shock. He had to make sure they weren't mistaken. He later said, 'I went to the ravine and about 10yds from the bridge saw what appeared to be a human arm. I went down to the water's edge and found various parts of a human body wrapped in a newspaper and a sheet. I immediately went straight back and informed the police.'

Constable James Fairweather was on duty at Moffat's police station, which occupied rooms in the Town Hall on High Street. It was a small, district station falling under the jurisdiction of Dumfriesshire Constabulary. Moffat was no hotbed of crime, nothing like Glasgow, 60 miles to the north-west, or Edinburgh, 50 miles away in the north-east. PC Fairweather could reasonably have expected a quiet Sunday shift. That was until Alfred Johnson arrived excitedly with disturbing information. The officer called the main police station at Dumfries asking for help.

Then he and Alfred set out for Gardenholme linn.

Sgt Robert Sloan drove from Dumfries as quickly as he could and met PC Fairweather and Alfred Johnson at the bridge at 3.40 p.m. He spoke with them both. He looked over the wall of the bridge, as Susan Johnson had done, into the gully below, and saw the human remains. He climbed over fencing at the top of the banking and clambered down to the edge of the stream, which ran east to west. He carefully made his way to where the bundles lay, about 66ft downstream from the base of the bridge. Speaking later, Sloan said, 'I found four bundles, two heads, a thigh bone, and two arms. The top of the fingers and top of the thumbs were missing, and there were also several pieces of flesh and skin lying loose.'

He could only ascertain the contents of the parcels by opening them, which he did with trepidation. Among the remains he found pieces of newspaper. Their significance made no impression on Sloan, but shortly they would prove critical in the police's investigation.

Sloan was a resilient officer. Three months earlier he had narrowly missed being run over in Moffat after attempting to stop a hit-and-run motorist. But now, as he stood in the remote ravine under the bridge, he was overwhelmed by the magnitude of the discovery. He needed yet more assistance. More police officers from the Constabulary arrived by 4.30 p.m., among them Inspector Henry Strath, who was based at Lockerbie a few miles to the north.

Approaching the scene, Strath could see Sloan in the stream with the remains. Sloan had taken notes and marked where the remains had been discovered. Strath inspected the horrific finds for himself. He noted that a human head was wrapped in a baby's romper, tied with twine. This too would be a significant piece of evidence.

The inspector searched the area around the stream, but it was starting to turn dark. Inspector Strath and Sergeant Sloan decided to remove the human remains to Moffat's small mortuary and resume a search of the area the following day. This was a monstrous discovery but none of them that evening had an inkling of the further horrific details that would emerge.

The following day, Monday, 30 September, Strath and Sloan were among a large party of police officers to conduct more thorough searches of Gardenholme linn and neighbouring areas, including the River Annan. Press photographs show officers in smart uniforms and caps, as though dressed for a parade rather than for retrieving decomposing parts of a human body.

More grisly discoveries were made, including a left forearm and hand, wrapped in part of a *Daily Herald*, dated 7 August, a left thigh and more scattered pieces of flesh. It was a harrowing experience for the officers and the sheer amount of human flesh and body parts accumulated at Moffat mortuary was staggering.

On that first day a preliminary examination was made of the remains by two local general practice doctors by the names of Dr David Huskie and Dr F.W. Pringle. PC James Fairweather noted down everything the doctors described as they removed body parts from each bundle.

The first details of the discovery were reported in the press, headlined as the 'Ravine Mystery'. Although the police had no clue at this stage how the bodies had come to be in the ravine, nevertheless other matters were already being considered. Such as: how many bodies were they dealing with? Who were the poor, unfortunate victims? And, tantalisingly, who was responsible?

Professor John Glaister was resting in bed after a busy week at the University of Glasgow, where he was Regius Professor of Forensic Medicine. Glaister, his wife, Muff, and their daughters were staying with friends for the weekend in Arbroath, in the north-east of Scotland. The break had been a welcome respite for Glaister and the last thing he wanted that morning was for work to disrupt his relaxation.

It was the morning after the discovery in the ravine.
Muff came into the bedroom carrying a newspaper. 'Have you seen the papers yet?' she asked. 'There's a very peculiar story about pieces of body found in a stream at Moffat.'

'I'm not interested,' Glaister replied and he yawned, as if to make the point.

Muff could tell this was not the time to pursue the conversation. 'Well, don't say I didn't tell you,' she said and left him to his 'semi-conscious daydreaming', as he would later put it.

Once he was up and dressed, Glaister picked up some of the details from the newspapers, but he was not intent on devoting too much energy to the ravine case. He had to return to Glasgow and work. He left Muff and Morag, his youngest daughter, with their Arbroath friends, while his other daughter, Joan, accompanied him as she was at school the following morning.

Reflecting later, Glaister wrote, 'The Moffat business, if in my mind at all, constituted only a vague curiosity.'

On Tuesday, 1 October, Glaister received a telephone message at Glasgow University: could he come to Moffat? Shortly afterwards, a police car collected him and set off to the Borders town, 60 miles away. The drive took just under three hours. Glaister soon had a sense of how much interest there was in the grisly ravine discovery. Moffat was normally a 'lonely spot', he noted, but as they neared the town, the traffic thickened unexpectedly.

'For the last mile of distance we were often forced to a crawl, caught up in a procession of vehicles, some of which were press cars but many of which were packed with sightseers, who had travelled down to stand as spectators,' he wrote.

Glaister was to be taken directly to the remote ravine at Gardenholme linn but due to the crowds, doing so was not possible without a local police escort. Stepping from the vehicle, he was struck by the large number of uniformed police officers and detectives in attendance. They had been drawn from several forces across the Borders area. Heading the investigation were Chief Constable William Black of Dumfriesshire Police and Assistant Chief Constable David Warnock of Glasgow Constabulary. Glaister was introduced to two of the detectives from Glasgow CID: Detective Lieutenant William Ewing and Detective Lieutenant Bertie Hammond, who was an expert in forensic fingerprinting. The two Moffat GPs, Dr Huskie and Dr Pringle, who had made an initial inspection of the remains were on the scene.

Significantly, Dr Gilbert Millar, a pathologist from Edinburgh University, had also been called upon.

Chief Constable Black told Glaister, 'There's very little fresh at the moment. The remains we have gathered have been taken to a local mortuary. But you'll want to have a look round here.'

Glaister and Millar spent a short time exploring the tree-lined linn. Describing the spot later, Glaister noted the ravine was 'thick with bracken and fern, leading down to the narrow boulder-strewn stream'.

One of the Moffat doctors informed Glaister and Millar, 'Most of the remains were found over there.' He pointed to the left bank below the bridge. Chillingly, the doctor concluded, 'From what I've seen of them there could still be many more portions waiting to be found.'

Glaister was 43. He was thin, with a long face and dark eyes. His hair was black, oiled back, but thinning, and he had a thick, black moustache. He wore round horn-rimmed spectacles over which inky speech-mark eyebrows hovered quizzically. A press photograph of his arrival at Moffat showed his beautifully knotted tie sitting under sharp wings of a gleaming white collar. Over his suit he wore a long double-breasted overcoat to protect against the Borders autumn chill, while the dome of his head was topped by a black bowler hat. He carried a small black briefcase, while his free hand was thrust deep into his overcoat pocket. He looked like one of the Thompson twins from Hergé's *Adventures of Tintin*, the strip cartoon that was becoming popular in Europe at the time.

After leaving the linn, the party headed for Moffat, a small market town composed of whitewashed stone buildings and coaching inns. There was a knot of police officers and press outside the tiny mortuary when they arrived. In addition to the senior police officers and detectives, there was the Procurator-Fiscal for Dumfriesshire, essentially the local coroner and public prosecutor, who investigated sudden deaths. A photograph of the party shows a huddle of men in long overcoats and wide-brimmed hats. They look like they have stepped out of a Humphrey Bogart movie. To keep the press at bay, Chief Constable Black briefed the newspaper reporters, who were eager for titbits of information.

A young police constable unlocked the door of the cramped mortuary in Moffat's plain old cemetery, whose most famous incumbent was John Loudon McAdam, the nineteenth-century inventor of the 'macadamisation' road-making process. Once inside, the two scientists for the first time laid eyes on the grisly remains of the bodies. Fingerprint expert Detective Lieutenant Hammond had a camera to record evidence. The police had taken great care during their investigation of the ravine, stream and surrounding area. They had made detailed notes on what had been recovered and precisely where in the gully under the bridge at Gardenholme it had been found. The remains had been brought to the mortuary by officers first on the scene, along with pieces of newspaper that were among the bundles recovered. One of the officers had placed the scraps of newsprint between pieces of blotting paper to help dry them. He had initially put them in front of a fire but had singed them.

The medical experts were met with, in Glaister's words, 'the majority of the portions … in a heap on one mortuary table, and in the same apartment was a trestle containing debris, and it was supposed there might be small portions of tissue there. The debris consisted of twigs, leaves, and certain forms of animal life that had developed on the remains'. In a report he wrote later, Hammond noted the remains were 'a black mass seething with maggots, and stench overpowering'.

Given the cramped working conditions and the manner in which the bodies were presented, Glaister and Millar made no more than a cursory examination. They quickly concluded that to make sense of the remains they would need to remove them to a laboratory. They decided the best place was the University of Edinburgh's Department of Anatomy. This respected faculty was overseen by the eminent pathologist Professor Sydney Smith, who was known to the newspaper-reading public for his work as an expert witness in several high-profile criminal trials. Smith was out of the country at the time visiting his native New Zealand.

Before their removal, Glaister made a precise inventory of human remains found in and around Gardenholme linn and the nearby River Annan since Sunday, 29 September. It made for grim reading. He recorded:

> Of the four bundles recovered during the initial search, the first was wrapped in a blouse and contained two upper arms and four pieces of flesh; the second bundle comprised two thigh bones, two legs from which most flesh had been stripped, and nine pieces of flesh, all wrapped in a pillow-case; the third was a piece of cotton sheeting containing seventeen portions of flesh; the fourth parcel, also wrapped in cotton sheeting, consisted of a human trunk, two legs with the feet tied with the hem of a cotton sheet and some wisps of straw and cotton wool. In addition, other packages opened to reveal two heads, one of which was wrapped in a child's rompers; a quantity of cotton wool and sections from the *Daily Herald* of 6 August 1935; two forearms with hands attached but minus the top joints of the fingers and thumbs; and several pieces of skin and flesh. One part was wrapped in the *Sunday Graphic* dated 15 September.

This final detail would prove crucial in the coming days.

The remains amounted to seventy separate pieces. Keenly aware that the police were desperate for leads and professional guidance, Glaister and Millar had to make a quick assessment. 'Knowing discoveries might still be made, the first thing we had to try to decide was how many bodies were involved,' Glaister wrote. After an 'arbitrary separation of these tragic remains', the two experts believed they were dealing with the bodies of two people, and although there were so many dismembered parts, on balance they believed it was no more than two. They were also of the opinion that the bodies had been dismembered by someone who had knowledge of human anatomy and had gone to great lengths to make identification difficult. From the two heads the butcher had cut away the noses, lips and ears, removed the eyes and extracted some teeth post-mortem. The sex organs had also been removed. The trunk, however, was evidently of a female, as was the less mutilated of the two heads. The other head had certain male characteristics.

Glaister and Millar instructed officers to put the remains into two separate boxes for their transportation. As the professors departed Moffat they left detectives with the notion that the bodies were those of a man and a woman. These conclusions would soon be made public when they were reported in the press.

Among the unholy mess of body tissue that Glaister and Millar inspected there was one bizarre and inexplicable item not reported to the press: a cyclops eye, almost perfectly preserved.

Neither scientist could say with any certainty if it were human.

The case was a sensation in the next day's newspapers. In time, the case would attract various headline-writers' nicknames, the most potent of which was perhaps the 'Jigsaw Murders'. In the golden age of detective novels, particularly those by the Queen of Crime, Agatha Christie, this latest, real-life murder mystery was irresistible. In the coming days, weeks and months, the Moffat case would fill countless column inches in newspapers around the world, keeping hungry journalists busy and morbidly fascinated readers on tenterhooks. Central to this fascination were key questions. First, who were the victims? And vitally, who was the killer?

Initially, Scottish police were bullish, telling reporters they were close to identifying the bodies. By Friday, 4 October, it was reported:

> Police investigating the Scottish ravine mystery were more hopeful to-day, and it was confidently anticipated that identification would be established within the next forty-eight hours of the two mutilated bodies found at Gardenholme linn, near Moffat, on Sunday.
>
> Following a midnight conference in Edinburgh between Crown Law Officers, Police Chiefs and pathologists, a new line of investigation was begun in various districts in the East and West of Scotland.
>
> The police, however, were very reticent regarding their inquiries.

Bertie Hammond's report of that first day's investigation suggested police were considering the possibility that the bodies were those of holiday-makers visiting the area.

It is unclear what this 'new line of investigation' was, but the direction of the police's inquiries would turn soon enough when the significance of one of the pieces of newspaper retrieved from Gardenholme linn was realised in the succeeding days.

A hundred miles south, in the town of Lancaster in the north of England, Dr Buck Ruxton read about the sensational discovery at Moffat. Dr Ruxton's wife Isabella and their children's nanny Mary had been missing for almost two weeks. He had told friends and acquaintances that his wife had left him and had taken Mary with her to pay for an abortion. He said he believed they had gone to Edinburgh, where Isabella's sisters lived. But when the newspapers began to report the discovery of two bodies in the Scottish Borders, tongues began to wag in Lancaster that they were those of Isabella and Mary.

Ruxton showed his copy of the *Daily Express* to his charlady Agnes Oxley; it bore the headline 'Ravine Murder'. 'Do you see, Mrs Oxley,' he said, 'it is a man and a woman, it is not our two.'

But the truth was the two *were* Isabella Ruxton and Mary Jane Rogerson. Dr Ruxton had murdered them both. He had been thorough in the disposal of their bodies. Surely there was nothing incriminating that could lead the police to his door at 2 Dalton Square? Perhaps the newspaper report confirmed in his mind that he had committed the perfect murder.

Dr Ruxton might have convinced himself the matter was at an end. In reality, it was only just beginning.

PART ONE
EDINBURGH

1

HAKIM AND ISABELLA

The man who would become Buck Ruxton sat in the restaurant, oblivious to the whir of activity around him and to the human bustle and rumble of trams on Princes Street outside. For Gabriel Hakim, a handsome, 28-year-old Indian immigrant medical student, the universe was reduced to a single point of interest: the young woman whom he had become besotted with. He could make the simple act of eating a meal last an eternity if it allowed him to gaze at her.

She was the restaurant's manager, in her mid-twenties and self-assured, issuing instructions to the waitresses and concerning herself with the satisfaction of the customers. Some people thought she was haughty but Hakim was charmed. She was not beautiful, but she was striking: tall, muscular and slightly masculine, with grey-blue deep-set eyes, high forehead and cheekbones, prominent teeth and a full jaw. She dressed smartly, wearing her soft, brown hair in a contemporary popular style. Her skin was exquisitely pale. Even though mixed-race couples were not unheard of in 1920s Britain, nevertheless prejudice against someone with dark skin like Hakim was commonplace and he would no doubt have been conscious of the risks he might run in showing interest in the woman. It did not matter. He was smitten.

The woman's name was Isabella Kerr. She was about to change his life.

Hakim was a recent arrival in Edinburgh. He was a post-graduate student at the city's famous university medical school, regarded the best in the world as a febrile melting pot of innovation for the finest medical minds of the era. He also worked as a chemical assistant in the Eye Department of Edinburgh's Royal Infirmary. He was keen to integrate into the society in which he found himself, and was drawn to the bright lights of Princes Street. It was the beating heart of Edinburgh and the hub of its social life.

It unfurled like an expensive carpet outside the Victorian splendour of Waverley railway station, from which visitors emerged into the vibrant, modern city. A place of smart hotels, exclusive department stores and expensive restaurants, it was where Edinburgh's citizens with money in their pockets frequented. Jenners department store was an Edinburgh institution, the 'Harrods of the north', while the New British Hotel, or the NB, sat impressively above Waverley station. There were very few buildings on the south side of the street, which afforded panoramic views of the jagged outline of the Old Town and the castle. The attractive public parks of Princes Street Gardens linked Edinburgh's old and new towns. It was as if the city's divided personalities were locked in an existential fight, separated only by the gardens' gentility, making it a carefully manicured haven for families and courting couples. In truth the gardens had been laid out in the eighteenth and nineteenth centuries after Edinburgh's original cesspit, Nor Loch, a giant festering stew of human waste, had been drained.

Edinburgh's dark reputation was cemented a century before Hakim met Isabella by the deeds of William Burke and William Hare, whose exploits inspired Robert Louis Stevenson to write the story *The Body Snatcher.*

Burke and Hare were Irish immigrants who had come to the mainland to find work. Each had been employed as a labourer in the construction of the Edinburgh and Glasgow Union Canal around 1815 and they may well have been acquainted at the time. Their employment came to an end once the canal opened in 1822. In time, both men would find themselves in Edinburgh trying to eke out a living.

Eventually, they would find nefarious employment with Dr Robert Knox of Edinburgh Medical College.

The burgeoning medical school was dependent upon corpses for research and experimentation. The school was entitled to only five cadavers each year, far fewer than the number required by Knox for dissection. With such limited supply, this created a demand for more dead bodies and gave rise to the grim trade in body snatching. Knox illegally paid for hastily exhumed corpses, often stolen from Edinburgh cemeteries, notably Greyfriars Kirkyard (a kirk being a Scottish word for church), in the heart of the Old Town, close to the Royal Mile, the Grassmarket and importantly the medical school. The cadavers had to be recently deceased, as they were useless to physicians if badly decomposed. Body snatching quickly became notorious in Edinburgh and grieving relatives of the recently interred would keep watch in the graveyard overnight to ensure no unscrupulous nocturnal visitor desecrated the fresh grave. Some families invested in mort-safes at Greyfriars. These cage-like structures were placed over tomb-stones to deter grave-robbers by making access to the remains interred within nigh-on impossible. Watch-groups were also established to patrol the kirkyards at night. A watchtower for this purpose was constructed at the city's St Cuthbert's Churchyard.

These safeguards were effective and helped to cut the number of bodies dug up from their graves. The supply of usable corpses might have dried up; the demand – and offer of payment – for them, however, did not.

What Burke and Hare did next demonstrated a quite chilling entrepreneurial zeal.

In 1827, after they became acquainted, Burke and his wife moved in with Hare and his wife at their lodgings in Tanners Close in the west of Edinburgh. When a lodger died of dropsy, the two men, bemoaning their meagre income, decided to sell the body to a physician. Under the cover of darkness they took the corpse to Dr Robert Knox, who paid them £7 10s for their trouble. As they left, an assistant of Knox said they would be welcome at Knox's door whenever they had another delivery for the good doctor.

Seeing a business opportunity, the men realised they could not rely on natural deaths as a steady source of income. To sustain a regular supply of bodies, they would have to target the living. And so began Burke and Hare's murderous enterprise.

During the winter of 1827 and much of 1828, they are believed to have committed sixteen murders in Edinburgh. The victims were apparently mostly lodgers at Hare's house, often itinerant workers passing through Edinburgh, and latterly prostitutes. Their crimes were exposed when a body was found under Burke's bed at Tanners Close. Burke and Hare exonerated Dr Knox at their trial, saying he was unaware of their enterprise. Hare turned King's evidence: that is, was granted immunity in return for testifying against Burke. He was released and, advisedly, made a hasty escape from Edinburgh. It is thought he stayed at a hotel in Moffat on his journey. There were sightings of him years later in the English town of Carlisle.

As for Burke, he took the rap for the crimes. He was hanged in Edinburgh on 28 January 1829. His body was duly dissected for research purposes at the medical school, while his skin was put to a rather macabre use. It was turned into the covers of a book. His skeleton is still on display at the Anatomical Museum at the medical school.

✷

Hakim first encountered Isabella earlier in 1927 at a cafeteria in Leith, a small port north of Edinburgh on the Firth of Forth coast. He would go there each day to eat, finding Isabella the pull rather than the cuisine. He was captivated, sitting for hours gazing at her. When she took a new job at the restaurant on Princes Street, Hakim changed his dining routine too, choosing to eat each day at the new establishment, one of countless on Princes Street.

His infatuation did not go unnoticed by Isabella. She was charmed by the exotic foreigner who spoke broken English with a high-pitched voice and who would grab people excitedly by the shoulders when engaged in conversation. His dark skin, handsome looks and smart clothes reminded her of Hollywood movie idol Rudolph Valentino, who died tragically young the previous year.

It was not long before they fell in love.

Edinburgh society might have accepted the mixed-race couple, but had they known that Hakim and Isabella were also both still married to other people, there might have been a scandal.

2

A MAN IN A HURRY

From the very beginning, Hakim was an outsider who craved acceptance.

He was born Bukhtyar Chompa Rustomji Ratanji Hakim in Bombay in 1899 to wealthy parents. His father, a doctor, was an Indian Parsi, while his mother was French: from the start he was conscious of this duality. He was neither truly Indian, nor truly French. His life would be characterised by attempts to rewrite the past, and an apparent quest for acceptance could explain his compulsion to reinvent and renew himself, like a chameleon adapting to new surroundings.

He was sensitive, prone to overthinking things, and could be emotional and temperamental. He was also intensely intelligent. Well educated in Bombay, he attended Sir Jamshetji Jeejibhoy Parsi Benevolent School in the city's commercial district of Fort. After passing his matriculation examination, he joined one of India's oldest educational institutions, Wilson College, in Bombay in 1915 when he was 16. From the start he had a sense of his own entitlement, which could flare up when he felt he was not shown his due respect.

His dream was to become a doctor, and at 19 he went to England to study medicine at London University in September 1918. It was in the final months of the First World War and it was a tense time in London where daily news reports of the thousands of young men killed on the battlefields of northern Europe left a generation of devastated and broken-hearted communities. Many thousands of those young servicemen who laid down their lives were Hakim's fellow countrymen, serving in the Indian Army, which played a hugely significant role in the eventual defeat of the German Empire.

Within a year Hakim had matriculated and in July 1919 he was back in Bombay studying at the Grant Medical School, where he completed his studies in 1922, earning his Medicinae Baccalaureus Baccalaureus Chirurgiae, or MBBS, in October, equivalent to a Bachelor of Medicine and Bachelor of Surgery.

Hakim was a star student and left Grant Medical School with a letter of recommendation:

Police Hospital, Bombay. 30/12/22
    Mr. Bakhtyar Rustomji Hakim obtained first place in the Medical Jurisprudence, Toxicology and Mental Diseases examination at the Final M.B.B.S. in October 1922 from a total number of students of 180. His record in other departments being on a par with this I have no hesitation in writing for him a letter of recommendation and good wishes for his future success.
    (Sd) [Signed] W. Nunan, M.D., Professor, Medical Jurisprudence, Grant Medical College, Bombay. Police Surgeon, Bombay.

Medical jurisprudence is the branch of medicine involving the application of medical knowledge to legal problems. Hakim's professional qualifications would lend a certain irony to the shocking events of autumn 1935.

In 1923, he offered his talents to the Indian Army's Medical Service, where he obtained a temporary commission as captain on 29 October. After being stationed in hospitals at Bombay and Deolali, a small British Army transit camp, he left on 4 November 1925 for Iraq, where he was stationed in Baghdad.

Hakim was restless, perhaps prone to feelings of frustration when he perceived progress in his life to be too slow. This could be attributed to his keen intelligence. These personality traits and his desire to become a doctor no doubt drove him to relinquish the country of his birth and to travel to foreign shores.

On 30 July 1926, Captain Hakim took ninety days' leave and made another visit to England, before being demobbed. On 28 October, he relinquished his commission. He decided to settle in Britain, metamorphosing into Dr Gabriel Hakim – the name perhaps an affectation designed to create mystique – and began attending medical courses at London's University College Hospital.

His time in England was not a happy one; his English was not good – Indian and French were his native tongues – and he struggled with his studies. His parents funded his education as they had done previously, but this time their motivation was not one of benevolence.

When he came ashore in England with a new name and a fresh start, he was also leaving behind a wife he did not love in Bombay.

It had been an arranged marriage, to a Parsi woman from a wealthy family, Motibal Jehangirji Ghadiali, in May 1925. Hakim had been working as medical officer at the hospital in Bombay at the time. A few months after the marriage, Hakim had been serving with the Indian Army's Medical Service and was transferred to Iraq. Although he wrote to his bride from Baghdad, it soon became apparent he was not committed to their union.

His parents were offended. By paying for his education in England they were trying to avert humiliation.

In 1927 he took the fateful step of moving to Edinburgh, hoping to obtain a Fellowship of the Royal Colleges of Surgeons.

Hakim had a new name and bright prospects; he had a past that he would rather forget. He was a man divided. It is apt that he found himself in Edinburgh, a city of two halves. On the one hand there was the New Town, a genteel world of tearooms, department stores and art galleries; on the other, an Old Town with a murderous past. The city was a Jekyll and Hyde, its Hyde-self as dark and hard as the rock beneath the imperious castle. It was no coincidence that Robert Louis Stevenson had the city, his birthplace, in mind when he wrote the definitive horror story of a divided self.

It would not be known for many years, but for a few months in 1927, as the Indian medical student and Isabella did their courting in the city's damp, foreboding streets or rode the tramcars, they may have crossed paths with the brilliant forensic scientist whose team seven years later would be faced with solving the twentieth century's most macabre, murderous jigsaw puzzle.

The forensic scientist's name was Professor Sydney Smith.

3

SMITH

Professor Sydney Smith looked at the evidence and declared, 'It looks like murder to me.'

The New Zealand-born Smith was 44, portly, with thinning sandy-coloured hair and the smiling eyes of a man of good humour. He was a senior lecturer in forensic medicine at the University of Cairo, having studied at Edinburgh two decades earlier. It was August 1926 and he was on his annual summer visit to Edinburgh and had been asked by his former tutor at the university, Harvey Littlejohn, to consider the details of a case he had been involved in. It concerned the apparent suicide of 55-year-old Mrs Bertha Merrett, who had died of a single bullet wound to the head in Edinburgh Royal Infirmary on 1 April that year. The police believed she had taken her own life, basing their conclusions on interviews with her 17-year-old son, Donald, and her housemaid, a young married woman called Sutherland.

According to their accounts, Mrs Merrett and Donald had just finished breakfast in the sitting room at their flat at 31 Buckingham Terrace when the maid arrived. After the dining table had been cleared, Mrs Merrett sat down to write letters, while Donald sat reading a book near the open door. Mrs Sutherland was working in the kitchen, which was at the rear of the flat. It was from there that she heard the gunshot followed by a scream and a thud. Donald rushed into the kitchen to bring Mrs Sutherland into the sitting room to find Mrs Merrett lying on the floor with blood pouring from her head. Donald told the maid that his mother had tried to kill herself.

So convinced were the police of this explanation that they neglected to secure one vital piece of evidence.

They failed to ask Mrs Merrett what had happened.

She had survived for two weeks in the hospital following the shooting and briefly regained consciousness. During this time she had made a number of statements to hospital staff. And yet the police took none of them into consideration.

A post-mortem on Mrs Merrett's body was performed four days after her death by Professor Littlejohn, the 63-year-old head of the Forensic Medicine department at Edinburgh University, a popular and eminent lecturer known for his dramatic presentation style, needle-sharp tongue and caustic wit. He concluded that the bullet wound was consistent with suicide, corroborating Donald's story. But the case niggled away at Littlejohn. Something was not quite right.

Having accepted Littlejohn's invitation that summer, Smith's reading of the facts would confirm Littlejohn was right to have doubts: there was something suspicious about Mrs Merrett's death.

Edinburgh's is one of the oldest universities in the world, dating from the mid-sixteenth century, while its medical school was at the time unrivalled. This fame was in no small part due to the brilliant Dr Joseph Bell, a surgeon at the Royal Infirmary, who was noted for his powers of deduction.

When Sydney Smith studied medicine at Edinburgh in the 1910s, he was taught by one of Bell's students, George Chiene, who lectured in surgery. In his bestselling memoirs, *Mostly Murder*, published decades later, Smith noted that Chiene 'encouraged his students to look for more than the conventional signs and symptoms before making a diagnosis'. Chiene learned this technique of taking the known facts and making a logical diagnostic leap from Bell, who could diagnose not only a patient's disease but also his or her occupation and character merely from their appearance.

Bell once demonstrated his remarkable talent to a class of medical students. After briefly glancing at his patient, he said, 'This man is a left-handed cobbler.' The patient gasped; the students were dumbfounded. Then Bell explained his deductions.

'The worn places on his trousers could only have been made by resting a lapstone between his knees. The right side is more worn than the left because he hammers the leather with his left hand.'

As Smith observed, 'like a conjuring trick, it always seemed miraculous until it was explained, and then it was almost absurdly simple'.

On another occasion, Bell asked a patient, 'Did you enjoy your walk over the golf-links to-day, as you came in from the south side of the town?' This was a remarkable question because the patient was a complete stranger to Bell. Bell's assistant could only marvel at his brilliance when he revealed how he had been able to make such an accurate observation. 'On a showery day such as this the reddish clay at bare parts of the golf-course adheres to the boot and a tiny part is bound to remain. There is no such clay anywhere else.'

A guest at a dinner party attended by Bell once remarked, 'Dr Bell might almost be Sherlock Holmes.'

Bell replied, 'Madam, I *am* Sherlock Holmes.'

The assistant who had so marvelled at Bell's ingenuity was Arthur Conan Doyle, the creator of Sherlock Holmes, who studied under Bell at the university and later qualified as a doctor while at Edinburgh.

Harvey Littlejohn was also a student of Bell's. He had gone on to become Regius Professor of Forensic Medicine at Edinburgh, following in the footsteps of his distinguished father, Henry Littlejohn. Between them, the Littlejohns dominated forensic medicine at Edinburgh University from the end of the nineteenth century until the early part of the twentieth. Another famous scientific dynasty did the same during the same period at Scotland's other great university, Glasgow. Their name was Glaister.

Smith first encountered Littlejohn in the early part of the 1910s when he arrived in Edinburgh from his native New Zealand on a prestigious Vans Dunlop Scholarship to study botany and zoology, but he quickly switched to medicine, graduating with first-class honours in 1912 with bachelor degrees in medicine and surgery. He followed this with a research scholarship and received a Diploma in Public Health the following year. Littlejohn had been so impressed with Smith that he recommended the young Kiwi for the post of assistant at the university's department of forensic medicine. Littlejohn's faith in the golden boy from New Zealand proved well placed as Smith obtained his doctorate in 1914 with a gold medal as well as winning a prestigious prize.

That summer in 1926, Littlejohn had asked Smith to look at the evidence from the Merrett shooting because he was becoming an established forensic expert in the field of guns and ballistics and was the author of a respected work on the subject, for which Harvey Littlejohn had written the foreword. Smith – who was meant to be enjoying a vacation with his wife and two young daughters in Edinburgh – was only too happy to oblige his old teacher.

In his report after the post-mortem, Littlejohn noted the position of the wound in Mrs Merrett's right ear and described the path taken by the bullet, all of which was consistent with a suicide attempt. He had been suspicious, however, because there was nothing to indicate how far away from the head the gun had been held. In other words, there was no proof Mrs Merrett had fired the weapon.

When Mrs Merrett had come around in the days after the shooting, she told the doctors and nurses of what she could remember. She said she had been writing a letter at her desk at her first-floor flat at 31 Buckingham Terrace. Her son, Donald, was standing beside her. 'Suddenly something burst in my head, just like a pistol shot,' she is reported to have said. The medical staff reported that she had shown no knowledge of the firearm. The doctor who first examined her when she was admitted into hospital saw no evidence of blackening or burning of the skin, nor any smell of burnt gunpowder. There was also an absence of torn flesh around the entrance wound. These points were confirmed by a second doctor, who dressed Mrs Merrett's injuries. They had made such meticulous observations specifically to determine whether the gun had been fired at close range. They found no evidence that it had.

All of this pointed to a rather different explanation for Mrs Merrett's injuries than that of suicide. This would also call into question the evidence given by her son and that of the housemaid.

Having weighed the evidence, Smith concluded that it appeared Mrs Merrett had been murdered. There was one obvious course to take, Smith advised his former teacher: 'Why don't you make some experiments with the weapon that killed her? Find out if a discharge close to the skin would cause powder marks.'

That August, Littlejohn did as Smith recommended and put the evidence of John Donald Merrett to the test.

He took the six-cartridge .25 Spanish automatic pistol and, using the same type of ammunition as that which killed Mrs Merrett, fired it at cardboard targets, measuring the distances between the barrel and the cardboard. Next, he took a human leg, recently amputated from an accident victim, and he repeated the experiment with the gun, firing into the flesh of the severed limb.

Littlejohn worked on the theory that anybody attempting to shoot the pistol at their own head would be inclined to hold the barrel of the gun close to the skull, and certainly not more than 3in away. He tested this theory, to see what the effect was of firing the gun into the human flesh from this distance. The Spanish automatic pistol left definite powder and burning marks around the wound in the skin. Littlejohn repeated the test, this time from a distance of 6in: the shot again left marks.

It was only when he fired the weapon from 9in that Littlejohn found the gun left no trace of powder or burning. He reasoned that it was not logical for somebody to try to shoot themselves with a firearm held at such an unnatural distance from the head. And given that Mrs Merrett had no powder or burning marks, Littlejohn had no option but to conclude that somebody else had fired the pistol.

Littlejohn accepted his mistake. He wrote a second report, categorically ruling out accident and suicide attempt and suggesting foul-play.

Smith wrote in his memoirs that he was perplexed why it took Littlejohn a further five months to make his revised report public; the delay perhaps said something about Littlejohn's shaken confidence.

By January 1927, Merrett had been charged with murdering his mother and forging cheques from her account made out to him. His trial was held in February and Littlejohn was called as an expert witness.

Smith later believed that Littlejohn's change of mind cast doubt on his authority and reputation when his evidence was tested at Merrett's trial; Smith was saddened to see the effect this had on his former teacher.

Adding to Littlejohn's professional discomfort was the fact that giving evidence in Merrett's defence was the most famous and the most feared expert witness in the country: Home Office pathologist Sir Bernard Spilsbury. He normally gave evidence for the prosecution and a great number of murderers were convicted on his evidence, including the notorious Dr Crippen nearly two decades earlier. In the Merrett case, however, Spilsbury was making a rare appearance for the defence of Donald Merrett. By his side was ballistics expert Robert Churchill. Together they often gave evidence in cases involving a shooting. Smith would become well acquainted with Spilsbury in the coming years in his own capacity as an expert witness. In his memoirs he described Spilsbury and Churchill as dogmatic and stubborn: 'they were indeed a formidable team – terrifying when they made a mistake'.

Merrett's trial began on 1 February 1927 at Edinburgh's High Court of Justiciary in Parliament Square, Scotland's supreme criminal court. Donald Merrett was brought from Edinburgh's prison to face charges of murdering his mother and of trying to cash forged cheques at the Clydesdale Bank on George Street in the city.

When he was called to give evidence for the Crown's prosecution case, Littlejohn repeated the main points of his second report into Mrs Merrett's injuries: in his opinion both accident and suicide were inconceivable.

He also had to concede that he had changed his mind over the plausibility of the victim having shot herself. Inevitably, this point was exploited by

Merrett's legal team, led by the brilliant barrister Craigie Aitchison KC, who chose to quote from a book on ballistics to score a point while Littlejohn was on the stand. Adding to his discomfort was the fact that the book was the very one written by Smith and for which Littlejohn had provided the foreword.

The passage written by Smith that Aitchison read out in the High Court was this: 'Although automatic pistols produce wounds identical with wounds from revolvers, it should be remembered that automatic ammunition is always charged with smokeless powder and that absence of blackening and burning in close discharges is relatively common.'

Aitchison claimed that because Littlejohn had written the book's foreword he must have endorsed its contents, including the quoted passage. Yet, here he was giving evidence in court to the contrary. Littlejohn did not accept this point, but the effect must have been stinging. Smith later noted that there was another passage in the same section of the book clarifying that the only way to test the theory of blackening and burning to a wound being left behind after being discharged at close range was to conduct an experiment, which is exactly what Littlejohn had done. Unsurprisingly, Aitchison and the defence team failed to mention this reference in the book.

When it was Spilsbury and Churchill's turn to give evidence, they told the court they had conducted similar experiments as those done by Littlejohn at Smith's urging. They said that no marking was left behind when the gun was fired at close range. Spilsbury confidently told the trial that it was entirely possible that Mrs Merrett could have shot herself and he concluded that in his opinion she had.

The one advantage Littlejohn's experiments had that Spilsbury and Churchill's did not was the fact that Littlejohn had used the actual weapon that had killed Mrs Merrett. The trial's judge, Lord Alness, warned the jury that because of this the experiment by Spilsbury and Churchill was effectively worthless.

As it turned out, the police's bungling of the investigation following Mrs Merrett's death – their failure to interview her when she was conscious – and their unshakeable conviction that it was suicide, led to the jury returning a verdict of not proven on the charge of murder against Donald Merrett. On the matter of the forged cheques, however, he was found guilty and was sent to prison for twelve months.

Littlejohn might have been vindicated in his conclusions, but the experience, particularly the circus surrounding the high-profile case, the attendant newspaper interest and the tainting of his reputation took its toll on the 64-year-old scientist.

The great Spilsbury had been shown to be wrong. As Sydney Smith had noted in his memoirs, Spilsbury and Churchill were 'terrifying' when they made mistakes. Smith's own path would cross that of Spilsbury's soon enough, when he would encounter his wrath.

Smith had been convinced of Merrett's guilt. After he heard the outcome of the trial, he told Littlejohn, 'That is not the last we'll hear of young Merrett.'

His words would prove prophetic. Merrett was a man who desired a life of extravagance and did not care how he achieved it. Over the years he tried smuggling, gambling and gun-running, before joining the Navy during the Second World War under the assumed name of Ronald Chesney. He reached the rank of lieutenant-commander, taking charge of a gunboat in the Mediterranean. In 1954 he killed his wife and her mother in a bungled attempt to get his hands on their money. He tried to hide his crimes as accidents – in much the same way he had done with his own mother – but the police were soon on his tail and were on the verge of arresting him when Merrett shot himself dead.

In the summer of 1927 Smith visited Littlejohn as he usually did during his annual vacation to Edinburgh. It was exactly a year since Littlejohn had asked him to look at the Merrett case and six months since Merrett's trial. On this occasion, however, Littlejohn was in hospital. Smith was shocked to see the toll the case had taken on his former teacher. He later noted that it had caused Littlejohn 'a great deal of worry and anxiety'.

As Smith sat with Littlejohn in his hospital room, the older man had a request to make of his one-time student. Smith was shocked when Littlejohn made him promise that he would leave Cairo and return to Scotland to take over the chair of Forensic Medicine at Edinburgh University as his successor. Smith replied that he hoped Littlejohn would be in the post for many years to come. But with the certainty perhaps only a forensic scientist could muster, Littlejohn had snapped back, 'Don't be a sentimental fool, Smith – you've seen, and I've seen, hundreds of cases like mine. You know perfectly well that one of these mornings soon the nurse will come in and find me dead. Will you come back and take my place?' Smith politely agreed he would consider it very carefully, but would not discuss it further.

Ten days later, in mid-August, as Smith was on his way back to Egypt, he received news that would turn his life on its head: Littlejohn was dead.

He felt compelled to honour his promise, but just because Littlejohn had wanted him as his successor did not mean he would automatically inherit the post. It was a Regius Chair, which means that appointments are made by the Crown and not by the university, although the university does play an advisory role in the decision-making. Back in Cairo, Smith must have sensed Littlejohn's hand at work when he received a letter from Edinburgh's Dean of the Faculty of Medicine. It was inviting him to apply for the prestigious job.

And so he found himself back in Edinburgh with mixed emotions on the first day of April 1928. If he had any doubts about his return, the date – April Fool's Day – deepened the feeling. Smith and his family were relinquishing the sun of Cairo. However, it was a practical move to allow Smith more time with his children, who were being privately educated in Britain. It would also end the painful separation he experienced at the beginning of each term when his wife and the girls left him alone in Egypt.

As he would later note, he had always viewed Edinburgh as a 'cold and cheerless' place. In comparison with the heat of Egypt, the Scottish capital's inclement weather came off a poor second. Admittedly, he had studied in the city and subsequently spent a number of years working at the university. But despite regular visits, it had been fourteen years since he had actually lived there. To top it all, he was taking a huge pay cut in order to take up this new job – his Edinburgh pay would be less than half of what he earned in Cairo, where his salary was also tax-free.

Despite his qualms over the weather and his salary, Smith's intellectual and professional curiosity would soon be piqued after arriving back in Edinburgh. A murder case, soon to feature on the front pages of every newspaper in the land, would call upon his talents, in particular his expertise in firearms. He would also find himself in the same position as Littlejohn had recently been in: he would clash with the feared Spilsbury in a court of law.

In vacating the post at Cairo, Smith paved the way for a bright, young Scottish forensic scientist keen to make his mark: in 1928, John Glaister packed his belongings and departed for the heat and mystery of Egypt as Smith's successor.

It was as if fate were moving the pieces in Smith's future team around a chess board in readiness for the events of 1935.

4

ISABELLA

Isabella Proudfoot Kerr was not originally from Edinburgh, but from the small town of Whitburn in West Lothian, which lies equidistant between Edinburgh and Glasgow. She was two years younger than Hakim, having been born in the tiny village of Camelon, near Falkirk, in March 1901, but then moved with her family to Whitburn, originally a small farming and weaving community that grew around a burn, or small river, that ran through it. By the time of her birth, coal mining had become the town's main source of industry, dominated by the giant Polkemmet Colliery, whose seams and tunnels ran like arteries below the West Lothian landscape.

Little is known of Isabella's early life, but her parents were John Kerr and Elisabeth Stewart; she had three sisters, Jeanie, Eleen and Lizzie, who were much older; a brother, John; and she went to school in Whitburn.

When she was 19 she met and fell in love with a Dutch merchant seaman called Teunis Cornelius Van Ess, who had emigrated to the United States, had become a naturalised American and whose home was in San Francisco. He met Isabella on leave in Edinburgh while working on the *Golden Gate*, a traditional three-mast rigged sailing ship, which was docked at Leith for a few days.

Isabella and Van Ess's relationship was truly a whirlwind. Within days of meeting, infatuated with each other, hasty and impetuous, they decided to marry. On 19 March 1920, they arrived at the register office at Gayfield Square in Edinburgh, not far from Leith. Neither had family in attendance. Isabella's family were not happy with the relationship, feeling that she was impulsive; marrying an itinerant seaman was not the 'done thing'. In their eyes she was bringing shame on the family. Instead Isabella and Van Ess called on acquaintances to act as witnesses. Van Ess asked a fellow merchant seaman from the *Golden Gate*, Willem Meyer, while Isabella asked Agnes Goodfellow Hopkirk, who worked alongside her at the restaurant at Leith. At the time, Isabella was living with one of her older sisters, Lizzie Trench, at 7 Heriot Mount, a small cobbled street of towering tenement buildings, at the end of which were steps that led to Holyrood Park.

Isabella and Van Ess's relationship lasted only days, no more than a week or two at most. Inevitably, Van Ess returned to the *Golden Gate* and set sail from Leith, abandoning his new bride, with little prospect or means of easy communication.

Isabella soon reverted from Mrs Van Ess back to her maiden name of Kerr; the couple, however, remained married.

Isabella's family remained unhappy. They felt her head had been turned by a foreign sailor. The hasty marriage was put down to Isabella's flighty nature. For years afterwards, the family talked about the shame she had brought upon them through her impulsive nature with men.

It would be the same conclusion they would draw when, a decade later, she met and fell in love with an Indian medical student.

And so she was Isabella Kerr when she met Dr Gabriel Hakim. From the very start there was a strong mutual attraction between them and they were soon friends; Isabella was so taken with Hakim that she introduced him to her sisters. It was not long before they were lovers. They must have made a striking couple around Edinburgh: the tall, muscular Scottish woman, with a high forehead and prominent teeth, and the slightly built Indian medical student with a shock of black hair, who was full of nervous energy and spoke quickly in a high-pitched voice.

Their relationship was tempestuous from the start. Both were impulsive. Isabella had shown how quickly she could become infatuated with a man in her brief time with Van Ess; admittedly she had been 19 at the time. She had fallen in love with Hakim quickly, too. She learned soon that Hakim was capricious, incapable of controlling his passionate temper. It would burn bright and hot but cool quickly, leaving Hakim contrite and remorseful, his usual good manners returning, accompanied by effusive apologies.

The lovers would discover that a volatile and violently unpredictable relationship could be a heady aphrodisiac.

They had their first argument not long after they met, setting the tenor for their relationship. On 31 August 1927, Isabella wrote a letter to Hakim apologising and 'begging his pardon' for having been rude to him.

Hakim kept a diary from 1919 and would continue to do so for the rest of his life. Mostly they were small, pocket diaries; he was not given to

writing lengthy entries, instead he would scribble a couple of sentences to
record the day's highlights. The entries would be longer if he found himself
in an emotional state, pouring out his feelings.

In October 1927, he confided his private thoughts in its pages: 'Isabella
and I had a heart-to-heart talk. I told Kerr [Isabella] not to misunderstand my friendship and to consider me as nothing but a mere friend.' By
December, however, Hakim wrote that he and Isabella were 'head over
heels' in love. 'She told me she was already married to a Dutchman, named
Van Ess, and confided in me her unhappy life with him. Thank God she
was only with him a week or two. Oh Lord, grant Kerr a good and happy
and prosperous life. Amen.'

Within a few days their relationship had strengthened and Hakim's occa-
sional diary references to Isabella as Kerr had ceased; she had become 'my
darling Belle'.

He bought his first gift for her, a frock that cost £5, a considerable sum
and one he, as a medical student, could hardly afford. 'I do not begrudge it,'
he wrote in his diary.

The lovers took a short trip to Rothesay, the main town on the
beautifully remote Isle of Bute off the west coast of Scotland. It was a
rugged, windswept, romantic place in which two young lovers could spend
time together. It was also a long way from the hubbub of Edinburgh and the
inevitable wagging tongues. Hakim regarded the trip as their honeymoon,
even though they were never to marry. 'I love Scotland and the Scots,'
he wrote.

Isabella never wore a wedding ring, but once she and Hakim became
a couple she did sport a 'wish-bone' ring on the index finger of her left
hand; such rings were popular at the time and were deemed to be symbols
of good luck. She could hardly have known how unlucky her time with
Hakim would be.

GLAISTER:
'DEAD MEN DO TELL TALES'

John Glaister lost out to Smith on the post at Edinburgh in main due to lack of experience. Smith was nine years older, had spent a decade in Cairo, and was Harvey Littlejohn's personal choice as successor. Glaister had presented impressive credentials and letters of recommendation, including one from his father, the great Professor John Glaister senior, which was icily formal, appropriate for a man who was a Victorian to his bones. Whatever disappointment Glaister might have felt, Sydney Smith's old job at Cairo University was nevertheless a very satisfactory consolation prize: the Egyptian climate was appealing, as was the revelation that he would not have to pay income tax.

Glaister might well have felt his early life had been akin to that of an understudy, but the role he was preparing for was that of a noted forensic scientist. A talented mimic and actor, particularly in light comedy roles, Glaister had harboured ambitions to train at the Academy of Dramatic Art before going on the stage as a professional actor. But whatever dreams he nurtured, there was a different course set for him. Young Glaister remembered his father, originally a doctor and a police surgeon – 'a self-made man' – as a 'thin, wiry, energetic figure, ebullient in character, with high cheekbones and a very small dark "imperial" [moustache] which was always immaculately trimmed'.

The Glaisters were comfortably off. They lived in a large house in the affluent Townhead area of Glasgow. Glaister junior was the youngest of six children, and he grew up surrounded by servants and with a father who was mostly absent due to his important work. The young Glaister would wander around the rooms of the big house, lost in his own playful world.

'It might have become a lonely childhood, but for the games I invented,' he said later. The one room in the house that was out of bounds, however, was his father's lab, where the distinguished Victorian scientist locked himself away, working for long hours.

Perhaps Glaister's curiosity about his father's job during these childhood explorations and the mystery of what took place behind the locked door were what set the youngster on his true course.

He first saw death as a child when he was taken to see his grandfather's body before his funeral, which was a Scottish custom at the time. The event affected Glaister: he thought the body looked more like a wax effigy than the grandparent he had known. It was an experience that would prepare him for his future work.

In 1899, at the outbreak of the Boer War, Glaister's father was appointed Regius Professor of Forensic Medicine at Glasgow University. Remarkably, the post would be held by one John Glaister or another, father and son, from that time until 1962. In time they became known as 'Old John' and 'Young John'.

Glaister's father had come from humble beginnings. Once he had enough money to educate his children privately, he chose not to. Glaister said his father regarded public schools as 'educationally greatly overrated'. Perhaps the great man felt that, as he had risen to the top of his profession from inauspicious roots through hard work, so his children should do the same.

This sort of pressure did not sit easily with the younger Glaister.

One evening his father summoned him into his study. Glaister knew what was coming. His father looked at him for a moment, removed the cheroot he was smoking from his lips, frowned, and said, 'I don't think you're making much progress at school, are you?'

'No,' replied Glaister.

'Your reports aren't good, you know.'

'No.'

'You're not concentrating, my boy. Stay in at nights a little more and do some work for a change!'

Glaister plucked up the courage to tell his father that he was so far behind in his studies, he should leave school and study under a tutor.

His father considered the idea. He then asked his son, 'John, have you ever considered seriously what you plan to do when you have finished school?'

Glaister now had to expose to the cold light of his father's study his true ambitions. 'I'd like to go on the stage. I want to go to London and study at the Academy of Dramatic Art.'

His father puffed on the cheroot as he ruminated on the advice he was about to deliver. 'Forget it. Let's suppose you went to the university and chose a proper career. What would it be?'

Glaister, still clinging to his dream of performing for a living, thought he might become a barrister. 'I had formed the impression, still unbroken, that a certain histrionic ability was one of the hallmarks of a successful courtroom personality,' he later wrote.

He and his father discussed this idea; the machinery of fate was clicking into gear. The family was rooted in the medical profession. Glaister's older brother, Joe, had already followed their father into the field. Glaister senior had shown it was possible to combine a medical career with a burgeoning reputation in the field of medical law and jurisprudence, and also as an expert witness at high-profile murder cases. He felt that a similar trajectory would be appropriate for his youngest son. The die was cast.

Glaister might not have won the right to go on the stage, but he did walk out of his father's study with one little victory: his father allowed him to leave school and choose a tutor.

The long journey to emerging from his father's shadow had begun.

Glaister began to apply himself in his studies and he arrived at Glasgow University as an undergraduate in the dying golden years of the Edwardian era before the spectre of the First World War descended upon Europe.

At university, Glaister found himself a curiosity. His fellow students were keen to see how 'Young John' would behave when attending lectures given by 'Old John'. As it turned out, the young Glaister was afforded no special privileges by the older Glaister. He was 'just another blob of student material in the eyes of his father', Glaister later noted.

Then the Great War erupted across Europe in 1914. When it became clear it 'wasn't going to be over by Christmas', as Glaister later put it, qualified doctors rather than students were required on the front line. So Glaister remained at university in Glasgow. He and his peers would eventually tend to casualties when they returned to Scotland. When he qualified as a doctor in March 1916, he was commissioned in the Royal Army Medical Corps and underwent his army training at Ripon in Yorkshire.

Once training was completed, Glaister did active service with the Royal Army Medical Corps in France and Palestine at field hospitals and clearing stations, which were military medical facilities just beyond the range of enemy artillery behind the front line used to treat wounded soldiers.

Glaister had found his calling, but his heart remained in Scotland with the love of his life. Her name was Isobel Lindsay, or 'Muff' to everybody who knew her well. Her father, Sir John Lindsay, had been the town clerk of Glasgow and it was at a dance at the City Chambers that Glaister had first met her, when she was aged 11 and he was 15. Five years later, romance bloomed between them and they became engaged to be married.

Their wedding was set for May 1918. Glaister secured leave from his duties, landed in London, telegraphed Muff that he was on his way home to Scotland, and then spent the night in his hotel watching a Zeppelin raid on the English capital. Shortly after, on 25 May 1918, Glaister and Muff were married at Glasgow Cathedral. As the celebrating wedding party emerged from the cathedral, they passed a cameraman from the British Moving Picture News. A handsome Glaister, sporting an impressive moustache like his father, was dressed smartly in his army uniform and cap, while Muff looked beautiful in her Edwardian wedding gown and veil. A guard of honour was formed by ten men in various military uniforms, creating an arch with their swords. Glaister and Muff looked overjoyed, unable to contain their smiles. The procession filed past the camera in the stuttering piece of ancient footage, leaving for posterity a glimpse of Glaister's parents, Professor John Glaister senior and Mary, as well as Muff's parents, Sir John and Lady Charlotte Elizabeth Lindsay.

After the war, and newly married, Glaister wanted to move into the field of medico-legal work, but he was unsure if he could support himself and his new bride during the required study period. It was Muff who persuaded him. He later wrote of his beloved wife, 'Behind every man, it has been said, there stands a woman. Both in private and public life few men can have been more fortunate than I have realised myself to be in having such a partner.'

Glaister found himself busy studying in the parallel fields of medicine and law. It also led to his working with his father. Just like the days when Glaister was attending lectures given by his father, now it was the police that became accustomed to 'Old John' answering requests for assistance, with 'Young John' at his heels. Glaister later wrote of their working relationship, 'I found him a dominant but pleasant chief who at first kept me on a tight rein with definite and detailed instructions as to the work I was to carry out.' In time, the father began to let the son stand on his own two feet. 'Gradually … the reins began to loosen a little.'

It truly was the family business. Glaister learned his trade at the side of his father, watching as he performed post-mortems. But the conditions in which this delicate, sensitive work was done were not ideal.

Glaister described them as 'appalling'.

Glasgow's city mortuary was in an old building within the Central Police Office. Glaister and his father could be surrounded by slabs upon which were resting as many as five decomposing cadavers that had been pulled from the bone-chilling murk of the River Clyde. The room was filthy, antiquated and poorly lit. Undertaking work in such conditions was testing, to say the least, Glaister wrote. And as if that were not challenging enough, the Glaisters on occasion had to concentrate while the Glasgow City police band blared and fanfared their way through their regular practice session in a neighbouring room.

The 1920s was a grim time in Glasgow. The country was in a state of shock following the Great War; communities had been ripped apart, a whole generation of young men had been extinguished. Poverty stalked the streets and slums of major cities, including Glasgow. Crime grew out of the misery and hardship like a weed grows between the cracks of a pavement. Glaister characterised it this way: 'There was an obvious reason: the grim poverty which formed the domestic environment in which so many people had to live out their lives, an environment which could grind all but the strongest hopes to dust and often left only an animal-like sense of values.'

The Glaisters' work gave them a daily account of the consequences, the harm done by the weapons used in brawls: axes, cut-throat and safety razors, 'peaky-blinder' razor blades secreted in the peaks of caps, bicycle chains, broken bottles, chisels and heavy-rubber coshes.

Glaister pitied the families of victims who had to attend the city mortuary, or one of the other facilities he and his father used to perform post-mortems. Some were little more than ancient lock-ups, with doors that sagged. Many times Glaister worried that local children might get a glimpse through the gaps in the doors of the gruesome work being performed inside.

In 1926, Glaister and his father helped Sir Harvey Littlejohn in the Donald Merrett murder case, which Professor Sydney Smith had offered his views upon. The Glaisters assisted Littlejohn in the tests to establish at what distance blackening ceased when a gun was fired.

The paths of Professors John Glaister and Sydney Smith, a decade away from the Jigsaw Murders, had, if not exactly crossed, at the very least come close to touching.

Glaister now threw himself into his career. All thoughts of a life on the stage were behind him and he got on with the business of death. There was much to learn. Where he had once indulged his talents in learning how to entertain an audience, now he concerned himself with the tools of the trade and craft of his new profession.

'Dead men *do* tell tales,' he would later write in his memoirs, 'though first it is necessary to learn the language, a language with a vocabulary constantly being expanded by the advances of modern research and technology. The language and its medium, forensic medicine, still has many facets to be explored and problems to be conquered.'

The first time Glaister gave evidence as an expert witness in court was alongside his father. Both were appearing as Crown witnesses at the High Court of Justiciary in Edinburgh in 1926, when Glaister was 34. They had been summonsed to present their expert opinions on blood, a subject upon which Glaister had based his doctorate.

The experience was one that was a watershed in the reputation of the Glaister family in the medical world. It was also a hint that 'Young John' might be ready to take over from 'Old John'.

His father took to the stand to expound on his expertise in the field of blood tests. The defence barrister put it to the distinguished scientist, 'Why then, Professor Glaister, did you say in a textbook that these tests were at a stage where they could not be completely relied upon?'

Glaister's father was clearly in trouble. The defence had found a weakness and were prepared to exploit it. The attack threatened to undermine his authority before the court and the presiding judge. He responded, 'My views have changed since then because of the further work I have seen done. Alterations will be made to the next edition of the textbook.'

This was dynamite for the defence, who put it to Glaister senior that if he could change his mind once, how could the judge or jury know whether he might not change it once more?

Glaister was due to follow his father into the witness box. He had not had the benefit of being present to hear his father's evidence. The defence's questioning opened gently – Glaister later termed it 'mild' – designed to explore how thorough his research into the classification of blood had been. With the gaze of the entire courtroom on him, Glaister came to a dreadful realisation. It was all a ploy. The defence were cleverly allowing him to establish himself as an expert; but doing this would result in his father being damned as knowing very little about blood tests, and as a man who relied on his son's judgement.

Glaister, no doubt uncomfortable because of the line of questioning and the scrutiny of his father, replied, 'I carried out all of these tests in this case. But in each instance they were checked and corroborated by my father.'

The incident unnerved Glaister and it stuck in his memory. He later wrote, 'The trap had come close to springing – but it had been avoided.'

Glaister took refuge from his work in the protective cocoon of family life, which was woven around him by Muff. But while she may have provided this idyllic place of retreat, nevertheless she was quick to point out his responsibilities with regard to his work. Never was this illustrated more than when a disturbing discovery interrupted their summer holiday in 1927.

Glaister was exhausted after a hectic time during which he had given evidence at a number of criminal trials. He needed a break, to forget the smell and sight of death.

So the Glaisters booked a holiday at the Ayrshire seaside and golf resort of Troon, on the coast to the south-west of Glasgow. The couple checked into their hotel on the Saturday afternoon at the start of their break. They had taken their wire-haired terrier, Roy, with them, and planned to go for long, tranquil strolls along the beach, allowing the sea breeze to blow away the concerns of the past months. Glaister and Muff were devoted dog-lovers and there was always a pet in the family throughout their married life and years of parenthood. Due to Glaister's work commitments, they often relied on students at Glasgow University to walk their current dog of the day and Glaister would later proudly tell whoever was listening that their most distinguished dog-walker had been Isobel Barnett. Glaister described her as an 'exceptionally good medical student and a prizewinner in my class'. She later became a famous television personality in Britain thanks to her appearances on the panel show, *What's My Line?*

Once Glaister and Muff had unpacked in their hotel room, he suggested they go for a walk along Troon's beach before returning for dinner. 'Good… and we'll take Roy,' said Muff.

Glaister, Muff and Roy set off along the soft, silky sands, following the course of the grassed dunes, beginning to relax, looking forward to the holiday that lay ahead. Suddenly, Roy fell behind. He was frantically sniffing at the bottom of a sand dune. Glaister was unconcerned: this was what dogs did. 'Oh, he's probably found a dead seagull,' he said. He whistled and shouted at the terrier to come to heel. The dog looked up at his master briefly, but then returned to his frantic sniffing. Frustrated, Glaister had to traipse back to fetch Roy. 'Come on —' Glaister began to say, but stopped short suddenly. Roy had certainly found something of interest. Glaister instantly recognised what it was. It was as if death followed him everywhere.

Lying in the dune was the body of a newborn child.

To most people, such a discovery would have been a traumatic, disturbing and upsetting one. But Glaister was not most people when it came to a dead body. He was a forensic scientist. And he was a tired one who had come away on holiday to a seaside resort in the hope of a break from the concerns of the dead. As his terrier continued to make a fuss over the child's body, and with his wife waiting further along the sands, Glaister's mind went into a whir. He dreaded getting involved; he knew what would lie ahead, the questions, the paperwork, the tiring administration. He could kiss goodbye to a relaxing break. So he began to reason to himself the notion of leaving the body undisturbed. He told himself: I am an innocent passer-by who happened to have an inquisitive dog. It would not be long before there would be other people strolling along the beach with equally inquisitive dogs.

Glaister began to ease sand over the little body with his foot. Muff appeared at his side and saw what was going on. She was alarmed. 'You can't do that,' she scolded her husband. 'You'll need to report this to the police.'

He knew protesting was futile, but he did so nevertheless: 'Somebody else will … it's bound to be found. We're down here for a rest. You know what'll happen if I get involved … our holiday will vanish in a puff of police reports.'

'We'll have to report this,' Muff insisted. 'If you don't, I will.'

Glaister knew who the wise one was in their marriage: he listened to Muff.

They returned to the hotel and Glaister telephoned Troon police station. He gave them a description of where the body was. The officer took down the details and then asked the question the scientist had been dreading: 'And your name, sir?'

He knew what would happen as soon as his name was known. He tried to avoid it: 'Oh, I'm just a visitor … down for a day or two. You don't need to bother about that, do you?'

'We need your name, sir,' insisted the police officer.

And so he gave the most famous name in forensic science in Scotland, but slurred it slightly, hoping not to draw attention to it. The officer asked him to spell it.

'Glaister, Dr Glaister.'

After a moment when recognition dawned on the officer, the reply came, 'Now, that's nice and handy, sir. You won't mind giving us a wee bit of a hand over this, will you?'

The next few days of Glaister's holiday vanished in 'a puff of police reports'. He conducted an examination of the body but was unable to establish whether the child had been born alive or not. Neither was he able to explain how or why the body had been hidden in the sand. The police were unable to proceed any further.

6

RUXTON RISING

The slim, handsome, charming young foreign doctor was also a jealous, deeply controlling man. The signs were there even in the early days of their acquaintance, when Isabella was working in the cafeteria at the top of Leith Street in Edinburgh. She was impressed by his looks and ambitious talk of becoming a successful doctor, with his own practice and a healthy income. But Hakim became infatuated with Isabella. He would burn with jealousy if she smiled at another male customer in the cafeteria. He wanted all of her attention, all of the time.

Perhaps his obsession with her had a detrimental effect on his studies as he failed the exams for his Fellowship of the Royal Colleges of Surgeons. Nevertheless, his medical qualifications acquired in Bombay and London were enough to allow him to go into general practice. Wanting to provide a future for himself and Isabella, and perhaps with a sense of shame over his exam failure, he decided to leave Isabella in Edinburgh and head to London to make some money. He arrived as a penniless former medical student late in 1927 and survived by living off the generosity of Indian acquaintances already in the capital city. He was not too proud to borrow money and his loose attitude to his finances, exacerbated by a weakness for gambling on horses, would persist for the rest of his life.

He initially secured eight weeks of sustained employment, as an assistant to a doctor who was based at Forest Road in Walthamstow, in north-east London. For a time he worked as a locum for a Dr Manek Motofram, a fellow Parsi medic, and also as an assistant to a Dr B.R. Rygate, of 126 Cannon Street Road in Stepney in London's East End. He impressed his employer with his diligence and hard work and was popular with his patients, slowly establishing a reputation as a compassionate medic.

‡

Being separated from Isabella took its toll. He composed reams of poetry, which he sent to her in Edinburgh, declaring his love for her. He wrote in his diary:

> My happiness is dawning on me! To all whom it may concern I hereby put on record my sincere appreciation of a very marvellous sense of devotion towards me of my beloved and noble Belle. Her warm welcome, patient suffering and faith in God have been an inspiration to me oft-times when despair has overpowered me. Her industry has made many of my rough paths smooth. Long live my Belle! Amen.

All the while he was working long hours, trying to save money to allow him to return to his lover. Their love burned bright across the divide.

Isabella – by now Belle to Hakim; she called him affectionately 'Bommie', perhaps short for Bombay – eventually left Edinburgh and joined him in London.

Hakim did not seek a divorce from his wife in Bombay. As a Parsi, he was forbidden from marrying outside of his faith, so going through with a divorce and marrying Isabella was out of the question.

His wife, now Motibal Hakim, remained fond of him, even after his bad treatment of her and what would happen in the autumn of 1935. She later said, 'It was in 1928 that he suddenly left for England, and I never had a chance of seeing him again. He explained he wished to further his medical knowledge and improve his position.'

His letters to her after 1927 became irregular. She later said, 'In February 1928, I received a cablegram asking for £300. My people were against sending anything, but he was my husband and I persuaded them.' Her father, Jehangirji Ghadiali, was wealthy. Ghadiali means 'watch maker' and Jehangirji Ghadiali was well known and respected for the repair work he undertook on the huge Rajabhai Tower clock at Bombay University.

No doubt worried about the state of his daughter's marriage to Hakim, Jehangirji instructed his solicitor to send his son-in-law 1,000 rupees, which was around £80 sterling, significantly below the figure Hakim had in mind. Jehangirji also sent a message to Hakim via Thomas Cook and Sons of Edinburgh with strict instructions on how the money was to be spent: Hakim should use the funds to pay for his immediate passage home to India.

Motibal Hakim later observed, 'He had all along, of course, promised to return to me as soon as he could.'

It is unclear why Hakim asked his in-laws for the money, but it is likely he wanted financial assistance in helping Isabella to secure her divorce from Van Ess. This was a costly business and it no doubt left the spendthrift Hakim short of cash.

Hakim wanted Isabella free of that other man. She was his 'Belle'. No other man would have her.

The Ghadiali family never heard from Hakim again, for he never wrote to them and every effort they made to trace him – including inquiries through the Parsi Association of England – turned up a blank. Efforts by his in-laws to trace Hakim would have been doomed to failure anyway because around this time he had chosen to metamorphose once more.

On 19 April 1929, like a butterfly emerging from its cocoon, Gabriel Hakim changed his name by deed poll to Buck Ruxton.

DEATH ON THE NILE

Life in Cairo was good to Glaister, Muff and the girls.

The city had developed beyond all recognition since he had last visited a decade earlier during his army service. He was impressed to see new, luxury apartments, office blocks and plush hotels populating impressive tree-lined boulevards. He would write of his impressions that 'Cairo was freely regarded by its inhabitants as one of the most cosmopolitan cities in the world'. He and Muff would sample the finer side of Cairo during their time there. They were afforded the luxury of servants and a personal cook. They attended parties and receptions at hotels, clubs and government buildings. They were entertained at the private theatre within the Abdin Palace, a historic royal home that became the residence of the Egyptian president.

Much like the duality of Edinburgh, there was another side to the Egyptian capital, however, a side composed of slums where lives of misery and grinding poverty were lived out, a million miles away from the high-life the Glaisters were enjoying. Dilapidated houseboats – home to poor Egyptians – pocked the surface of the Nile, encircling Gezira Island, the location of Cairo's most expensive hotels and accommodation, and nick-named the 'septic rosary' due to the foul and disease-ridden effluent that was discharged into the river.

While he enjoyed the spoils of the work he had been employed to do in Cairo, it was from this other, darker part of the city that Glaister's work emanated. The Egyptian government's desire to establish a first-rate medico-legal department at the university to cope with the staggering amount of death was a priority. One of the carrots that had been dangled in front of Glaister – besides the lack of income tax – was the promise of more medico-legal cases in a week in Egypt than he would encounter in a year if he stayed in Scotland.

✢

Within a short space of time he found he and his assistants were performing up to 150 autopsies every month. He later wrote, 'To use a hackneyed
phrase, life was cheap around Cairo. Violent death was commonplace.'

Two years into their new life in Egypt, Glaister received a communication that would once more change the course of his life.

He received a letter from his father urging him to take the Regius Chair
of Forensic Medicine at Glasgow University. 'Old John' was stepping down,
retiring from the post he had held since 1898. Glaister could see that whoever took the job had a huge task ahead, not least because he – and the
post was almost certainly to be filled by a man – would be compared to the
legendary erstwhile incumbent. The fact that Glaister was his son would
make the challenge even greater.

Glaister once more turned to the person who gave him the soundest,
wisest counsel: Muff. They both loved the lives they had built in Egypt;
they had two young daughters who adored living there. But Glaister sensed
things were changing. At the time Egypt was 'for the European', as he
put it, offering a privileged life and a healthy income. Egyptian national-
ism was on the rise, however, and he sensed that the country would seek
its freedom.

His mind was made up and, on 8 September 1931, he received a telegram confirming he had been appointed to the Regius Chair. He and
Muff packed their belongings and headed home to Scotland with their
young family.

There must have been a sense of pride for Glaister, returning to his
birthplace to such a prestigious position and following in the footsteps of
his father. Perhaps he thought back to that conversation with his father in
his study all those years earlier and reflected upon how far he had come. He
had made his father proud.

Fate can be cruel. Glaister's happiness was to be short-lived.

Late in 1932, almost a year after his new appointment in Scotland,
Glaister was back in Egypt at Cairo University. At the request of the
Egyptian government he was to spend three months of each year during
Glasgow University's non-teaching term in Cairo sharing his expertise.
Glaister snapped up the offer – the prospect of spending three months
out of twelve in the sunshine of Egypt seemed a pleasant arrangement, a
welcome contrast to the chill of Glasgow.

He and Muff set sail for Cairo that September. Their daughters remained in Scotland at their boarding schools. Glaister later noted that the trip began with a holiday atmosphere; his duties involved giving a few lectures and supervising the university's new forensic medicine department. To top it all, they were provided with comfortable quarters in a hotel at Gezira, the island on the Nile in central Cairo, the 'septic rosary'. But events took a dark turn. Muff received a telegram to say that her brother had fallen seriously ill. She set off for Britain immediately, leaving Glaister to follow her in due course. Her brother had soon recovered once she arrived home, but it was not worth her returning to Cairo for the remaining few weeks of Glaister's time there.

On his return journey to Britain, Glaister was playing bridge in one of the upper deck saloons of the ship when a steward brought him a telegram. He told his bridge companions that it was likely to be a message from his wife confirming that she would meet him in London. Without further thought, he finished playing his cards.

But the cable had very different news to what he was expecting.

Both his parents had died within two hours of each other on 18 December, having contracted influenza. 'There was nothing I could do but wait until the ship reached Plymouth, its first British call,' he later wrote. When he disembarked at Plymouth he found the newspapers full of reports of his parents' deaths, and also of his return to Britain. The newspapers also informed him that the 'flu epidemic was sweeping the country.

Tired and grieving, Glaister finally arrived in Glasgow on the morning of 22 December. Both of his daughters had gone down with the 'flu but soon recovered. Within days Muff caught it and eventually Glaister himself went down with a bout. He arrived home on the day of his parents' funeral service, held at the University Chapel. A large congregation attended, to pay their respects to John Glaister senior, regarded as one of the finest and most influential forensic scientists of the age.

There was now only one Professor John Glaister. Only time would tell if 'Young John' would measure up to the standards set by 'Old John' and whether he would step out from his father's shadow.

8

SEXUAL JEALOUSY

Dr Buck Ruxton could not shake the jealous thoughts of Isabella and Van Ess from his troubled mind. Early in their relationship Isabella had told him of the marriage, but no matter how many times she reassured him, Ruxton could not be convinced. He poured his pain and suspicions into his diaries, while venting his temper on Isabella and tightening his control.

While she was in Edinburgh and Ruxton in London, she wrote to tell him she planned to travel to Holland – Van Ess's homeland – to see through her divorce from her estranged husband. Ruxton wrote back, outlining his demands on the matter. The letter was long and rambling and read as though it had been written in an incandescent rage. It was a chilling peek into the dynamics and power-play of their relationship.

He wrote to Isabella:

My ever beloved, devoted, and truthful Belle:
   Listen very, very carefully, and please obey without question. The occasion forces me to take the fullest possible privilege I possess of dealing with you. I have gone into the matter thoroughly, and have come to the following conclusions:–

   (1) I shall never be ashamed of you. Reason – because I know you inside out, and you are all my trust. Conclusion – throw off your worries and be proud.

   (2) You may do what you like in this matter in Edinburgh, but you shall not cross British borders and lay your feet on Dutch soil. (Spend any amount in Edinburgh.) Reasons – (a) You are officially at present Dutch, and if you are on Dutch soil where is the guarantee that the opposite party won't molest you by detaining you there? (b) Scottish laws cannot prevail in Holland, and if the opposite party tricks you, no lawyer on earth can get you back in Britain. Scottish laws will be paralysed to get you from the clutches of Dutch regulations – and I am not prepared to lose you.

The last sentence is not a joke. I mean it sincerely.

You are a damned fool if you think of setting foot in Holland. Conclusions – I command you not to go to Holland, and if ever you think of doing so you lose me forever. I shall die of a broken heart. What's the earthly reason of your presence there?

Whatever you wish to do in Edinburgh, I am prepared to stand by your side, but do not go contrary to my wishes; nay, I command you.

I regret to have to assume such high-handedness, but I see no other way to protect you. What more do you want than my assurance and written guarantee that I am never going to be ashamed of you?

Trying to get out of the frying-pan, you are getting into the fire. I can never allow you to do such a silly thing. You are very cheap and so is your lawyer – that cheap that you want to do away with your troubles for £20.

You have no idea of the sleepless nights I have. I can neither read nor sleep, and your foolish adventure is the cause.

In the name of God, in the name of our holy love, in the name of our Prophet, I command you not to go to Holland. I will never permit you to have your own way and afterwards be sorry for myself.

My Belle, suppose those scoundrels play you a trick and you are detained in Holland. What an anxiety for us all in Britain! Funny Dutch laws: damn them all.

You shall not cross British borders if you are my dear and obedient Belle. Even if you do not want to be obedient, I want you to obey me.

I am shouting at you not to go there, and I am in my full temper. My love forever!

Promise me with love you won't go there.

Always yours, and yours only, Bommie [Isabella's nickname for Ruxton].

Isabella ignored Ruxton and went to Holland.

PART TWO
BRILLIANT MINDS

9

SHERLOCK HOLMES MADE FLESH

Criminal forensic pathology came into its own in the twentieth century. The image of the infallible, scalpel-brandishing pathologist was seared into the popular public imagination largely because of one man: Sir Bernard Spilsbury.

At a time when Smith and Glaister were establishing themselves, the shadow of Spilsbury loomed large over everything they did. He was the yardstick by which all others were measured. To the common man and woman who read the popular newspapers of the day, Sir Bernard was Sherlock Holmes made flesh.

'The word Spilsbury is simply a name to the general public. It tends to connote violent or mysterious death,' wrote Bentley Purchase, the coroner for St Pancras Coroner's Court in London, one of Spilsbury's close working colleagues.

Spilsbury's reputation in the popular imagination was due to the key murder cases in which he was involved. Chief among these were the cases of Dr Crippen in 1910 and the 'Brides in the Bath' case of 1915. These were sensational criminal cases that electrified the public through the pages of the popular press and turned Spilsbury into a superhero forensic detective.

Spilsbury became so well known to the public that he was caricatured in the great British humour magazine *Punch*. Celebrated cartoonist George Belcher drew a serious-looking Spilsbury dressed in wing-collar shirt, waistcoat, dress trousers and shoes and spats. His shirt sleeves were rolled up. He looked dressed for a formal dinner. Over this he wore a white apron, like a butcher's. In his gloved hand he delicately held a long, thin, ultra sharp scalpel.

Belcher appended the following lines beneath his drawing:

When arsenic has closed your eyes,
This certain hope your corpse may rest in:–
Sir B. will kindly analyse
The contents of your large intestine.

Yet of the 25,000 post-mortems conducted during his long career, around 250 – just 1 per cent – were linked to murder. The rest were routine operations performed in hospitals and at coroners' courts.

Bentley Purchase wrote, 'Spilsbury as I saw him was a man who had no room for half-truths.' Spilsbury never spoke about his cases, Purchase observed, except to correct falsehoods of misinformed individuals. 'In public affairs he showed no interest: looking back on it, I think the only facet towards the public was the ascertainment of truth and the demonstration of justice,' he wrote.

When giving evidence in the witness box of a criminal court, Spilsbury used simple words and phrases; he wanted his meaning to be plain, for there to be no room for ambiguity. He was obsessed with the truth being understood. This facility to communicate clearly and without artifice in order to convey objective truth was achieved because of an uncommon quality Spilsbury possessed.

'He thought before he spoke,' wrote Purchase.

This resulted in Spilsbury gaining a reputation for being aloof. 'He never made conversation for its own sake,' Purchase wrote, adding, 'If asked a question, he made sure that he understood it before he answered it. He next made sure that his answer was also understood.'

It also made him a fearsome figure in the courtroom; defence barristers' hearts would sink if they knew Spilsbury was giving evidence for the prosecution. In time, his professional and public reputation became unassailable and his judgement perceived to be infallible. If ever his judgement were questioned, Spilsbury was a formidable opponent.

In 1929, Professor Sydney Smith – just as Professor John Glaister junior had done a couple of years earlier – would discover first hand the wrath of Spilsbury.

Medical jurisprudence – that is, the application of forensic knowledge in a legal context – is centuries old and can be traced back to 3000 BC Egypt, when Imhotep acted both as chief justice in the court of Pharaoh Djoser as well as court physician; he was effectively history's first known medico-legal expert. This natural link between medicine and the legal field continued in early Greek and Roman society. In modern times, Germany and France were early hothouses for the development of the discipline. Britain was slower in coming to the field; in 1807 the first dedicated university chair was established at Edinburgh. This natural affinity between forensic science and the law was not always obvious and at the time a Member of Parliament stood up in the House of Commons opposing the move in Edinburgh on the grounds that he did not understand what medico-jurisprudence was. Alfred Swaine Taylor was perhaps the first influential figure in the field in Britain. In 1834, he was appointed to the Chair of Forensic Medicine at Guy's Hospital Medical School, a handsome set of buildings arranged in a courtyard in the borough of Southwark in central London. It was Taylor who first set down on paper the early modern discoveries in the field that would still be practised by Spilsbury, Smith and Glaister a century later.

In Edinburgh it became the practice that the Professor of Medical Jurisprudence also performed the functions of the Chief Surgeon to the City Police. In England, it was common for pathologists to be Home Office approved.

Spilsbury became the most famous such holder of the position.

Bernard Spilsbury was born in 1877 in the town of Royal Leamington Spa in Warwickshire, in the English Midlands. His father, James, was a manufacturing chemist. Spilsbury's childhood was comfortable and he was happy. He grew up to be tall – he stood 6ft 2in – and handsome, with light-brown hair, steely grey eyes and a slim, clean-cut face.

After graduating with his degree in natural science from Oxford in 1899, Spilsbury found his interests had shifted from general medical practice to the new and emerging field of forensic pathology. To this end, he went to study at St Mary's Hospital in Paddington, London.

It seemed highly appropriate that someone so single-minded and determined to do things his own way should choose a field still relatively untouched by others' fingerprints. With his customary confidence, Spilsbury knew he could be a pioneer in this nascent scientific area.

According to his biographers Douglas Browne and E. V. Tullett, Spilsbury had fixed views from a young age. 'Unlike many, he changed few of them in later life. Some might be called prejudices, for they were part of his inheritance and make-up; others were the result of reflection, and this with him was always a careful and logical process,' they wrote.

Bernard Spilsbury stood on the cusp of great public acclaim in 1910, which marked the end of the Edwardian era and the dawn of a seemingly brave new technological and enlightened age. That year was historic in many ways: it witnessed the appearance of Halley's Comet, whose spectacular light-dripping tail is seen every seventy-five years or so, while the fight of the Suffragettes reached fever pitch in England with the Black Friday march on the Houses of Parliament by 300 women demanding the right to vote.

It was also the year of the notorious murder trial of Dr Hawley Harvey Crippen, the case that would introduce the world to Bernard Spilsbury.

Mild-mannered widower Crippen was an American homeopath and medicine dispenser who married a loud, brash music hall singer, Cora Turner, who used the stage name Belle Elmore, and moved to England in 1897 to live at 39 Hilldrop Crescent in Camden, London. The Crippens' marriage was not a happy one: where Cora was vivacious, gregarious and attention seeking, Crippen was quiet, reserved and withdrawn, a small, nondescript figure with a bald head, sandy moustache and protruding watery eyes behind thick-lensed spectacles.

In January 1910, Cora went missing after a party at Hilldrop Crescent. Publicly, Crippen said she had returned to her native United States; later he said she had died and been cremated in California. When news of her disappearance reached the police, Crippen was interviewed and he said he had lied about her death to avoid the embarrassment that she had actually run off with another man.

In a panic, Crippen and his mistress Ethel Le Neve ran away together. What Crippen did not know, however, was that the police had been satisfied with his explanation during the interview. Now, the couple's disappearance aroused suspicion. Detectives from Scotland Yard dug up the cellar at Crippen's Hilldrop Crescent home and discovered human remains. The hunt was on to find Crippen and Le Neve. The world's newspapers were filled with speculation about where the wanted couple were; descriptions were issued.

Crippen and Le Neve were recognised by the captain of a transatlantic liner, the SS *Montrose*, as passengers on his ship. Le Neve was disguised as a boy. The captain informed the authorities, sending a telegraph using new-fangled Marconi wireless equipment; soon Chief Inspector Dew of Scotland Yard had travelled from London to Liverpool, where he hopped aboard a second ship, the SS *Laurentic*, a faster ship due in Montreal before the *Montrose*, in hot pursuit of his quarry.

Dew and the captain of the *Montrose*, Henry Kendall, kept up a constant but covert correspondence via wireless in the tense hours as the *Laurentic* advanced on the *Montrose*, until both ships were in the Gulf of St Lawrence, which leads to Montreal. Arrangements had to be made for Dew to board the *Montrose* without arousing Crippen's suspicion. On 31 July, the SS *Montrose* pulled into the quay at Father Point for the purpose of letting aboard the ship's pilot who would guide the ship safely into the harbour at Montreal.

The 'pilot', smartly dressed in a gold-braided uniform, boarded and tapped Crippen on the shoulder, saying, 'Good morning, Doctor Crippen. Do you know me? I'm Chief Inspector Dew from Scotland Yard.'

Crippen reportedly replied, 'Thank God it's over. The suspense has been too great. I couldn't stand it any longer.'

Spilsbury was preparing to go on holiday with his wife, Edith, and their young son, Alan, to Minehead, a seaside resort in Somerset, when the newspapers first featured stories about Crippen. When human remains were discovered in the cellar at Hilldrop Crescent, Spilsbury was called upon to help with the medical aspect of the police investigation, undertaken by a team from St Mary's Hospital. Spilsbury took notes on the remains that had been recovered from Crippen's house. There was no head, no bones and all of the limbs were missing. There were pieces of skin, one of which appeared to have an operation scar. Prior to her marriage to Crippen, Cora had undergone an operation that would have resulted in such a scar.

Spilsbury and his associates were of the opinion that the remains were those of Mrs Crippen. Spilsbury was called to give evidence at Crippen's trial, the first occasion he had done so. Well dressed, with a red carnation in his buttonhole, the tall, handsome Spilsbury spoke calmly and confidently, and became something of a media sensation, as the newspapers portrayed him as a medical detective of the first order.

Crippen's defence suggested that Spilsbury and his colleagues had been swayed by newspaper reports of Cora's operation in reaching their conclusion.

In a firm, clear and assertive tone, Spilsbury told the Old Bailey: 'I have absolutely no doubt in my own mind as regards the scar … I have my microscopic slides here, and I shall send for a microscope in case it should be wanted.'

He had stood firm; those who witnessed it took his performance as a defiant rebuke to anyone who might suggest he was not at all times completely objective in his assessment. Crippen would be convicted of the murder of Mrs Crippen and sent to the gallows.

As Spilsbury left the witness box, word was whispered around the court: 'There is a coming man.'

That is to say, a medico-legal star was born.

10

DECREE ABSOLUTE

Sitting in her room at the Central Hotel in Rotterdam in Holland in October 1928, Isabella wrote to Ruxton:

> My Beloved Bommie – Again another day gone. Love, to me it is like another year. I'm simply just pushing in time I go to bed so early I cannot sleep. You understand? I'm afraid to go out when dark, so there is nothing left but bed.
>
> I have lived one thousand times over all our past joys and pray God to let me be beside you very soon. The one thing I love here is the bathroom. Each bedroom has a bathroom and so beautiful.
>
> If you were here, dear, I think you would live in the bathroom. The staff are all exceedingly nice, and most attentive, but with it all I would rather live in a room with my Bommie. I'm so lonely, dear.
>
> All my love, darling. I am breaking my heart for a sight of you. – Always, your Belle.

She had gone to Holland against Ruxton's orders but she had done it to seek a divorce from her husband Van Ess. She wanted to be free from the mistake she had made when she was 19. She wanted to be free to be with Ruxton.

Isabella's marriage to Van Ess was dissolved in Rotterdam on 9 October 1928. She truly was his 'Belle'.

II

A NAME FORGED IN MURDER

In the decade after the Crippen case, Spilsbury was unassailable. He was a stickler for detail and with his gritty determination he dramatically revolutionised the field of forensic medicine. He was knighted in 1923.

A newspaper reporter observed Spilsbury at work at Wandsworth Prison in 1924 when he performed a post-mortem on a convicted murderer following execution. The reporter said Spilsbury arrived, carrying his famous black bag, ready to examine the corpse of Patrick Mahon, who had murdered his mistress, Emily Kaye, dismembered the body and hidden the parts in hat boxes, luggage and biscuit tins in her bungalow in Sussex. It was a case that would be a point of reference for experts and the press when the human remains were discovered at the Devil's Beef Tub in 1935.

Spilsbury, dressed in preparation, opened his black bag. The usual procedure was to cut open the prisoner's neck to confirm hanging as the cause of death. Spilsbury did not do this. Instead, with his scalpel he opened Mahon's body up entirely from the head down, before undertaking a complete and thorough examination. In addition, he spent an hour inspecting Mahon's brain, removing a sample to take away for further inspection. The reporter noted that the coroner, Bentley Purchase, who was also in attendance, made the suggestion that Spilsbury was, perhaps, being over-thorough.

'I must do this in my own way,' Spilsbury informed the coroner sharply.

Spilsbury had been horrified when he had arrived at the Sussex bungalow in the Mahon case to find officers had scooped up the bloodied body parts of victim Emily Kaye with their bare hands. He knew things had to change and instigated innovations that changed the course of police work in the collection of evidence at murder scenes. Spilsbury was credited with devising the 'murder bag', or forensic kit used in future by police officers. It included rubber gloves, tape, compass and portable fingerprint utensils.

✣

As Home Office pathologist he had a unique advantage as an expert witness in criminal cases, which added to his mystique. It was as if his mere presence in a courtroom assured his verdict was taken as the true narrative. He started to believe his own hype and to consider himself infallible.

The almost-mythical status that Spilsbury had attained was well illustrated in the words of Lord Alnes, the judge presiding over the 1927 Merrett case in which Sydney Smith, John Glaister and Harvey Littlejohn had been involved. In guiding the jury, Lord Alness said:

> I need not remind you that in this case we have had the great and learned assistance of Sir Bernard Spilsbury. I do not dispute that Professor Littlejohn and Professor Glaister are men of eminence, but I do not hesitate to say that there is no name in Britain, there is no name in Europe, on medico-legal questions on the same plane as the name of Sir Bernard Spilsbury.

How could Smith or Glaister or anyone else for that matter compete with the mighty Spilsbury?

Smith's and Glaister's paths would inevitably cross with Spilsbury's over the coming years in a number of cases. Each occasion left Smith and Glaister stronger as a result, if at the time they were not easy experiences.

The first time Smith was burned by Spilsbury was in the autumn of 1929 in the treacherous case of Sidney Fox, which was similar to the Merrett trial but, if anything, even more disturbing.

Smith would be giving evidence for the defence. Spilsbury was the Crown's expert witness. 'The stage was set for our first major clash in court,' Smith wrote later.

HAPPY FAMILIES

In the autumn of 1929, Ruxton and Isabella were living in Grove Park Road, Lee, in south-east London, close to Eltham and Lewisham. It was a year since Isabella had divorced Van Ess. Although she and Ruxton were never to marry, she adopted his name and called herself Mrs Ruxton. Ruxton's religion might have prevented him from divorcing his own wife, but that did not mean he had to tell the world he and Isabella were unmarried. Creating the illusion of a legal union became necessary to the scandal-averse Ruxton when his and Isabella's first child was born.

Dr and Mrs Ruxton presented to the world a daughter, Elizabeth Ava Stewart Ruxton, who was born on 27 August 1929. They were now a proper family.

Despite tensions between Isabella and her family over her marriage to Van Ess, she was on good terms with her older sisters in Edinburgh and would make regular visits to Scotland with baby Elizabeth to stay with them.

Meanwhile, Ruxton was keen to lay down roots and find stability for his new family. He began actively looking for a medical practice that he could buy.

13

FOX

Sidney Harry Fox was rotten to the core, 'a bad hat', as Professor Sydney Smith later described him. Fox was in trouble with the law from a young age: first admonished by police at 12, sent to prison at 19. Eschewing a law-abiding path, the undoubtedly plausible and charming Fox instead chose a career in deception as a swindler and forger. It was a hand-to-mouth existence, travelling from town to town, staying in one cheap, seedy hotel room after another, made all the more precarious because his mother Rosaline travelled with him. Travelling without luggage, the pair would flit their digs, leaving a trail of dud cheques and unsettled bills behind them before their creditors could do anything about it.

In October 1929, Fox's luck ran out as he and his mother stumbled from one financial scrape to another.

From 12 to 15 October, Fox and his mother stayed at the County Hotel in Canterbury, a historic, Tudor-style coaching inn. When they checked out of the hotel, the proprietor Frank Mason challenged Fox about his unpaid bill. Fox replied he had no money, but would return later to collect his car and settle his account, once he had taken his mother to the Kent port town of Dover, around 20 miles south-east of Canterbury.

Mason was unimpressed and warned Fox he would inform the police to question him at Dover. Later that afternoon, Mason received £2 from Fox, wired telegraphically, but it was not enough to cover the bill for bed and board.

There was no family loyalty with Sidney Fox. When he and his mother arrived at the Hotel Metropole in Margate, Kent, on the south coast of England on Wednesday, 16 October 1929, he had terrible, dark thoughts in mind.

He and Rosaline settled into their new hotel accommodation, room 66, which had adjoining bedrooms. The hotel boasted that it was 'Well-sheltered from the north east', had 'magnificent views', and was 'handsomely and comfortably furnished', 'splendidly decorated', with 'lounges, electric lights', and an 'elevator'. As it faced Margate's jetty, no doubt Fox and his mother enjoyed bracing walks in the autumn air of the seaside resort, which is 15 miles north-east of Canterbury.

Fox was up to his usual conniving during their stay at the Metropole. He presented a cheque made out on Hotel Metropole notepaper and signed 'Rosaline Fox' to James Elgar Farmer at a chemist's in Margate, asking for it to be cashed. Farmer twice refused to cash it; he later discovered that the cheque had been cashed, presented for payment but not honoured.

Six days into their stay at Margate, Fox told his mother he had some business to attend to in London and took the train up to the capital. Unbeknown to his mother, Fox had taken out two insurance policies on her life. As both policies were about to expire, Fox went to extend them until midnight the following day.

Fox got the train back to Margate later the same day, 22 October, and returned to his mother at the Metropole.

The following day, 23 October, Fox and his mother ate dinner at the hotel and Fox treated Rosaline to a bottle of port, as a nightcap, before they retired to their room.

Later, Fox, dressed only in a shirt, came running down the hotel stairs shouting that there was a fire. A brave fellow guest rushed to help Rosaline and dragged her from the blazing room. As a crowd watched, efforts were made to revive her, but when two doctors arrived she was pronounced dead.

It was 11.40 p.m. – twenty minutes before the two life insurance policies were due to expire.

The following day, an inquest was held and a verdict of accidental death was returned. Fox's mother was buried five days later in her home village of Great Fransham in Norfolk. There was no further interest in the death; the police considered the matter closed.

All that was to change when Sidney Harry Fox went to claim the insurance payments on his mother's life.

The insurance companies, as a matter of course, looked into Fox's claims; insurance companies are very careful in making payments. An official at one of the companies, whose suspicions were aroused, sent a telegram to his head office: 'Extremely muddy water in this business.' They smelled a rat, and detectives at Scotland Yard in London were notified.

The police reopened the case into Mrs Fox's death.

Her body was exhumed eleven days after the funeral. Sir Bernard Spilsbury performed the post-mortem examination. He concluded that she had been strangled.

Detectives arrested Fox and subsequently charged him with the murder of his mother.

Fox's solicitor, seeking to secure forensic expertise matching Spilsbury's, invited Professor Sidney Smith to present evidence in Fox's defence at his trial.

'After examining the medical part of the case for the Crown,' Smith wrote, 'I agreed to appear in the role of expert witness.'

Smith had given evidence as an expert witness hundreds of times before, mostly for the Crown and usually in cases from Edinburgh, although he was often asked to look into cases elsewhere around the country.

Under the British legal system, the Crown allowed expert witnesses to be available to the defence, and in circumstances where defendants had no means to pay for their legal expenses, the Crown would cover this cost as well.

Smith had strong views on the role and conduct of the expert witness. He wrote:

> The attitude of a scientific witness should be the same whether he is called in by the Crown or by the defence. It is not for him to concern himself with the previous character of the accused or with other evidence in the case. As a scientist he should be completely detached: he must not let himself be influenced in any way by emotional considerations such as sympathy or antipathy. His sole function is to examine the facts which come to his knowledge in his special capacity, to decide what is the true or the most probable interpretation of them, and to indicate to the court that interpretation, along with the grounds on which it is based.

Smith was often asked why he should give evidence in defence of an accused who on the face of it seemed guilty or to be a 'scoundrel who was not worth saving'. He was always clear-minded on the matter and unequivocal in his response: 'the accused may not be worth saving, but the principles of justice always are'; in not doing things properly and fairly, then, 'you open the way to flouting the fundamental proposition of our law that every man is innocent until he is proved guilty'.

There was much circumstantial evidence against Fox: the life insurance policies taken out on his mother, the fire. Based on that alone, things did not look good for him.

None of that, however, was of interest to Smith. He could only concern himself with the medical evidence relating to Mrs Fox's death, and this was based entirely on the report Spilsbury had prepared following his post-mortem examination. When Smith read the report in preparation for the trial, his eye was caught by the report's conclusion: 'Cause of death: asphyxia due to manual strangulation.'

Spilsbury had already outlined this finding when he gave evidence at Fox's initial appearance on 9 January 1930 at Margate Magistrates' Court, in Kent, at which Fox was indicted for trial at Sussex Assizes in Lewes, in March.

At this preliminary court hearing, Fox's solicitor George Hindle questioned Spilsbury's evidence. He asked the esteemed forensic pathologist for the Crown: 'Is it not extraordinary that there were no marks of violence on the neck?'

Speaking in his clear, unambiguous manner, Spilsbury had replied: 'It is unusual in a case of manual strangulation, but that is another matter.'

The lack of marks on Mrs Fox's neck perturbed Smith.

On Saturday, 8 March, Smith visited Spilsbury's laboratory at University College Hospital, on Gower Street, close to Euston railway station in London, an elegant building designed by famed architect Alfred Waterhouse, renowned for his Gothic-influenced designs for London's Natural History Museum, in South Kensington, and Manchester Town Hall. Many years later, during the Second World War, crime writer Agatha Christie would work as a pharmacy assistant at the hospital, learning much about poisons, which would later prove invaluable knowledge for such books as 1961's *The Pale Horse* in which the odourless thallium is used to devastating and fiendish ends. In January 1950, writer Eric Arthur Blair would die in room 65 of the hospital. Blair was better known to the world by his pen name: George Orwell.

Smith was accompanied to Spilsbury's lab by Dr Robert Brontë, formerly the Crown Pathologist for All Ireland, who was also due to give evidence in Fox's defence. Brontë was a turtle-faced man of ramrod-straight posture who dressed elegantly in winged-collar shirts and bow-ties and a bowler hat. Originally from Armagh in Northern Ireland, he was from the same family line (the name originally being Brunty) as the famous writer sisters, Charlotte, Emily and Anne, of Haworth in Yorkshire, whose father Patrick hailed from County Down. In 1918, Dr Brontë had been appointed Spilsbury's assistant at the Home Office and together their collaborative evidence had been crucial in a number of murder cases.

Brontë was clever, mercurial and sharp-witted, quick at making friends and allies, but could also be combative, pushy, self-opinionated and boastful. He did not keep good health; he drove a specially adapted car and would be dead within two years of the Fox case at the age of 52. Given his temperament and strong will, it was inevitable that he would come into conflict with Spilsbury.

According to Smith, however, Spilsbury was most helpful and courteous as he showed him the bodily samples he had taken at the exhumation of Mrs Fox's remains. These included the larynx, which Smith was especially keen to inspect. Smith regarded Spilsbury's theory of strangulation as 'flimsy' and believed Spilsbury was relying solely on the larynx evidence to make his case to incriminate Fox. Spilsbury's theory relied upon there being a bruise on the larynx.

Smith's views on manual strangulation were clear. He wrote:

A person being strangled fights like mad. Even if the victim is a feeble old woman, Nature will supply her with unsuspected additional strength to help her in her fight for life. She will struggle furiously to wrench the strangler's hands away from her throat. She may fail, but some marks of the struggle will remain. Nearly always there will be scratches about the neck.

Yet Spilsbury's report had noted there was no trace of external injury at all.

As Smith examined the larynx, Spilsbury said nothing, just stood silently next to him. Smith was looking for a bruise. 'There was none to be seen,' he later wrote. There was discolouration from putrefaction, but no bruising at all. Brontë next examined the larynx. He shook his head.

After some time, Smith said, 'I can't see any sign of a bruise, Spilsbury.'

'Nor can I,' said Brontë.

Spilsbury looked at them. He agreed: 'No. You can't see it now. But it was there when I exhumed the body.'

Smith later wrote, 'That fairly staggered me. The larynx had been preserved in formalin ever since the exhumation.'

He asked Spilsbury, 'Where's the bruise gone, then?'

'It became obscure before I put the larynx in formalin,' Spilsbury informed Smith and Brontë. 'That is why I did not take a section.'

Smith regarded this last admission as an important oversight by Spilsbury: a microscopical section would have shown whether the discoloration Spilsbury had seen was a bruise or not. A bruise is the result of small vessels breaking and blood extruding into surrounding tissue and clotting: once this has happened, the blood cannot be removed by changes in the body post-mortem. 'To get a bruise the size of a half-crown quite a lot of blood would have to be extruded,' Smith noted. Such a sample of the larynx in question could have confirmed what Spilsbury had seen was indeed a bruise. 'Personally I was pretty sure it was not' was Smith's assessment. He told Spilsbury so: 'I don't see how a bruise of that size could have just disappeared.'

Spilsbury repeated, 'It became obscure. It was there. I saw it myself.'

Smith, however, was not giving up, despite the great man's reputation. 'Spilsbury, I don't doubt that you saw something,' he said. 'But I put it to you that it might not have been a bruise. It could have been a patch of discoloration from post-mortem staining or putrefaction.'

On this point, Brontë was in agreement, nodded, and said. 'We all know how difficult it is to diagnose a bruise with the naked eye after partial putrefaction has occurred.'

If Spilsbury was rattled by this dissent in his own laboratory, he did not show it. According to Smith, he 'listened attentively and was very polite, but he would not argue the point'. Smith concluded, 'I had the feeling that nothing I said would make any difference, that his mind was closed.'

Smith later realised why Spilsbury was so dogmatic:

Had I known him then as well as I came to later I would have realised why I was wasting my time. He could not change his opinion now because he had already given it. He had described the alleged bruise in his report and given evidence about it before the magistrates. His belief in himself was so strong that he could not conceive the possibility of error either in his observation or interpretation.

The three of them examined further injuries. Once more, Smith questioned Spilsbury's findings; again it was an alleged bruise, on the thyroid gland.

'I cannot accept that as a bruise,' Smith informed Spilsbury.

'Nor can I,' Brontë said.

Spilsbury stayed silent.

A third dissenter came in the form of Dr Henry Weir, a renowned pathologist who was due to support Spilsbury's evidence on behalf of the Crown. He did not believe it was a bruise, either. The four men discussed the matter in Spilsbury's laboratory and after some time Smith was convinced that Spilsbury now conceded they were right and that he had been wrong on this point.

Brontë, however, who knew Spilsbury better, put Smith right as they left the laboratory and stepped out onto Gower Street.

'You wait till we're in court.'

14

COURTROOM CLASH

And so the scene was set for Sidney Fox's trial.

Spilsbury was the highest-profile witness appearing for the Crown; Smith was among a number appearing in Fox's defence. Smith had given evidence at trials hundreds of times. Generally, if the case was in or around Edinburgh, he would appear for the Crown; if it was elsewhere, he would give his services to the defence.

The trial began on Wednesday, 12 March, in the assize court in the town of Lewes on the Sussex coast. It was a few days after Smith had visited Spilsbury's laboratory.

The Crown's case for the prosecution was that Sidney Harry Fox had strangled his mother for the purpose of claiming on the life insurance policies he had taken out, and had set fire to the room to hide his crime.

Standing in the witness box, Spilsbury repeated his belief that the cause of death was asphyxia due to manual strangulation. He explained that he had examined Mrs Fox's body, looking for soot on the lining of her air passages. He had also checked her blood for carbon monoxide poisoning. In each case the test results were negative. This, in his view, was evidence she had not died from suffocation caused by the smoke.

Under cross-examination, he agreed that he had never come across such a case where there were fewer signs of bruising but this did not mean his professional opinion was wrong. 'The injuries could, in my opinion, only have been produced by strangulation by the hand,' he told the crowded courtroom. He elaborated: firm pressure from the thumb and fingers to the larynx could have produced bruising.

Spilsbury used a delicate porcelain model of a human neck and mouth to describe his theory about Mrs Fox's death to the jury, pointing to the exact spot where he said he found a bruise 'about the size of half a crown' at the back of her larynx.

Smith, who sat in the courtroom observing him, noted that when he spoke, Spilsbury used verbs such as 'could' and 'might'. 'The theory sounded so plausible that the unwary could forget it was only a theory, not hard fact,' he wrote later.

Smith agreed with Spilsbury on the conclusion that Mrs Fox had not died through suffocation caused by smoke. He later wrote: 'In my opinion she had not died of asphyxia at all. I thought she might very well have died of heart failure brought on by sudden exertion or fright. The shock of waking up and finding the room full of smoke, and the effort to get out of bed and escape, might well have put a fatal additional strain on her already weakened heart.'

Such a theory, if true, would mean that Sidney Harry Fox was innocent.

In the coming days, Smith prepared to present his own expert opinion on behalf of Fox's defence. In all the hundreds of cases at which he had previously given evidence, he had always been treated with respect and courtesy. The Fox case would prove a stinging experience, as he put it, 'my first experience of the clashes between counsel and expert witness that are a feature of British criminal courts'.

Smith stood in the witness box and told the courtroom that, in his opinion, 'there was not sufficient medical evidence to support a charge of strangulation'.

The following day, however, he was to be cross-examined by the prosecution's counsel Sir William Jowitt, the celebrated and notoriously tough Attorney General, the chief legal adviser to the Crown.

Smith's opinion of Sir William was not a high one. He later wrote: 'He seemed determined to hang Fox. It is, of course, not the proper function of the Crown counsel to press the case against the accused.'

Smith believed that Jowitt's attitude and treatment of the medical evidence relating to Spilsbury's 'half-crown bruise' was open to criticism as he had told the jury in his remarks that a bruise inside the throat could only be present if an outside one were too, stating that it was. Jowitt had concluded: 'This much is plain: the inside bruise is there. It is there −.' But Smith knew it was not there; Spilsbury himself had also testified that the bruise had vanished.

Smith was on his guard as he stepped back into the witness box to prepare to be grilled by Jowitt. He knew he would be hauled over the coals, and he was.

'You stated in your evidence that you had a very long experience in cases involving manual strangulation,' Jowitt said.

'Yes,' Smith replied.

'Were there cases of strangulation by a young man of an old woman as the old woman lay in bed?'

'I have had many cases of strangulation of elderly men and elderly women.'

Jowitt tightened the screw: 'Will you try to answer my question?'

Smith steeled himself and responded, 'I will think of the special conditions for one moment. Yes, I have had.'

'Do you mean to tell us you had not considered that question before you came to give evidence in this case?'

'I have considered the question,' replied Smith.

'Then I take it you have brought your notes of a person being strangled in bed.'

'No, I have not.'

'Was there one case, or more than one case?'

Jowitt was on the attack; Smith had to speak slowly and carefully, to navigate the traps Jowitt was laying.

'I have had many cases of a somewhat similar nature. May I explain?'

'Please answer my question. It may be difficult for a gentleman who gives lectures to answer questions, but I want you to answer mine,' scolded Jowitt.

The sparring between the two continued, with Jowitt pressing his questions on Smith in a 'hectoring way', as Smith later described it. The tension rose in the courtroom and Smith found himself forced into silence as Jowitt jabbed at him.

'Do you think that is being quite candid with me?' Jowitt asked. When Smith did not reply, he tried again: 'If the answer is "No", say "No". You are not trying to make it difficult for me, are you? I want you to try to help.'

Unaccustomed to such provocation whilst in the witness box, Smith responded: 'I am, to the best of my ability, but you won't give me an opportunity of putting you right. If I begin to explain, you say, "Please answer my question." It makes it very difficult.'

Jowitt tried to draw Smith, to make it seem that he was belittling Spilsbury by implying that distinguishing between bruises and discoloration marks was an elementary skill that was taught to assistants.

'Do you put Sir Bernard Spilsbury on a par with one of your assistants?' Jowitt taunted Smith.

Smith maintained that there were many flaws in Spilsbury's evidence in relation to the lack of a bruise, even though Spilsbury claimed to have seen one. Spilsbury's reputation was such, and Jowitt had done such a good job of preserving it, that things were not looking good for Sidney Harry Fox. The defendant did not help himself, either, when he gave a poor performance in the witness box.

Nevertheless, the judge in the trial, Mr Justice Rowlatt, in his summing-up cast doubt on the evidence of Spilsbury. He told the jury:

> There were no external indications of asphyxia. There were no external marks on the throat. Sir Bernard Spilsbury has said it was quite possible there would be none, but you and I might think it difficult to believe it. As regards the brittle bone in the throat known as the hyoid, it is a very curious coincidence that the bone was not broken in this case. That is a very strong point in favour of the accused. As to the mark at the back of the larynx, alleged by the prosecution to be a bruise, there is no doubt that Sir Bernard Spilsbury saw some object there. It is unfortunate that those tissues could not have been preserved for others to see. The defence have said – and are justified in saying it – that the point rests on the testimony of what one skilled man observed, and observed at one moment only.

Smith would later comment that the judge had not grasped the 'dangerously high esteem in which that one skilled man was held'. He noted: 'Perhaps Spilsbury did not fully realise that fame brings responsibility as well as honour. I do not think the jury would have returned the verdict they did if his evidence had been given by anyone else but Spilsbury.'

The judge's summing-up complete, the jury retired to deliberate its verdict; an hour and ten minutes later the twelve returned. Fox was ordered to stand; the courtroom fell silent.

'Guilty!' said the jury's foreman when asked what verdict they had reached.

Stunned, Fox was able to say only this: 'My lord, I did not murder my mother. I am innocent.'

Smith later wrote that he believed Fox had been innocent.

He would not have put it past Fox to have murdered his mother – the evidence of the insurance renewals was highly suspicious. But Smith believed Fox had been wrongly convicted for strangling his mother. He believed there was no evidence of that fact.

Sidney Harry Fox was hanged on 8 April 1930 at Maidstone gaol in Kent.

The clash with Spilsbury and the steamrollering of what he perceived to be the truth in service of one man's ego stung Smith but he came away from it wiser and, even after many years' experience as an expert witness, with less respect for Spilsbury. He never took for granted the fact that one was always learning in the field of forensic pathology, or that one could be wrong. It was not a weakness to admit so and to change one's mind.

It was a quality that would stand him in good stead when his team was presented with the remains from Moffat six years later.

15

A NORTH COUNTRY PRACTICE

As 1929 came to a close, stability was at the forefront of Ruxton's thinking. They were entering a new decade, the 1930s. He had a common-law wife and a young child to support. He had begun to build a reputation as a hard-working and popular doctor during his time in London. But now he wanted to strike out on his own. He wanted to make a mark on the world as a doctor. He was not alone; in the late 1920s and early 1930s, many doctors and medics from South Asia headed for Britain and, in particular, the industrial north where patient panels were largely working class and there was much demand for their talents.

Ruxton's pulse quickened when he saw there was a practice for sale in Lancaster in the north of England. It was a long way from London. But it would allow him to make a fresh start with Isabella and baby Elizabeth. And they could easily make trips to see Isabella's family in Edinburgh. The panel of patients was made up of mostly working-class people but there was a sizeable number of well-off middle-class families, which appealed to Ruxton's social ambitions.

So he entered into negotiations to purchase the practice at 2 Dalton Square from a Dr Gonsalves. In April 1930, the deal done, Ruxton watched with pride as the nameplate bearing his name was screwed to the wall outside the front door.

Prospects were good, but money was tight, so while Ruxton set about establishing himself in Lancaster, Isabella took Elizabeth with her to Edinburgh for a time so that she could earn some extra money working as the manager of Woolworths cafeteria on Princes Street.

The practice, a smart three-storey Georgian stone house built around 1784, would serve both as Ruxton's surgery and as a home for his new – if temporarily remote – family. For the ambitious Ruxton, the emerging medical professional, the property was perfect: it oozed respectability, success and ambition.

Fate would decree that this would be the last home in which Ruxton and Isabella lived. Number 2 Dalton Square was destined to enter the annals of murderous addresses in British criminal history.

PART THREE
HYDE

THE RAJAH OF DALTON SQUARE

Ruxton and Isabella began a new chapter in their lives.

Ruxton's restless spirit and white-hot ambition drove him forward. He had come a long way and the journey had been arduous and sometimes painful. He was determined to make Lancaster a success. He would work hard, harder than he had ever worked before. Ruxton and to a degree the times in which they lived expected Isabella to fulfil the role of the wife of a well-to-do doctor and mother to their baby daughter and to oversee the running of the household at 2 Dalton Square. But she had been an independent woman in Scotland before she met Ruxton. She had been the manager of a number of cafés. Despite Ruxton's controlling nature, Isabella would never surrender her sense of her own worth and would forever harbour ambitions of pursuing her own business ideas.

Dr and Mrs Ruxton were certainly a novelty when they arrived in this northern English town in 1930: he the foreign, handsome young doctor, she his vivacious, striking-looking wife with the charming Scottish accent. He was most likely the first Indian doctor Lancaster people had seen. There is no evidence he experienced prejudice from local people based on his skin colour and culture. Soon the Ruxtons were a popular and well-respected part of the fabric of life in Lancaster. Isabella quickly made friends and acquaintances, while Ruxton, perhaps due to his natural reserve and lack of English as his native tongue, found it more difficult.

Dalton Square was a bustling place, a focal point in the town. One of the town's main roads ran past the square, bringing a constant stream of motorcars, buses and lorries. (The Lancaster Corporation Tramways ceased its tram service in the town in the month Ruxton arrived in Lancaster.)

The Ruxton home stood on the north edge of the cobbled square, whose centrepiece was a Queen Victoria statue set on Portland stone. The memorial stood in an oval walled garden. The square was a mix of businesses and residential property. Ruxton's home had a Britannic Assurance office on one side, the County Cinema on the other. Beautifully kempt flowerbeds with exploding colours encircled the Queen Victoria statue and were a popular place of escape for residents seeking a moment of tranquillity.

On the opposing edge of the square, directly opposite Ruxton's house, was Lancaster Town Hall (the town would not become a city until 1937). Inside the Town Hall was the local police court. Below street level, underneath the grand rooms of the Town Hall, were the police station and cells. This latter detail is unlikely to have troubled Ruxton at the time.

The civic business of Lancaster Corporation was conducted within the magnificent chamber of the Town Hall, which had been paid for by James Williamson, the Lord Ashton, in 1909. Lord Ashton was a wildly successful Lancaster industrialist who had made his vast fortune in linoleum. In the 1890s, to provide employment for the men of Lancaster, he paid for a former stone quarry high on the hill in the south of the town to be transformed into an exquisite ornamental Victorian park for the edification of the Lancaster population. The site was close to an old Lancaster community known as Golgotha village, comprising a number of workers' cottages and a Quaker burial ground. The spot was also where the notorious Pendle witches were hanged after being tried at Lancaster Castle in 1612. The lino king named the place after himself, Williamson Park.

Between 1907 and 1909, Lord Ashton kept the workmen on salary and commissioned a folly in memory of his late second wife, Jessy. He spent £87,000 on the work. Today that figure would be in the region of £8.2 million, indicating the size of Lord Ashton's fortune. This breathtaking structure, complete with grand sweeping marble staircase, resembles the Taj Mahal and became a dominating landmark, seen from all directions for miles around. When Lancaster Corporation outgrew its previous offices in Market Square, Lord Ashton offered to pay for new premises. Work began in Dalton Square and Lord Ashton took great pride in opening the new Town Hall, twenty years before Ruxton arrived in Lancaster.

Next door to Ruxton's surgery was the County Cinema, complete with portico entrance and billboard featuring giant posters of the movie stars of the day, which would be changed with the turnover of each week's selection of films. It was one of many picturehouses in the town. For such a compact place, Dalton Square boasted not one but two cinemas. Besides the County, there was also the Palace Theatre, on the western flank of the square. Because the Palace had only a small stage and had essentially been built as a cinema rather than a theatre, it did not have the capacity of the

County. The County secreted a cavernous interior belied by its modest frontage on Dalton Square. Ruxton and Isabella regularly went to see films at the County.

A dizzyingly tall chimney could be seen from Ruxton's house, beyond the Town Hall in the south of the town. This belonged to Storey Brothers and Co., a textiles printing business that was a major employer in Lancaster. Thirty-six years after Ruxton's arrival, the chimney collapsed, killing two workmen and injuring twelve others.

Number 2 Dalton Square must have seemed like Buckingham Palace to Ruxton and Isabella. It was perfect: room enough for Ruxton's medical practice and ample space on two floors upstairs for a comfortable family life. The nameplate outside read:

Dr B. Ruxton
Hours
2–4 p.m. 6.30–8 p.m.

Callers could press one of two bells, one for the surgery during the day, the other for the Ruxton family at night.

Ruxton used three of the four rooms on the ground floor for his general medical practice: a surgery, a waiting room, and a consultation room. The final room was a kitchen. The Ruxtons used the middle floor for living quarters: two living rooms and a dining room. On the top floor were the bedrooms. In time, Ruxton and Isabella slept in separate rooms; baby Elizabeth slept in her mother's room, and when two more children were born, they too slept in Isabella's room. A final bedroom would in time be used as their maid's bedroom.

Ruxton and Isabella filled their new home with expensive and ostentatious furniture and decorations made from the finest materials: marble, alabaster, walnut, mahogany. The walls were lined like an art gallery with oil paintings. Many of these pictures were scenes of the Scottish Highlands and mountains, a reminder to Isabella of home.

Ruxton had a taste for the exotic. Perhaps he was trying to emphasise his foreignness to the people of Lancaster. Throughout the house were touches of the East: Oriental rugs, animal skins, and Moorish and Egyptian furniture. These mingled with items reflecting his ancestry, such as French-influenced timepieces and chinaware. Lastly, he and Isabella invested in expensive traditional English items such as Chesterfield suites and the finest-quality Axminster carpets.

The morning room, on the first floor, no doubt where Ruxton liked to relax, reflected his dual heritage with Oriental and French china vases. The walls were decorated with a mounted wolf skin. Ruxton and Isabella would listen to radio broadcasts on a walnut wireless set while sitting in this room.

They kept an eye on the local auctions of antiques and desirable items. 'Clifton Hall sale,' Ruxton wrote in his diary. 'Bought marble statue of Prince Consort and Queen Victoria Rosewood cabinet.' Two weeks later he noted: 'Bought from Hest Bank Lodge sale: Statue Indian slave girl holding a torch … Binoculars. Plated ware. Dresden China figures and fruit bowl. Fresh linen.'

Not long after they had arrived at Dalton Square in 1930, Ruxton wanted his Belle to be immortalised in oils and commissioned a portrait painter. Isabella found herself self-consciously posing for a painting that imitated Giorgione's *The Reading Madonna*. Ruxton insisted on being present at all the sittings; he wanted to ensure that nothing inappropriate took place between the painter and Isabella. He could not bear the thought of her spending time alone with another man.

Ruxton was keen to make a statement to the world. He filled his medical consulting room with luxurious carpets and exotic ottomans. At one end stood an exquisitely carved chest made of sandalwood, while in the corners stood low tables ornately embellished with filigree – gold and silver ornamental wire – and mother-of-pearl. Ruxton decorated each of the tables with bric-a-brac and ornaments he had collected. He decorated the room a deep blue colour that was peppered with gold stars in a style that was described at the time as 'Oriental'. Ruxton took great pride in his rooms and would boastfully tell anybody who would listen that they were the envy of every other doctor in Lancaster. He loved nothing more than seeing the reaction of his patients when they were shown into his consulting room for the first time. As they walked in, he would be seated in a high-backed chair extravagantly upholstered in red. In his mind he was a king sitting on his throne and his patients the courtiers ushered into his palace. When he was consulting a patient he would not leave his seat to give instructions to his dispenser; instead, he used a speaking tube that ran down through a hole in the floor next to his chair and through to the dispensary across the hall.

The plain-speaking folk of Lancaster nicknamed Ruxton 'the Rajah' – the King.

SUCCESS

The people of Lancaster fell for Ruxton's charms.

He soon had one of the largest panels of patients in the town. These were the days before the National Health Service when you paid for your own medical treatment. Many poorer families were unable to. Ruxton did not ignore them; over the years, stories would be handed down of his kindness to sick patients he treated without charge.

It was well known that if Ruxton encountered a patient in the street who was unwell, he would drive them to his surgery for treatment out of hours and would not ask for a penny.

Many young patients later in life would remember Dr Ruxton's medical skill and kindness and would never hear a bad word said about him, even after what was to happen in the autumn of 1935.

Ruxton once treated a little boy called Jim Stewart who was seriously ill. Jim lived at 9 Castle Hill, an old house in one of the narrow cobbled streets in the shadow of Lancaster's medieval castle. Later in life, Jim Stewart would tell the story of how Dr Ruxton saved his life.

One young girl would spend the rest of her life telling people the doctor had 'given her back her life'. She came from a large, extremely poor working-class family in Lancaster. From a very young age she was losing her sight. Her parents, not expecting her to have many prospects, chose not to send her to school. Instead they sent her to do menial work on a remote farm on the edge of Lancaster. Due to her poor eyesight, the young girl was given the task of feeding swill to the farmer's pigs. Although she was unable to distinguish the contents of the swill by sight, she found it unusually fragrant: it was leftovers from local cafés and restaurants. Her spirits would leap whenever she made out pink shapes in the pig-feed: she knew these were delicious, if slightly stale, pink wafer biscuits. To an underprivileged working-class girl they were heaven.

The farmer's family were patients of Dr Ruxton. On one of his visits to the farm, Ruxton noticed the small girl feeding the pigs. He asked why she was not at school, and her circumstances were explained to him. Concerned for the child and, sensing that he might be able to help, he opened his medic's bag and took out his little torch. He asked the girl to stand still in front of him and he knelt down and shone the beam of light into each eye in turn.

'Can you bring the girl to my surgery on Saturday?' he asked the farmer. This was the one day when the girl would not be feeding the pigs at the farm.

Ruxton had a particular interest in diseases of the eye. During his time in Edinburgh he had worked in the Eye Department at the university. In his consulting room at Dalton Square were several books on ophthalmology.

That Saturday, in his surgery, Ruxton operated on the girl. When he was done he swaddled her face in bandages and told her parents to let the girl rest.

Later in life, the girl – by then a grown woman – would recount the moment the bandages were finally unwrapped. She could see! 'Dr Ruxton gave me my life back,' she said.

Another recipient of Dr Ruxton's kindness was PC Norman Wilson. Wilson was a young officer with Lancaster Borough Police, in his late twenties when he came to know Dr Ruxton, who was for a time Lancaster's police surgeon. On one occasion PC Wilson's nose was broken in the line of duty. One evening, he was on duty, standing on the corner of Dalton Square near Ruxton's house. The doctor fell into conversation with him and asked what was wrong with the young bobby's nose. PC Wilson explained what had happened; Ruxton took him into his surgery and reset it.

The policeman never received a bill from Ruxton.

Ruxton's hard work and kindness to patients soon endeared him to the people of Lancaster, who were fascinated by the Indian doctor with the film-star looks. He soon built up a large and successful panel of patients. Some of his success can be attributed to the range of medical specialisms he offered, including ophthalmology and dentistry. Patients in agony with toothache could visit Dr Ruxton to have the offending tooth pulled.

The rewards for Dr Ruxton's endeavours were rich. In time he saw his income rising to £3,500, a significant amount.

As Ruxton became more successful, he and Isabella took on a number of servants to help with the running of the home and medical practice, and to help Isabella with their children, as a second daughter, Diana, was born on 1 January 1931. The Ruxtons did not skimp on their home help, employing an army of charwomen (cleaners) and maids. In the coming years there would be a turnover of staff, but central to the slick running of the Ruxton home was cook general Mrs Elizabeth Curwen, who lived in nearby George Street. Mrs Curwen, a thin, dark-haired woman, prepared all the family's meals and oversaw the housework at Dalton Square. In time, Ruxton would employ a nursemaid or nanny specifically to look after the children as well as perform other duties around the home. Ruxton did not wish for Isabella – the wife of a doctor – to concern herself with such mundane domestic chores. Ruxton also employed a dispenser to measure out and make up prescriptions for his patients.

Each morning, Ruxton would rise at 7.10 a.m. to let in his charlady Mrs Agnes Oxley and to collect his mail, before returning to bed to read his letters. Mrs Oxley would bring him coffee and toast, before he would prepare for the day's surgery ahead. Isabella and the children in their separate bedroom would rise in their own time; the servants would help Isabella to get the children ready.

Ruxton had little free time, but out of hours on Wednesdays and Sundays, he and Isabella would take the children for a drive to the Lake District.

As he and Isabella became better known, their circle of friends grew. They became good friends with an insurance superintendent, James Jefferson and his wife, who lived at 51 South Road in Morecambe. The Jeffersons had a young son who was roughly the same age as their daughter, Elizabeth. The Ruxtons and Jeffersons would go for day trips together, often in Ruxton's car.

Ruxton's was one of only a few single-run general practices in Lancaster. He forged a professional relationship with Dr Leonard Mather, whose surgery was at 20 Spring Bank on South Road, five minutes from Dalton Square. Mather was the same age as Ruxton, originally from Manchester, and a bachelor. Like Ruxton, he preferred single general practice rather than entering into a partnership. The two doctors became acquaintances and struck up a beneficial working relationship. Mather would later describe it this way: 'He looked after my work when I went away and I looked after his, when he went away. The scheme worked very well.'

Another friend was a dentist from Morecambe, Herbert Anderson, who was almost twenty years older than Ruxton. Anderson was a Yorkshireman, born in 1879 in Leeds on the other side of the Pennines from Lancashire. He moved to Morecambe in his twenties, married his wife Ethel in 1906 and had two daughters, Elsie and Beatrice. By the early 1930s when they became friendly with Ruxton and Isabella, the Andersons were living at West Royd, 126 Balmoral Road, a comfortable detached house with a steepled roof in a leafy part of Morecambe's West End. Ruxton would have approved; it was the sort of home and work environment he was seeking to establish himself.

Anderson was just the sort of respectable professional figure Ruxton looked up to and aspired to emulate.

Anderson's dental surgery was in Ffrances Passage in Lancaster, just off Dalton Square. Whenever Ruxton was conducting some minor dental work, such as extracting a tooth, he would consult Anderson over the use of ether as an anaesthetic, which Ruxton kept at Dalton Square.

Ruxton and Isabella became close friends with the Andersons and they attended many social events together, while the Andersons became very fond of the Ruxton children. Ruxton affectionately called the dentist 'Andy'.

PENANCE

Outwardly Ruxton and Isabella seemed the perfect couple: a healthy income, a beautiful home, two beautiful daughters and a comfortable life with servants. But Ruxton's stifling jealousy and controlling nature took its toll on Isabella. He was unpredictable; his temper volatile and frightening. After a flare-up, he would rapidly calm down and immediately regret his words and deeds. The gentle, charming man Isabella had fallen in love with would once more be standing in front of her. She and Ruxton would fall into each other's arms. And then into bed. Against her better nature, Isabella seemed incapable of resisting Ruxton.

The toxic cycle would begin again.

Isabella slipped easily into the social world of Lancaster with her outgoing personality and talent for making friends. She became well known around the town for the children's parties she organised for Elizabeth and Diana and the friends they made on Dalton Square.

She craved company and loved to go out dancing in Lancaster. Although Ruxton would accompany her, he was reserved and sometimes reluctant to go out in the evening after a long day at work. Isabella did not let this deter her; sometimes she would go out alone and meet friends.

This would inflame Ruxton's jealousy as he began to suspect she was meeting other men.

The merest thing could trigger his fury, whether real or imagined, and the likelihood was that Ruxton saw betrayal where there was none. When they returned from a night out, he would be incandescent, accusing her of dancing with another man. How dare she disrespect him so, cavorting with another man in such a public way? In the culture in which he had been raised respect was a central tenet and if a member of the family transgressed, a penance must be paid.

Isabella was frequently forced to perform an act of penance.

On one occasion, Ruxton made her take off her shoes and compelled her to run, barefoot, up and down the stairs of 2 Dalton Square fifty times.

Chillingly, he stood at the bottom brandishing an unsheathed knife until she had completed his demands.

Another time, Ruxton sat on the throne in his grand Oriental room, the lord and master of Dalton Square, the high and mighty ruler of the Lancaster surgery, and made her enter his court stripped almost naked, forcing her to kneel before him and kiss his feet.

The dark side of the Ruxtons' relationship disturbed the servants, who witnessed what went on at 2 Dalton Square. Turnover became an issue as one maid after another left because of the toxic atmosphere.

Charlotte Smith worked for six months as a 'day woman' or general maid. One Sunday, as she worked in the kitchen, Isabella came downstairs crying and holding her left arm. When Smith looked, she could see it was badly bruised. Isabella told Ruxton she would leave him, but he scolded her, saying she would not. He told Smith to make sure Isabella did not go off with the children as she was not fit to have them.

Another charlady, Mrs Agnes Oxley, cleaned Ruxton's surgery, waiting room and the hall, ensuring it was spick and span for the doctor's patients. She would also help the maid with some of the cooking, making the beds and also dressing the children.

She too became perturbed by the atmosphere in the house.

One day, she was with Isabella in her bedroom, helping to dress the children. Ruxton came into the room and rather sharply told Isabella that she was wanted downstairs. Isabella replied that she did not feel like seeing anybody that morning.

'For the second time, you are wanted down the stairs,' he ordered her.

When she repeated her feelings, Ruxton said: 'For the third and last time, I want you down the stairs.' Isabella stood up to go downstairs. As she left the room, she said to Ruxton, 'Where have you got that knife?'

When Mrs Oxley went downstairs, she could not find Isabella or Ruxton. Ruxton returned and instructed his maid 'not to let the children out of her sight'.

What the servants witnessed is likely only the tip of the iceberg. The distress and humiliation Isabella suffered when she was left alone with Ruxton can only be imagined.

Late in 1931, Isabella and Ruxton were expecting a third child. Elizabeth and Diana must have chattered excitedly, speculating on whether they would have a brother or sister. It was everything Ruxton wanted: a growing family.

Isabella felt differently. She was not the same person she had been when she had first met Ruxton. She had lost her sparkle. Ruxton's jealousy and abusive behaviour had done that to her. One of her sisters visiting from Edinburgh had recently been shocked to see how drab Isabella had become.

Isabella felt trapped. With two daughters and another child on the way, leaving Ruxton would take immense courage. There was only one way out.

In the dying months of the year, Isabella's sister Jeanie Nelson received a disturbing telegram from Ruxton urging her to come to Lancaster immediately.

Ruxton met her at the front door of 2 Dalton Square. He took her into his consulting room with the blue walls and stars. Mrs Nelson, a widow who was fifteen years older than Isabella and looked on her sister more with a maternal eye, was shocked when he told her that Isabella had tried to gas herself. Mrs Nelson knew that Isabella was a bright and vivacious person and not given to thoughts of taking her own life. She asked Ruxton if he were the cause of her misery. Ruxton was indignant; he denied he was at fault and said he was a loving husband. Isabella was trying to ruin him, he claimed, even after he was loving and kind to her. He became extremely excited, Mrs Nelson would later recall, and refused to allow her to go upstairs to see her sister.

At last Ruxton calmed; he accompanied Mrs Nelson upstairs to see Isabella, but even then was controlling. He demanded that Isabella tell Mrs Nelson the truth. By which he meant his truth.

Isabella said the gassing had been an accident. Ruxton refused to believe this and slapped her face as she lay in her bed. 'Come on now, the truth,' Ruxton said. 'You must tell the truth.' Mrs Nelson was shocked; she could see Ruxton was pushing Isabella to admit she wanted to kill herself.

Isabella, pregnant, tired and weary, was distressed. She asked Mrs Nelson to take her and the two girls back to Edinburgh with her, away from Ruxton and that house.

Ruxton was in a violent rage. He threatened Mrs Nelson and Isabella that he would cut the throats of them both and of his daughters if they tried to leave.

Ruxton calmed down. The Hyde side of his personality was ushered away; the kindly Dr Jekyll regained control.

Mrs Nelson stayed the night and the following morning she returned to Edinburgh. Ruxton relented and agreed Isabella should go with her, taking their daughters too for a holiday. He took them all to the railway station at Lancaster Castle to see them off.

It would not be the last attempt Isabella would make on her life.

LOSS

Heartache loomed.

In the spring of 1932 Isabella was heavily pregnant. Excitement was palpable in the house; Elizabeth and Diana eagerly awaited their sibling's imminent arrival. Ruxton made preparations for Isabella to travel to Edinburgh to have the baby. He felt she would receive the best care there.

But on the evening of Sunday, 17 April 1932, Isabella fell in the bedroom she shared with Elizabeth and Diana. Ruxton would later tell the nurse-maid, Jane Grierson, that Isabella had been running up the stairs when she slipped.

Isabella was bleeding profusely.

In a panic, Ruxton telephoned the one person he knew he could trust.

It was almost dawn when Dr Leonard Mather was awakened by his telephone ringing at South Road.

'It was Ruxton at the other end,' Mather later wrote, 'very excited, asking me to go at once as his wife was bleeding. I went almost straight away in my bull-nosed Morris Cowley car.'

Mather, familiar with 2 Dalton Square from his cover of the practice in Ruxton's absence, strode through the hall and up the staircase. The first light of day was streaming in through the windows.

'There was Mrs Ruxton in bed,' Mather wrote. 'On a side-table was a full-term baby boy – stillborn.'

Mather could see the child was beyond resuscitation. 'Her after-birth was still in situ but the haemorrhage was easy to control.'

Later Ruxton gave Dr Mather one of his tables from 2 Dalton Square as a token of his appreciation of his treatment of Isabella.

A desperate pall fell over the Ruxton household and Isabella's mental state deteriorated in the summer and autumn of 1932. Ruxton recorded it all in his diary.

On 10 July, Isabella threatened suicide. 'I had to lock up my dispensary and poisonous drugs for safety,' he wrote.

The following day, 'She went out and told a woman she had taken poison.'

Towards the end of September, he noted, 'Isabella left clothes hanging on a rack near coal-fire in children's bedroom. On my politely drawing her attention to it she positively asserted that it was not dangerous.'

Another day that month, Ruxton wrote: 'She flew into a temper and threw a cup of tea at me in presence of her sister, and made false allegations against my morality. God free this woman of her wild temper and obstinacy.'

On 11 October, Isabella called Ruxton 'nair' in front of her sister, he claimed. He took this term, a reference to a ruling Hindu caste, as a racial insult. 'She did not wish to withdraw her word,' he wrote.

Ruxton came from a more privileged background than Isabella. A sneering tone creeped into his diary.

'Isabella called me "dirty low-born",' he wrote a week later. 'I kept quiet – made allowances for her low upbringing and her past.' This latter point was a sour comment on Isabella's marriage to Van Ess.

Isabella tried to kill herself on 15 November by swallowing around forty tablets. 'She was very ill,' wrote Ruxton. 'I severely censured a man for having supplied the pills to my wife, and told him not to give her anything without my permission in writing.'

Despite Ruxton's healthy income, he and Isabella were constantly short of money, the consequence of extravagant spending and reckless gambling.

As master of the house, Ruxton spent as he chose but would casti-gate Isabella for what he considered her frivolous purchases. He fumed when invoices in her name plopped through the letterbox from the shops of Lancaster. Isabella, who loved beautiful clothes, nevertheless dressed rather shabbily, no doubt because Ruxton discouraged her from buying new items.

Meanwhile, Ruxton was freely spending huge sums. By his own admis-sion, he was a 'particular man'. 'Three hundred and sixty five days a year I take a bath,' he said. Each day he insisted that a clean shirt, underwear and socks were laid out for him; such extravagant demands, unusual at the time when most families considered a weekly bath and clothes washing sufficient, came at a cost, and Ruxton's laundry bills – he sent out his own clothes to be laundered – were astronomical.

He could not bear darkness. As soon as dusk fell, Ruxton switched on every light in the house, making their home twinkle across the gloom of Dalton Square like the famous Blackpool illuminations.

Ruxton could not bear to be considered ordinary; he believed that how he chose to spend his money was a statement of who he was. He masked any sense of inferiority behind his pristine new name and expensive clothes, and so his new home had to reflect this image too.

He was besotted with bright, primary colours. When he had enough money to buy his first car he had it painted in white enamel and the wheels bright blue. When he redecorated the house, it was he – not Isabella – who instructed the workmen to open cans of green and yellow paint for the outside, and to dip their brushes into exquisite tones of red and white inside.

RUMOURS

Rumours about the Ruxtons' constant arguments began to circulate Lancaster. Talk was that Isabella was associating with other men. This gossip may have been started – unwittingly or otherwise – by Ruxton himself, who frequently told others that Isabella was being unfaithful. She certainly socialised with other men when she and Ruxton went out to dinners and dances. But this did not make her unfaithful.

Ruxton, however, viewed events through a poisoned green lens.

Sometimes his temper boiled over in public and an unsuspecting patient might get a glimpse into the heart of the Ruxton home.

One woman patient who was sitting with him in his consulting room became alarmed by his agitated state when talk turned to the gossip about Isabella. Shaken by what she had witnessed, she later described the scene to her friends. She said he had a 'wild look in his eyes' and pointed a trembling finger at her. In an uptight state, he said: 'You know some of the police. You must go to them and ask them to stop this interference with my wife.'

It was impossible for the Ruxtons to keep their arguments secret with so many staff employed at Dalton Square. Vera Shelton worked as a maid until May 1935, and slept in the maid's bedroom on the top floor. At about half-past eleven one night she heard a bang and her name being called by Isabella. Vera rushed into her mistress's bedroom to find Ruxton grabbing her. Isabella told Vera to get Ruxton away from her. The doctor ran out of the room, calling Isabella a 'prostitute', and then ran downstairs. Vera quickly locked Isabella's bedroom door; she could see a bruise on Isabella's arm and her nightdress was torn. There was a broken telephone lying on the bedroom floor.

On another occasion, one Sunday afternoon, Vera witnessed another row after Ruxton accused Isabella of opening a private letter of his, which she denied. 'I will shout it around the square,' yelled Ruxton, 'You are opening my letters.'

Eliza Hunter, a young woman who was employed as a domestic servant at 2 Dalton Square, also shared the maid's bedroom for a time. She eventually had to leave her employment because, as she later put it, 'my health was down owing to the doctor's conduct' and because of the constant rows between him and Isabella.

Many times she witnessed Ruxton's domestic abuse of Isabella.

Two months after she had been working there, Eliza saw Isabella pack her clothes and walk out of the house. Ruxton told her that Isabella would not come back alive, that he would bring her back to the mortuary. Ruxton asked one of the maids if she would now be mother to his children.

One day, Eliza was attending to some chore in the backyard at Dalton Square when she heard Isabella calling her. When she went into the kitchen, she saw Ruxton with a knife standing in front of Isabella. Mrs Ruxton said Ruxton had held the knife against her throat; Ruxton tried to conceal the knife and denied he had one. He went into the surgery's waiting room and when he returned he denied again having had a knife, even when Eliza said she had seen it.

When Eliza was making up Ruxton's bed on one occasion, she found a heavy service pistol under his pillow.

On another occasion, Eliza witnessed a scene similar to the one Vera Shelton saw. Eliza rushed into Isabella's room one night when her name was called. Ruxton had his hands around his wife's throat and she was making strangling sounds. Ruxton told the young servant to get out as it was a matter between him and his wife.

The strangest aspect of the Ruxtons' relationship was how quickly they put such violent domestic quarrels behind them. No sooner had Ruxton threatened Isabella with a knife than he was contrite, charming and affectionate again and Isabella appeared to return to her normal self. Vera Shelton remembered on one occasion following a violent row they went for a drive in the car, 'the best of friends'.

But this apparent happiness never lasted long. The same toxic cycle would start over.

On one occasion Ruxton wrote in his diary that Isabella had a 'violent temper and is somewhat selfish'. After one of their fallings-out, he went to his study to calm down. He took up his diary and let the emotion pour forth in a great tidal wave. He wrote down the stinging words he claimed Isabella hurled at him. He wrote that Isabella had spat the following at him: 'I pity your poor mother. God pity her. She could not really suffer such a son. She deserves a gold medal for having suffered you as such. I would not weep for you when you die, even if you were a prince.' Isabella had then dashed up the stairs, Ruxton claimed, and locked herself in the bathroom. She would not come out; Ruxton tried to coax her out. She shouted at him that she was going to commit suicide. 'I was distracted,' Ruxton wrote in desperation in his diary.

Often the source of their arguments was lack of money. Worries over their finances weighed heavily on Ruxton. He noted in his diary:

> Gas bill for quarter came from the Corporation. I told Belle to be economical. Thereupon she got excited, and called me names. 'Rotten hypocrite' she said twice, and wanted to go away from me. She said, 'I do not wish to be reconciled this time,' and threatened to sue me for maintenance.

The following day, Isabella took Ruxton's chloroform bottle from his dispensary and went to the bedroom. She inhaled the mixture, and turned on the gas.

'Our maid,' Ruxton wrote, 'came and told me that something was wrong. All day I fought for her life.'

Ruxton was shaken by Isabella's latest suicide attempt.

Once she recovered she told him that she did not feel safe in his company. He replied that she was free to leave and go wherever she wished.

'However, I here and now place on record,' he wrote, 'the fact that although we might appear to live a cat and dog life, actually I worship my Belle, and at times we are very happy.'

Two days after he wrote this, Isabella went into their bedroom to speak to him. Ruxton perhaps thought she had come with her decision and feared she intended leaving him. She got on her knees and kissed his feet. Then she told him she was sorry for everything hurtful that she had said to him.

Within two days they were quarrelling again. 'She has threatened to make me "the talk of England",' Ruxton wrote. He claimed she criticised him over the cost of the Dalton Square practice. Their rows now flared up over the most trivial things. One was over who drove the car. 'She has thrown a flowerpot at me, a knife and a chair,' he told his diary.

Things could not continue at such a fever pitch. They needed a break from each other. It had worked for them before. So Isabella and the children went to stay with her sister, Jeanie Nelson, in Edinburgh.

It appeared to do the trick. She wrote to him:

> My dearest, beloved Bommie, I have an angel husband, and I am very grateful for it, but no matter whether you are angel or devil, I love you and will continue to love you lifelong.
>
> Dear, how I miss you. If my heart had been literally taken from my body and grafted to yours, I could not belong to you more completely.

There was a strange, poisonous bond between them, a mix of Ruxton's controlling personality and Isabella's inability to break free from him.

Ruxton wrote back that he would come to visit her in Edinburgh. She responded:

> My dearest, beloved Bommie, – I shall be at the station hours before time, and thinking all sorts of loving things. I want to take you in my arms again. I say here, with my hand on my heart, that I never have anything but the most tender feelings in the world for you.

Before his visit, Ruxton wrote to her, 'My beloved, faithful, and virtuous better-half. My pride and pretensions soar high when I read your letters. I want to assure you that I shall always keep an honourable manhood for you, and a stainless name free from shame for my Belle.'

She responded:

> My darling Bommie, I pray for you earnestly each night. Please keep a brave heart. I am not ignorant of your sacrifices or of how hard you work, or the circumstances or the conditions you work under.
>
> Very soon we will be united again, and then we three – you and I and our baby – will be so happy. We must indeed be grateful to the Almighty for our great gift of mutual love and understanding of each other.

After the heartache of the stillborn baby boy, she was expecting another child.

She wrote to Ruxton:

Each day our love matures, and becomes more beautiful. Surely it is a great blessing to feel we can trust each other in every way. That is not the happy lot of many.

Think of the winter of our lives, when sisters and brothers have their own interests, and perhaps we have lost touch with all old friends; when we are too worn and tired to turn round and seek new companionships: when the world generally has finished with us – what concerns are left then?

That is the time when 'Bommie' and Belle will draw up the chairs comfortably to a nice coal fire in a quaint wee cottage, sigh contentedly, and smile into each other's eyes – faded perhaps with the passing years, but still bright with fond love for each other.

Surely Bommie will then say to Belle, 'Belle, you were the sweetest girl in the race of life for me, and I did well to choose you for my own'.

And Belle will say in reply to Bommie: 'Well, Bommie, you certainly took a great risk in betting on me, but you gave that girl a supernatural confidence in herself. Without that confidence she would have stumbled and fallen before reaching heart's delight'.

Now, dear, don't think I am off my head writing all this. It is midnight, but I love you – Your loving Belle.

William Ruxton was born at 2 Dalton Square on 20 July 1933, a brother for Elizabeth and Diana. They called him 'Billy-Boy'.

Ruxton, besotted with his daughters, felt the family was complete. He and Isabella had a son to shower yet more love on. Elizabeth and Diana would have been transfixed by the crying bundle that dominated their mother's attention.

That autumn there would be another arrival at the Ruxton home.

Seventeen-year-old Mary Jane Rogerson was from Morecambe, the nearby seaside town. In October 1933 she began working as the Ruxtons' live-in nursemaid.

Her fate was sealed the moment she crossed the threshold of 2 Dalton Square.

MARY

The first thing you noticed about Mary Jane Rogerson was her smile. It radiated her kind and gentle personality. Everyone who knew her noticed it. She was a sincere and uncomplicated young woman on the cusp of life.

She was born in October 1915 at Overton, a village across the River Lune from Lancaster, close to the port of Heysham, where you could take a passenger ferry to the Isle of Man. Mary was born into a large family, not untypical for the day – she had eleven siblings. Her mother died when Mary was young. Nevertheless, she was doted on by her father, James, and stepmother Jessie.

She was not tall, standing 5ft, had light brown hair and blue eyes. Her stepmother would later say Mary had a 'slight glide' in one of her eyes, a condition that might also be described as a lazy eye.

The Rogersons lived at 139 Thornton Road in Morecambe. Things must have been a squeeze for Mr and Mrs Rogerson with a family of twelve and lodgers to accommodate in a small, stone end-of-terrace house, which was five minutes from the promenade and two minutes from the town's parish church.

Working as a nursemaid to the three Ruxton children meant Mary lived-in at Dalton Square. She visited her parents in Morecambe once a week, arriving religiously every Sunday with her dirty washing for stepmother Jessie. Later in the day she would return to the Ruxton home with clean clothes and a large bundle of newspapers that had been left lying around the Rogerson home by lodgers.

She soon adjusted to the routine and rhythm of Dalton Square, which was governed by the hustle and bustle of Ruxton's surgery and the comings and goings of patients. She was a small cog among many, keeping the well-oiled Ruxton machinery in motion.

As the days and weeks went by, Mary settled into life in Lancaster and became a popular figure around the town, often carrying out chores for Ruxton or Isabella.

Isabel Fryers, who worked at the palatial Co-operative store in the centre of Lancaster, often served Mary and would always remember the teenager as a sweet girl who 'wouldn't hurt a flea'.

Isabella got along famously with Mary, entrusting the teenager with the children, who loved her gentle manner. Mary served refreshments at Isabella's children's parties at Dalton Square. Elizabeth Ruxton was now almost six and had lots of young friends who came to play. These included the two Jackson children from number 13 Dalton Square. Their mother, Mrs Ethel Jackson, would walk them across the square to the Ruxton house. The parties were popular and Isabella made good friends with the mothers of the children who attended, and they later remembered her good humour and vivacious personality.

Theirs might have been a love–hate relationship, but there was never any question that Ruxton and Isabella doted on the children. Ruxton called them his 'wee mites'.

Most evenings before evening surgery, the doctor walked hand in hand with the girls to a nearby sweetshop. There he would let them choose their favourite confections, take some coins from his pocket and pay for a few ounces. They wouldn't forget Billy-Boy and would bring him back some treat.

One of Ruxton's patients, Miss Bessie Philbrook, became a trusted friend of the doctor and Isabella. She occasionally went to Dalton Square to take Elizabeth, Diana and Billy-Boy out for a walk. The Ruxtons gradually built up a large network of friends and acquaintances to whom they could turn in a time of need.

Despite these sunnier aspects of family life, the darkness was never far away.

Isabella's rhapsodic letters from Edinburgh might have temporarily lifted Ruxton's spirits and placed a sticking plaster over their ruptured relationship, but the bad times very quickly returned. 'Hardly is the ink dry on such letters before we are quarrelling again,' he confided in his diary.

Fastidious and precise, Ruxton was critical of Isabella's domestic conduct. 'I must write here,' he noted, 'that Belle is very untidy, and I reproached her with a reminder that her mother would not be proud.' Isabella was angry at being told this and, through tears, retorted: 'Those who talk of high birth and upbringing have, perhaps, not had a good upbringing themselves.'

In the spring Ruxton wrote: 'Belle has acquired an extraordinary craze. She has been chloroforming herself without any knowledge, and been very ill as a result. Her condition was not improved by the news her mother had died.'

One night, Ruxton went up to the children's room at the top of the house. He looked in on them, 'quite by accident'. Elizabeth, Diana and Billy-Boy were fast asleep.

'I found the gas-iron turned on and escaping into the children's room,' Ruxton wrote. 'I was just in time. A few minutes more and they would have been gassed where they lay in innocent sleep.'

He confronted Isabella, in a rage, and reproached her.

She did not care, she told him. She called him a 'dirty pig'.

'I have been unable to discover whether the gas was turned on accidentally or not,' Ruxton scribbled.

A week later Ruxton wrote that their maid had found Isabella lying unconscious in the bedroom. The gas was on again. The maid opened the windows and roused Isabella, saving her life.

'Day and night since then I have been on guard watching my Belle to prevent any attempt on her own life or the lives of the children,' he wrote. 'And I even went down to the cellar and turned the gas off at the main.'

The strain in the family home was palpable. Again Isabella decided to take a trip to Edinburgh for a break. This time the separation did not serve to remind her of her love for Ruxton.

He wrote in his diary:

Belle said that her love for me was not only lost, but that she now hated me. Again, I found the gas on in the children's room. On remonstrating with Isabella she said that her mind was taken off major things because I was fussy in little matters. What an impertinent excuse. She said she could not get on with my nature and threw the soup at me. God grant her sense! Amen!

Another entry read, 'Belle has said to me "I am going to ruin you. A doctor is a doctor everywhere in the world. I will expose you and destroy you. I will give you a shock. Go away before I murder you".'

He was concerned by what people would think. 'How can I possibly build up the practice in Lancaster, bring little children into the world and attend to the woes and hurts of other people?'

As 1934 dawned, another figure was to enter the Ruxtons' circle, triggering the chain of events that would lead to murder.

INTERLOPER

Robert Edmondson was a young solicitor at the Town Hall in Dalton Square. Known to all as Bobby, he was handsome and slim, and looked like a matinee movie idol with his dark, oiled-back hair. He dressed smartly in suit, tie and fedora hat and no doubt turned heads when he walked through the square to work in the town clerk's department of Lancaster Corporation.

He was a decade younger than Ruxton and Isabella, so it is likely that his parents first met the Indian doctor and his Scottish wife at an evening event, perhaps a dinner dance, in the Town Hall, where the well-to-do and influential members of society fluttered like moths round a flame. Bobby and his sister, Barbara, were soon introduced and the Ruxtons and Edmondsons became firm friends. Bobby and Barbara were regular social visitors to the Ruxton home. The ever sociable Isabella, in particular, became close to the younger Edmondsons.

Soon Ruxton's jealousy began to rise up inside him. Scenarios whirred in his mind like a cinema projector. He still could not shake thoughts of Isabella with Van Ess. Now there was a new, much younger man on the scene.

It did not help that there were whispers on the cobbled streets of Dalton Square that Isabella was a 'tramp' and a man-eater. Stories circulated of her cheating on the respected doctor; these stories would be passed down through generations of families, no doubt distorted by the mangle of time and faltering memories. Yet there was no evidence to damn Isabella, other than Ruxton's own accusations.

As usual, Ruxton kept a record of Isabella's apparent transgressions in his diary.

On Wednesday, 4 April, Isabella went out to a dance without Ruxton. He was not happy. That night he frantically scribbled his grievances in barely legible writing, spilling over onto Thursday. He wrote:

Isabella's dance. I worked for her the whole day. I even promised to stand by her in case of any financial loss. In return for this, she, whilst going to this dance, asked 'Am I to wait on you?['] instead of saying something like this:- 'Bommie dear I am waiting on you and wish us life together.' She went herself and did not even care to ask me to join later.

His wounded pride was seared into the diary, the ink branded into the paper with a white-hot anger. Ruxton no doubt sat stewing at home, dwelling on poisonous thoughts, waiting for her to return, waiting to confront her. He continued:

When she came home, she told me she did not dance a single dance. I made inquiries and found out she danced nearly the whole time. I even confronted her before two men with whom she danced.

When I said I was heart broken she said 'I do not care what you are. I am so disgusted with you'.

On the same page, Ruxton's obsession with Van Ess appeared to rear its head. The jealousy dripped off the page: 'When I asked Isabella … she ultimately admitted that she did sleep with him in this same bed but no misconduct took place.' It is likely to have been a reference to the Dutch sailor.

He concluded the diary entry thus: 'She said "He did push me and kiss me but no real actual sexual intercourse took place." She lived with him only for a week.'

Ruxton was not pacified.

He lost his temper.

He lashed out at Isabella.

The following day, Friday, 6 April, Isabella went to the police station across Dalton Square. She wished to lodge a complaint of attempted assault against Ruxton, she told officers. Detective Sergeant Walter Stainton went to look for Ruxton and found him in his car; he asked the doctor to come to the police station. When Ruxton saw Isabella there with the officers, he 'flew into a violent passion', according to Stainton, and told the detectives, 'My wife has been unfaithful. I will be justified in murdering her.'

It is not clear which man Ruxton meant, but it could have been Bobby Edmondson.

Stainton tried to pacify Ruxton and advised the doctor, 'Why don't you give a good hiding to that man?'

Ruxton wrote in his diary, 'I told the police all about her affairs with other men, whereupon Inspector [Thomas] Clark said "Nobody is more sorry for you than I am."

'Detective [William] Thompson said "Dr, I know you are heart broken but forgive and forget".'

Isabella threatened to leave Ruxton and go to Edinburgh, but changed her mind as the situation was defused by the officers. Ruxton claimed in his diary: 'in [the] presence of Detective Thompson [she] promised not to have anything to do with that man'.

No charge was brought against Ruxton. Were Isabella's allegations taken seriously by the police? The detectives' comments would suggest they were dismissed and Ruxton seen as the injured party in the incident.

The Ruxtons took several newspapers each week from newsagents in Lancaster, including the *News of the World* and the *Sunday Graphic*. They liked to keep abreast of domestic and international news. Then, as now, crime and punishment was a staple of these titles. Reporters sat each day in courts up and down the land, filing copy about salacious and shocking cases. Newspapers sold in the millions often on the back of such tawdry and tragic tales. The cases of Jack the Ripper and Dr Crippen were still in living memory and had appalled and thrilled newspaper readers in equal measure.

This was the golden age of detective fiction, and the queen of crime writers was Agatha Christie. She had enjoyed a decade of success and had been the subject of press fascination herself when she went missing in 1926. Her whereabouts became a national obsession, with newspapers asking: 'Where is Mrs Christie?' Papers printed grainy photographs of police searching ditches for the bestselling author of the Poirot and Miss Marple mysteries. Mrs Christie eventually turned up at the Swan Hotel at Harrogate in north Yorkshire, seemingly having suffered from a bout of memory loss. Much, much later it emerged that she had wanted to escape her failing marriage.

The year of 1934 was a fruitful one for Mrs Christie. She published six of her crime novels, including her most famous: *Murder on the Orient Express*. It featured her famous Belgian detective, Hercule Poirot. Her prolific writing often fed off real events and cases she read about in the newspapers. In particular, she was no doubt gripped that summer like the rest of the country by a bizarre case in Brighton, a resort on the south coast of England.

Two unrelated but equally gruesome murders would become known as the Brighton trunk murders. Central to the second murder was a brilliant English barrister called Norman Birkett. By the end of 1934, he was the most famous legal counsellor in the land.

As Dr Buck Ruxton sat in his Dalton Square drawing room reading about Birkett, he could hardly have known he would be calling on his services a little over a year later.

THE BRIGHTON TRUNK MURDER CASE

In the early hours of Tuesday, 18 July 1934, plain-clothes police officers recognised a man walking from London to Maidstone in Kent fitting the description of Toni Mancini, a 26-year-old petty criminal and pimp.

The whole of the country, it seemed, was looking for Mancini.

He stood 5ft 10in tall and his sallow skin, black slicked-down hair, scarred lip and cast in one eye made him a distinctive figure. The small-time crook had used many aliases in his time, including Antoni Pirillie, Luigi Mancini, Hyman Gold and Jack Notyre. Realising they had the most wanted man in Britain, the police took him to Brighton, where Mancini was charged with murder. Mancini's response was 'All I can say, sir, is that I am not guilty.'

Later, hundreds of people swirled outside Brighton's police court, many dressed in beach clothes and swimwear – it was the height of summer in the seaside resort – all desperate for a glimpse of the suspect. As Mancini was bundled into the court, the crowd booed and hissed. The scene reminded one senior police officer of the long-gone days of public executions.

A huge line of people waited in the hope of a place in the public gallery, but once it reached its capacity of sixty, most were turned away disappointed.

Court proceedings lasted precisely seven minutes.

Mancini was listed on the charge sheet as Jack Notyre, one of his aliases. He was charged as follows: feloniously, wilfully and of malice aforethought did kill and murder one Violet Saunders between May 7 and 15.

Court clerk Mr A.G. Walker called out: 'Jack Notyre.'

A stir in the public gallery. A few in the crowd, all women, stood to get a glimpse of Mancini as he stepped into the dock from the cells below, flanked by two guards. Police officers in the public gallery cried 'order!' and 'sit down'.

Mancini was dressed in a grey flannel shirt under a blue serge jacket and was tieless. His hands clasped the wooden rail of the dock. The two guards towered over his slight frame. The police applied for a remand of eight days to allow for further investigation. Mancini did not take his eyes off the string of officers who spoke before the court. The chairman of the magistrates granted the remand until Thursday, 26 July, and told Mancini he would remain in custody.

Mancini gave a quick glance around the court before stepping from the dock down the staircase that led to the cells below. His two towering jailers accompanied him.

The country was gripped and appalled by the events in Brighton that summer. The town was nicknamed the 'queen of slaughtering places' because of the two bizarre and, as it would turn out, unrelated killings forever known as the Brighton trunk murders. Toni Mancini was a person of interest to police in both cases.

The unsettling chain of events began on Wednesday, 6 June 1934, Derby Day, one of the most important dates in the horse-racing calendar.

Somebody deposited a pristine travel trunk in the left-luggage office of the handsome three-storey Italianate-style Brighton railway station. There the plywood trunk sat for eleven days until, on 17 June, baggage attendant William Joseph Vinnicombe noticed a ghastly smell emanating from the unclaimed luggage. Suspecting something terrible was inside, the station baggage attendant felt it was not his place to investigate any further. The trunk was removed to Brighton police station. When it was eventually opened, police officers recoiled in horror. Inside was the mutilated torso of a woman wrapped in brown paper and tied with a window sash cord. The head, arms and legs were all missing. Written on the brown paper in blue pencil was 'ford'. The front part of the word was obscured by blood that had seeped through the paper. Police were perplexed. The trunk had clearly been bought expressly for the purpose of concealing the body.

Police put out a nationwide appeal to railway stations for left-luggage staff to prepare for further gruesome discoveries; they suspected the killer would deposit the remaining body parts elsewhere. The police's hunch proved correct and shortly after a second travel trunk was discovered at King's Cross station in London. It too was starting to stink. Inside, police found two legs and severed feet.

All the body parts were, like the Brighton discovery, wrapped in brown paper.

Sir Bernard Spilsbury, the Home Office pathologist, conducted the post-mortem, noting that 'dismemberment [was] performed by a person with some, though not expert, appreciation of anatomy'.

When Spilsbury arrived in Brighton on Sunday, 15 July, following discovery of another trunk at 52 Kemp Street, near to Brighton railway station, gossip circulated in the town that it contained the missing head and arms of the poor woman in the first trunk.

The rumours were wrong.

Inside the black trunk was the body of an altogether different woman. This would become known as the second Brighton trunk murder.

Toni Mancini had been interviewed over the original 17 June trunk murder when Brighton police were working through their list of missing women and pursued the name of 42-year-old Violette Kaye, who was known to associate with Mancini. He was well known to police as a small-time petty crook who pimped for a number of prostitutes. He had a Mediterranean look but was in fact English and his real name was the rather less exotic Cecil Lois England.

Mancini had given police a description of her and told them she had left him.

Violette Kaye was ruled out as the victim whose torso was found in the left-luggage office as she was the wrong age.

Police had no idea when they dropped Mancini from their inquiries that his name and that of Violette Kaye would crop up again so soon afterwards.

24

DERBY DAY

Ruxton flicked through the racing pages of his newspaper, scanning the names of the horses, hoping for a flash of inspiration.

It was Wednesday, 6 June. Derby Day, the Epsom Derby, held in Surrey in the south of England. One of the highlights of horse racing's calendar. It was also the day that the first trunk had been deposited in the left-luggage office at Brighton railway station.

Ruxton was at home in Lancaster. He was an avid gambler, a passion he shared with Isabella, and he did not like to do things by halves. Today could be his lucky day and he did not want to miss out. He had over £100 ready to bet. All he needed were the right horses.

Ruxton studied the papers closely for each horse's form. In his diary he had noted three names for consideration: Windsor Lad, Easton and Columber, and by this latter name he scrawled a question mark. Underneath these he wrote:

I (Rajpipla)
II (Lord Woolay?)
III (Lord Glanley)

These names were those of the horses' owners. Rajpipla was the Maharaja of Rajpipla, a state in India during the British Raj.

The bookmakers' favourite of the nineteen runners was Colombo (Ruxton had it misspelled in his diary), which had won the 2000 Guineas in May. Windsor Lad was 15 to 2 joint second favourite.

Isabella also kept an eye on form and on that day she was travelling to Edinburgh to collect the children from relatives, where they had been staying. As she left, she had advised Ruxton to switch his money from Easton to her tip, a horse called Medieval Knight. She always had the knack of stirring Ruxton's passions and emotions. Her parting advice 'drove me crazy', Ruxton later confided in his diary.

At the last minute he switched his wager – £122 – persuaded by his wife. The tip, if successful, would give him a major pay day.

A crowd of up to 500,000 cheering and screaming punters watched the race on a dull day at Epsom, which had begun with sunshine. In keeping with tradition, there was a royal party in attendance, including the King and Queen, the Prince of Wales, the Duke and Duchess of York, the Princess Royal and the Duke of Gloucester. The monarch, George V, in particular, was a horse-racing fanatic. It was his horse, Anmer, that had killed suffragette Emily Davison twenty-one years earlier at the 1913 Derby at Epsom, when Davison stepped onto the racecourse as the horses and their mounts rounded Tattenham Corner, the final bend before the home straight.

Ruxton must have sat tensely listening to the race on his wireless. Meanwhile, Isabella was on the Edinburgh train, no doubt awaiting news of the Derby winner.

The nineteen horses and their riders braced themselves at the start, hooves clomping the earth and snorts like engine steam filling the air. Eyes were on the favourites Easton, Colombo, and Windsor Lad. The crack of the starting pistol sent the horses and their mounts hurtling at a great pelt, sods of earth fizzing through the air.

Ruxton may have gripped the arm of his seat.

Belting down the hill towards Tattenham Corner, Tiberius took the lead, pursued furiously by Windsor Lad, Easton, Primero, Colombo, and Patriot King. Windsor Lad edged forward and took the lead from Tiberius shortly after passing Tattenham Corner, with Easton in second place, just in front of Colombo.

Into the final furlong, and Windsor Lad was too far in front to be caught by either Easton or Colombo, and it was the Maharaja's Windsor Lad that romped home the unexpected winner, with Easton and Colombo second and third respectively, and Tiberius, the early leader, fourth.

Ruxton's horse, Medieval Knight, was an also-ran. Hopes of a big win were dashed.

He was stunned. He later wrote in his diary that Isabella learned of Windsor Lad's success – and therefore her husband's loss – on the train. One can only imagine her emotions at the prospect of coming home to his dark mood.

Ruxton had bet £122 on his chosen horses. In all, he lost £117. For the doctor with money troubles it was a disaster.

In his diary that night he wrote: 'Best lesson taught in my life.'

The identity of the woman in the trunk left at Brighton railway station on Derby Day remains a mystery to this day.

Police were luckier with the body found at 52 Kemp Street, however. The entire body had been secreted in the trunk, found at the foot of a bed. The dead woman was confirmed as Violette Kaye, the 42-year-old dancer and prostitute police had questioned Toni Mancini about earlier in the summer.

Mancini was in the frame. A full-scale manhunt began, which led to his eventual arrest in south London and court appearance in Brighton. The case was indicted for trial at Sussex Assizes in Lewes in December.

Mancini's solicitor knew it would take a remarkable barrister to convince a jury of his client's innocence.

He knew exactly the right person.

ENTER BIRKETT

Violette Kaye's real name was Violet Watts and she was sometimes known by the name Saunders, the name used in the murder charge levelled at Mancini. She had used the Kaye name when she was a professional dancer in London. When the work was thin, she also dabbled in prostitution. Mancini first met her in the capital. Despite their age difference – she was sixteen years older – there was an attraction between them. Both were living lives of deception, hiding behind false names, no doubt to evade the authorities. Perhaps that was one of the things that pulled them together.

In the autumn of 1933 they moved to Brighton, living together at a variety of addresses. When there was no work for either, Kaye would turn to prostitution, often supporting both of them from the proceeds. In 1934, Mancini secured work as a waiter at a Brighton café called the Skylark. It was a week before Violette went missing.

On 10 May, Kaye and Mancini had a violent row. She had been drinking heavily and accused him of flirting with a young waitress called Elizabeth Attrell at the Skylark. In the account he would later give in court, Mancini said Violette left after the argument. When he later returned to their basement flat at Park Crescent, he found her dead. He said that other men were frequent visitors of Violette and he believed one of them had murdered her.

He claimed he did not alert police because they would not believe him due to his own criminal background. In a state of panic, he had bought a new trunk and bundled Violette's body into it.

Then he had hauled the trunk to the address in Kemp Street.

The Epsom Derby had left Ruxton with money troubles.

The day after, Thursday, 7 June, he borrowed £100 from a Miss Webster, according to his diary. The next day, Friday, 8 June, he borrowed a further £33 from another friend.

These were considerable sums of money. Did he speak to Isabella about the loans? He did not relate whether he did in his diary.

He might have 'learned the lesson of his life', but it did not deter him from more gambling. On Tuesday, 31 July, he wrote: 'Backed Figaro on advice of Alec Norman [an acquaintance]. Placed a bet … £1 win and £1 placed. Got cheque for £17. Figaro came (14-1).'

And on Wednesday, 12 September, he noted: 'Backed Windsor Lad.' He had learned his lesson since the Derby, putting his faith in Windsor Lad and jockey Charlie Smirke. The race this time was the St Ledger and Ruxton's punt was rewarded when Windsor Lad won, making him one of the sensations of 1934.

Mancini's solicitor wanted Norman Birkett KC to defend his client at trial but there was one problem. Assize courts were held at least twice a year, presided over by judges. The counties of England and Wales were organised into circuits where cases were heard. Judges and barristers generally worked on set circuits. Birkett was not assigned to the Sussex Assizes circuit.

Birkett's agent travelled to Brighton to discuss the case with Mancini's solicitor. To navigate the problem, he would expect 50 guineas, plus a 100-guinea special fee and a daily 'refresher' of 10 guineas. A guinea was £1 and 1*s*. Birkett could expect to pocket a sizeable sum for the few days the trial would last.

The deal was done, the agent and the solicitor shook hands and, as the agent was leaving, he said, 'It's going to be a hard fight, isn't it?'

Mancini's solicitor, with complete faith in Birkett, replied, 'Yes, pretty difficult, but I'm certain we shall get a verdict.'

The *Western Daily Press* reported on Tuesday, 23 October that 'Mr Norman Birkett KC has accepted the brief for the defence of Jack Notyre (otherwise Toni Mancini) who is on remand charged with the murder of Violette Kaye, the victim of Brighton Trunk Mystery No 2.'

Norman Birkett was often likened to a bird, with his long, thin, beak-like face, and his habit of hunching his shoulders and folding his arms like wings in front of him as he spoke.

Miss Ellen Wilkinson, a sketch writer for the *Yorkshire Post*, made such a comparison in the Tuesday, 15 April 1930 edition. She said of Birkett, 'a man who can use his eyebrows as Norman Birkett does is a loss to the comic stage'. She continued, 'His voice is as musical as his choice of language is perfect. Always the correct pause at the comma and period, till I find myself unconsciously beating time as strong beat follows weak in regular six-eights. Not a moment's hesitation, never a halt for a word.' Miss Wilkinson gently mocked Birkett for having auburn hair (which she admitted to having, too), indicating that this fiery red colour led some to discount him as a serious orator. The piece was published at a time when Birkett was a regular speaker in Parliament as the MP for Nottingham East, a position he held in tandem with his legal practice.

Birkett was born in 1883 in Ulverston, a Lancashire town on the edge of the Lake District. Coincidentally, another red-haired boy was born in the town seven years later who did go on to the comic stage and was noted for using his eyebrows to great humorous effect: Stan Laurel. Birkett originally planned to become a Methodist minister and studied history and theology at Cambridge. He soon established a reputation as a powerful orator and impressed former American President Theodore Roosevelt, who was receiving an honorary degree from the university, with his speech to the Cambridge Union Society. When he turned away from plans of going into the Church, Birkett focused on becoming a barrister. While he prepared to take the bar exam, he worked as the personal secretary to George Cadbury junior, of the famous chocolate-manufacturing family, whose empire resided at the purpose-built community of Bournville near Birmingham. It was here that Birkett met his future wife, Ruth Nilsson. They were married in 1920 and had a daughter and a son, Linnea and Michael.

Despite his skill and talent in the courtroom during often gruesome and upsetting trials, Birkett was essentially a sensitive man, prone to dwell on courtroom exchanges and often being left upset, where perhaps other barristers might have been unmoved. One particularly sad and distressing case from his days as a junior barrister was heard at Lancaster Assizes, which were held in the castle, also the place where the Pendle witches were tried. The case involved a young mother who had suffocated her baby within moments of its birth. Today the court would treat this sensitively as a case of post-natal depression and deal with it appropriately. But in Birkett's early career, the judge directed the jury to convict the mother of murder, which they did. She was sentenced to be hanged.

Birkett could never shake from his memory the following scene. It still haunted him decades later and he recounted it in interviews just prior to his death in the 1960s.

The young mother, after being told she would be hanged by the neck until she was dead, began to moan and had to be carried out of the dock screaming, 'I am very sorry – I didn't intend doing it.'

Now Birkett faced what seemed like a huge challenge of defending a man everybody believed to be guilty: Toni Mancini.

26

MANCINI IN THE DOCK

Toni Mancini's trial opened at Lewes Winter Assizes on Monday, 10 December 1934. He was appearing under the name Jack Notyre.

The judge was Mr Justice Branson. Appearing for the Crown were Mr J.D. Cassels KC and Quintin Hogg, who would many years later become well known as Lord Hailsham. Representing Mancini was Birkett, with support from John Flowers KC and Eric Neve.

The expectation among legal people and the general public, though not stated in newspapers, was that Mancini would be found guilty. How could it be otherwise? He was a known criminal, who had been living with Violette Kaye and sponging off her earnings as a prostitute. Most damning of all, however, was the fact he had admitted knowing that she was dead all the while telling police that she had left him. He had also admitted to putting her body into the trunk.

Mancini's fate rested in the hands of one man, Norman Birkett, who was at the time, in legal circles at least, considered one of the finest criminal advocates in the land.

The court heard that the victim's sister, Olive Watts, had received a telegram the day after Violette went missing, that read: 'Going abroad. Good job. Sail Sunday. Will write. Vi.' It was handwritten in block capitals. A handwriting expert determined that the message bore a remarkable similarity to the hand that had written menus at the Skylark café in Brighton.

Those menus had been written by Toni Mancini.

On 14 May, Mancini, with the help of another man called Capelin, had moved his belongings on a hand-truck from Park Crescent to a basement

flat he had taken at Kemp Street, a slum area near the railway station. Chief among his effects was a large trunk.

Mancini had told witnesses he had left Violette – they were not getting along any more; he said she was constantly nagging him. Now she had gone to Montmartre in Paris, he said, and also bragged that he had beaten her, giving her a good hiding. To one witness, Mancini asked what was the point of beating a woman with your fists when using a hammer prevented you from injuring yourself? Police found a burnt hammerhead among rubbish at Park Crescent.

The large, mystery trunk, with large metal cup handles, had sat undisturbed in Mancini's basement room at 52 Kemp Street for the next two months.

The court heard how Mancini's landlady questioned him about the strange liquid running from the trunk in his room. He told her it was French polish.

On 15 July, police had questioned Mancini about Violette in relation to the first Brighton trunk murder, but he had successfully convinced them the body was not hers. Immediately after, he returned to his lodgings, packed a bag and left. By the following morning he was on the early train to London, having openly bragged in the intervening hours at a local dance hall that Kemp Street and Brighton would be famous.

Shortly afterwards, the stinking trunk in Mancini's room had been broken open by police to reveal the decomposing body of Violette Kaye inside.

Birkett knew the Crown would exploit Mancini's shadowy past. He could try to bury it. Or he could be clever, face it head on and use it to Mancini's advantage. Birkett's best hope was to dismantle the evidence of witnesses who had implicated Mancini.

He challenged the evidence of Capelin, the man who helped Mancini drag the trunk to Kemp Street. In his testimony, Capelin said Mancini told him the deadweight trunk contained china and clothing. Birkett highlighted this evidence, given in open court, pointing out that it contradicted what Capelin had originally told police.

In cross-examination of Capelin, Birkett said, 'I suppose you have read a great deal since then about this case?'

Capelin replied, 'Now and again I have.'

Birkett: 'Do you remember that you said, when you gave evidence before, "Nothing was said as to what was inside it"?'

Capelin: 'I am very sorry. I made a mistake.'

Birkett: 'Which do you mean is true – that nothing was said, or he said that there was china and clothes inside?'

Capelin: 'I mean nothing was said.'

Birkett's cross-examination of the landlord of Violette's flat at Park Crescent left the jury with the notion that other men were regular visitors. He was building a picture of her as a woman who associated with various men and also worked as a prostitute. He also coaxed the landlord into admitting that Mancini and Violette were always affectionate when he saw them.

The last witness for the Crown had been Sir Bernard Spilsbury, who concluded that Violette Kaye had suffered a depressed fracture of the skull caused by a violent blow with a blunt instrument. To make his point, Spilsbury had used a human skull, resting it on the ledge of the witness box, before producing the actual bone fragment from Violette's skull.

Fearless Birkett challenged Spilsbury in cross-examination and convincingly shook the great forensic pathologist's evidence, leaving the jury with the possibility that Violette Kaye, who was known to take drugs, might have fallen down the basement flat's steps and suffered a fractured skull while intoxicated.

It was time for Birkett to make his closing remarks. He rose from his seat and turned to the twelve men on the jury. 'This case is simply riddled with doubt,' he said.

'This man lived upon her earnings, and I have no word whatever to say in extenuation or justification. None,' he told the jury.

You are men of the world. Consider the associates of these people. We have been dealing with a class of men who pay eightpence for a shirt and women who pay one shilling and sixpence or less for a place in which to sleep. It is an underworld that makes the mind reel. It is imperative that you should have it well in mind that this is the background out of which these events have sprung.

He continued:

Defending counsel has a most solemn duty, as I and my colleagues know only too well. We have endeavoured, doubtless with many imperfections, to perform that task to the best of our ability. The ultimate responsibility – that rests upon you – and never let it be said, never let it be thought, that any word of mine should seek to deter you from doing that which you feel to be your duty. But now that the whole of the matter is before you, I think I am entitled to claim for this man a verdict of Not Guilty. And, members of the jury, in returning that verdict you will vindicate a principle of law, that people are not tried by newspapers, not tried by rumour, but tried by juries called to do justice and decide upon the evidence. I ask you for, I appeal to you for, and I claim from you, a verdict of Not Guilty.

Birkett paused.
    He looked at the jurors one by one.
    The courtroom was silent.
    Birkett spoke, his voice resonating around the room.
    'Stand firm,' he implored the jury.

27

BIRKETT'S REMARKABLE FEAT

Mr Justice Branson gave his final remarks to the jury in his summing-up, which took just under an hour. He told them:

> Can you imagine an innocent man dealing in this way with the woman whom he says he loved? According to him he comes in and finds this woman dead. Not yet cold, but to his idea, dead. Then he put her in the cupboard and nailed it up. What do you think of that as the action of an innocent man?

He continued, 'Give all the weight that you think proper to his statement that having been previously convicted as he was – not of any offence of violence – he felt that he would not get a fair deal from the police and therefore that he must conceal this body.'

The jurors retired to consider their verdict. They were out for the best part of two and a half hours. The court got to its feet when the twelve returned. Mr Justice Branson asked the foreman of the jury if they had reached a verdict. The foreman indicated that they had. The judge asked what their verdict was.

The foreman rose to his feet and announced, 'Not guilty.'

A stunned silence in the courtroom.

Mancini was dazed. He put his hand to his head and newspaper reporters noted that he 'seemed momentarily overcome'. He could not believe the verdict himself. His mother was waiting in a room outside the court. When she heard the news, she was also in disbelief. She told her son, 'Oh, my darling boy. My prayers have all been answered.' And then she fainted.

The first person to congratulate Birkett on his stunning success was Chief Inspector Robert Donaldson, the detective from Scotland Yard who had worked on the case. He shook Birkett's hand vigorously.

Birkett led Mancini and his solicitor into a side room of the court. The newly acquitted Mancini was in utter shock. He struggled to say much, other than 'Not guilty, Mr Birkett? Not guilty, Mr Birkett?'

Birkett, perhaps inwardly surprised at how effective he had been, simply said to Mancini, 'Now go home and look after your mother. She has stood by you and been a brick.'

Birkett was celebrated in the evening newspapers, and one of his legal colleagues, with whom he travelled to and from courts twenty years earlier, wrote in a letter: 'It will rank as one of the great defences in the annals of legal medical records …'

Birkett later commented on the press coverage he received. 'Strangely enough it has given me very little pleasure.' Of Mancini he said, 'He was a despicable and worthless creature.'

Sir Patrick Hastings, one of Britain's finest barristers and also one-time Attorney General (the country's chief legal adviser to the government of the day) under Ramsay MacDonald's Labour government in 1923, paid the most glowing tribute to Birkett's qualities as defence counsel.

Hastings, who knew Birkett well, wrote:

> If it had ever been my lot to decide to cut up a lady in small pieces and put her in an unwanted suitcase, I should without hesitation have placed my future in his hands. He would have satisfied the jury a) I was not there; b) that I had not cut up the lady; c) that if I had she thoroughly deserved it anyway.

A better testimonial could not have been written; Birkett could hardly have known that a year later his services would be called upon in a case whose circumstances were not so far removed from those described by Hastings.

In the aftermath of the sensational trial at Lewes, Toni Mancini became something of a *cause célèbre*.

On Friday, 28 December, a mere fourteen days after his acquittal, the *Daily Independent* reported that he had arrived in Glasgow and would appear at a fun fair and carnival at Stockwell Street in the city. The report also stated that Mancini would be delivering a series of lectures in the 'leading towns of the North and South of England and the Isle of Man under the auspices of Mr Erin A. Deane, Scottish entertainment caterer'.

Accompanying Mancini on the tour was his new bride, Miss Amelia May Wood, who had visited him and 'comforted' him while he was on remand ahead of his trial. They were married secretly at Wandsworth Register Office in London a week after his acquittal.

Nobody else was ever charged over the murder of Violette Kaye.

The story was not finished, however. The punchline would not be known for forty years, by which time, in 1976, Birkett was long dead.

POISONED COFFEE

In the autumn and winter of 1934 the entries in Ruxton's diary became increasingly paranoid over Isabella's friendship with Bobby Edmondson.

Isabella would sometimes accept a lift home from Bobby if she bumped into him at Lancaster's grand public swimming baths on Kingsway. She was usually accompanied by Ethel Anderson, dentist Herbert's wife, and Bobby would gallantly extend the offer of a lift to her too.

Ruxton read all kinds of suspicious sexual motives into Bobby's kindness. Yet his inner turmoil remained just that, internalised, finding expression only in the pages of his sour diary.

On Tuesday, 20 November, Ruxton noted: 'Isabella deliberately and openly went with Mr R. E. to the Palace Cinema, leaving me at home.' Ruxton committed his accusations to the page of his diary. He claimed Isabella said to Edmondson: 'Come on Bobby, we are going to the Palace Cinema.' Ruxton's ire was etched into the page: 'She uttered these words whilst asking Bobby to go with her, in my presence.'

Three days later, on Friday, 23 November, she again went out for the evening. Ruxton wrote, 'Isabella went to the Dance. I went with her and came home after supper. She never followed me but danced with others and came home at 10 minutes to 1 in the morning, though I had left at 10-30 p.m.'

The following day, Ruxton believed Isabella was trying to poison him. He wrote, 'My evening coffee tasted sharp. I immediately told Isabella that my coffee was rather peculiar in taste at bottom of cup. Soon after taking it I felt giddy. She left me alone in the house. I vomited the whole night.'

He wrote that she had deliberately put liquid morphine hydrochloride in his coffee. His pupils had been 'pin-points' after he had drunk it.

The day after that, Sunday, 25 November, Ruxton and Isabella spent the evening with their friends, Dr Anderson and his wife, Ethel, and another couple, the Harrisons.

In his diary, Ruxton added, '… and Bobby'.

Ruxton wrote that during the evening:

> Isabella sat all the time next to Bobby and though she knew I had been
> acutely ill the previous night, she did [not] inquire how I was feeling
> when I was sitting quietly and uninterestedly in a corner … She got up
> and began to dance.
>
> Isabella had a poison formula written in her bag and she asked Richard
> Harrison what was the action of nitroglycerine on the human body.

On Wednesday, 28 November, Ruxton wrote:

> Isabella came to me in the bathroom – saying that the bank manager had
> phoned her up to take some money to the bank to make up the overdraft.
> I gave her £10 in notes.
>
> She went away to Edin [Edinburgh] with it without letting me know.
> I waited and waited. I went to the bank. There was no trace of Isabella.
> She caused me misery and shocked my credit as the bank manager would
> not honour my cheque to the Lancaster Corporation without money.
> I borrowed £25 from Mr Beck.
>
> I felt this sort of treatment very bitterly at heart. I went to Edinburgh.
> I went to make certain inquiries. The servants had wired Isabella that
> I was following her to Edinburgh.
>
> I went to her sister's house and found her there. I went on my knees
> and begged her to go back with me to Lancaster but she refused to come
> home by the midnight train.
>
> <u>Hungry, languid and broken-hearted.</u>
>
> Isabella told a lie in the presence of her sister that she had deposited
> my money.

The following day, Thursday, 29 November, Ruxton wrote, 'Isabella came
home this afternoon.'

Christmas had a balming effect. Ruxton's diary described pleasant family
times, free from acrimony.

On Christmas Eve, he and Isabella held a party at Dalton Square for friends. They invited the Andersons, Jeffersons, Harrisons, Dunderdales and Edmondsons. The festivities lasted until five o'clock on Christmas morning. Ruxton wrote in his diary, 'Poor Isabella was run off her feet dancing, attendance upon visitors and catering for their amusements – My Beloved Belle.'

On Boxing Day, they took the children to a matinee performance of the pantomime *Dick Whittington* at the Winter Gardens on Morecambe's seafront, an elegant theatre touched by the genius of Frank Matcham, designer of the London Palladium.

In the evening Ruxton and Isabella went to a dinner dance at the resplendent Midland Hotel, with bay views to the snow-capped Lakeland hills beyond. The ice-white art deco hotel was less than a year old, resembled an ocean liner and was the hottest ticket for miles. Walking into the grand foyer, they were greeted by splendid Eric Gill sculptures and Eric Ravilious murals. Careless hours were whiled away in the company of Herbert and Ethel Anderson and another couple, Dr and Mrs Garden.

The following morning, the Gardens took tea with the Ruxtons at Dalton Square.

PART FOUR
MURDER

29

A NEW YEAR'S WISH

On Monday, 31 December 1934, Ruxton and Isabella went to celebrate New Year's Eve at the palatial, ivy-clad Elms Hotel at Bare in Morecambe.

They were joined by their friends the Jeffersons and Harrisons for the festive dinner and dance. In the past Thomas Harrison and his wife had visited Blackpool's illuminations with Ruxton and Isabella.

There was another guest who accompanied them: Bobby Edmondson.

The Elms Hotel was 'Morecambe's premier residential hotel', according to its publicity literature. It boasted a 'gentleman's smoke room, cocktail bar, mixed lounge, ample parking space' and four telephone lines primed and ready to take bookings. A decade later the hotel would welcome its most famous guests: Laurel and Hardy, who stayed during a tour of British music halls.

That New Year's Eve in 1934 there was dancing and 'frivolities', as Ruxton put it in his diary. When he and Isabella socialised with friends, they disguised the discord of Dalton Square. Isabella easily relaxed, throwing herself into the spirit of things. Ruxton was charming and charismatic, but below the surface was a smouldering intensity that later seeped into the pages of his diary. His eyes would rarely stray from Isabella; he secretly tracked whom she spoke to and mingled with, storing it away as toxic ammunition. Later, in the family rooms of Dalton Square the scores and slights were turned over, igniting the touch paper to another argument, exploding into theatrics and violence.

The year was coming to an end, the hours running down to the final minutes, the minutes spinning away to the final, last-gasp seconds of 1934. It had been a tumultuous twelve months, he and Isabella were raw but still together, held by the thread of the children.

Once 1935 had been ushered in, Ruxton, Isabella and their friends returned, tired, to Lancaster. At Dalton Square, Ruxton took out his pocket diary to record his final thoughts of the year.

He wrote, 'I was in the ballroom of the Elms at 12 midnight praying for all this world.'

30

1935

And so the curtain rose on the final act in the tragedy of the Ruxtons.

A calm descended over Dalton Square during January 1935; apparently there were no violent arguments, no brushes with the police. It is likely Ruxton and Isabella were emotionally exhausted. Perhaps as an act of conciliation, he paid for a glamorous portrait photograph to be taken of Isabella. It was five years since the oil painting of her that hung in Dalton Square and Ruxton wanted another permanent record of the mother of his children.

On 26 February, Isabella visited the studio of photographer Cecil Thomas at 22 Market Street in Lancaster. She wore a formal dress and a simple tiara. She and Ruxton must have been pleased with Thomas's photograph for it showed her smiling and looking relaxed.

A few short months later it would be splashed across the front pages of newspapers around the world.

The calm at Dalton Square continued, at least outwardly, but the truce between Ruxton and Isabella would not last. By spring, there would be another encounter with the police.

PC Wilson, the officer Ruxton had treated for a broken nose, was on duty at Lancaster police station on the evening of Monday, 27 May. According to Wilson's pocket notebook, he received a telephone message from Mrs Ruxton and called at the Ruxton home across Dalton Square.

He later wrote:

> On arrival I was met by Dr. Ruxton who was in a very excitable state and behaving like a man insane and threatening to commit two murders in Dalton Square tonight. Sergeant [Walter] Stainton then arrived and the Doctor calmed down. But stated his intention to come to the Police

Court on Monday morning and [to apply] for a summons against a man who had enticed away his wife's affections. We then came away leaving all quiet.

The man 'who had enticed away his wife's affections' was Bobby Edmondson.

Ruxton's jealousy was on the rise again.

In June, Ruxton and Isabella took their three children and the son of their friends, the Jeffersons, for a two-week holiday at a small farm in the Lake District.

The Ruxtons had visited the Cottage, whose owner Mrs Edith Holme ran a bed and breakfast business there, twice earlier in the month on day trips from Lancaster. Ruxton drove the first time, while Mr Jefferson followed behind in his own car on the second occasion. The farm was at a small hamlet called Seatle, near Grange-over-Sands, situated on the northern edge of Morecambe Bay. It was an area that Ruxton and Isabella loved to visit, although Ruxton often lost his way, taking lengthy detours.

Ruxton and Isabella did not stay for the two weeks, instead returning to Lancaster, but would visit each Wednesday and on the middle weekend to spend time with the children. They left the nanny, Mary Rogerson, to look after Elizabeth, Diana, Billy and the Jefferson boy. Mary relished the thought of two weeks surrounded by beautiful countryside, away from her duties at Dalton Square. She found the break relaxing, even allowing for little Billy-Boy, whose constant energy could be tiring.

In spare moments she sat at the farmhouse dining table and wrote to family and friends. These letters would become precious in only a matter of three months, providing rare glimpses into the heart and mind of a young woman on the cusp of adulthood, still in the first flush of life. One letter survived. It was written in an awkward blend of formal and informal language. It was addressed to a friend, Margaret Farrer.

'The weather has changed so the children can get out to play without worrying me,' Mary wrote. 'But I am staying this weekend out also and have got Billy to take care of which will mean more running about for me.' She was 'red raw' with sunburn, she wrote, and each night was bathing in buttermilk – no doubt from the farm, provided by Mrs Holme – which, she said, 'is supposed to give you a beautiful complexion "says me"'.

She explained that she had not 'had occasion' to wear a bathing costume which their mutual friend, also called Margaret, had kindly lent her.

Reflecting on the little holiday, Mary wrote: 'You say you don't feel like work, well I suppose you're right, because I don't know how I'll start work myself after such a lazy life.

'Anyhow, we'll just have to buckle into it with our heart and soul.'

After more about a dress Mrs Holme was helping her to make, Mary wound up the letter: 'Well, I must close now because the table is wanted for lunch. Give my love to "Margaret the Cook" [another friend]. Cheerio for now, Mary Rogerson. *Excuse my terrible writing.*'

Mrs Holme was very kind to Mary in those two weeks. As well as helping with Mary's dress, she gave her a pair of child's romper trousers for Billy to wear. They belonged to Mrs Holme's young son, but as the elastic had snapped, she had roughly tied the two pieces together with a distinct knot.

And Mrs Holme probably thought that was the last she would see of the rompers and the knotted elastic. She would be wrong.

But it was the last time she saw Mary Jane Rogerson.

31

SPYING ON THE LOVERS

The great mystery of Ruxton's suspicions about Bobby Edmondson was the fact that he never confronted the young solicitor on the matter. Instead, poisonous thoughts percolated in his mind before exploding into violence with Isabella.

By the autumn of 1935 he was becoming dangerously unhinged. Dark clouds were circling over 2 Dalton Square and Isabella's days on Earth were numbered.

On Saturday, 7 September, Isabella went to Edinburgh with the Edmondsons.

The trip was originally planned for August during school holidays; Isabella had invited Bobby's sister Barbara as the Edmondsons had relatives in Edinburgh. After it fell through, Isabella rearranged the trip and extended the invitation to Barbara's parents, Robert and Isobel, and Bobby was asked along to drive a second car.

The day before, Isabella finalised the arrangements with Bobby in Dalton Square as he strolled to work at the Town Hall.

Just after lunch on Saturday, Isabella drove Ruxton's car to the Edmondsons' home at 4 Ullswater Road, five minutes away. She went into the house and twenty minutes later, accompanied by Mrs Edmondson and Barbara, got back into the car and set off for Edinburgh. With his father in the passenger seat beside him, Bobby followed behind.

They headed north via Morecambe, along the coast road to the railway town of Carnforth and on to Kendal in the Lake District. From there it was a straight run to the Scottish border. They stopped at Penrith for petrol. The party broke their journey again just over the Scottish border at Gretna Green, famous for its blacksmith's where eloping lovers fled to get married.

The motorcars pushed on north to Moffat, where they made another stop, passed near the Devil's Beef Tub, before cutting eastwards, where they stopped at Penicuik a few miles south of the Scottish capital.

As Isabella's and Bobby's cars motored into Edinburgh they were unaware they had been followed.

In another car, a Morris Oxford hired from a garage in Morecambe, Ruxton had trailed them from Lancaster. Consumed with jealousy and suspicion, he believed Isabella had orchestrated the trip to sleep with Bobby in a hotel in Edinburgh.

32

ROOM 49

Plans to stay with Bobby's relatives evaporated as Mr Edmondson's aunt was unwell. Using her local knowledge, Isabella booked them all into the Adelphi Hotel in Leith, a couple of miles north of Edinburgh Old Town. Leith was, of course, where she had met Ruxton when she was manager of a cafeteria. The Adelphi was a smart Georgian stone building overlooking spectacular Calton Hill and close to Arthur's Seat. They booked four rooms, one for Mr and Mrs Edmondson, one for Barbara, one for Bobby and one for Isabella. Each signed the guestbook, Isabella as Mrs Ruxton. Then they carried their luggage to their rooms: Bobby to room 44; Isabella, room 49.

The visit was brief. The following day, Sunday, 8 September, Mr Edmondson paid all the room bills and they returned to Lancaster, arriving just after midnight.

Ruxton spent Saturday night in another hotel nearby. Early the following morning he went to the Adelphi. He saw his Hillman Minx parked next to Bobby's car. He went into reception and leafed through the guestbook. He saw Isabella's signature: Mrs Ruxton. He now had all the evidence he needed of Isabella's infidelity.

Isabella had precisely seven days to live.

PART FIVE
THE DEVIL'S PATHOLOGY

33

MURDER IN MIND

The following day, Monday, 9 September, Ruxton saw Bobby in Dalton Square. He stopped the young solicitor for a word. He was friendly towards the young man, betraying none of the anguish he felt. Ruxton asked how the trip to Edinburgh had gone, perhaps showing a little too much interest in who had travelled with him and Isabella, and where they had stayed.

Isabella had told Ruxton she had slept at her sister's house, not at the Adelphi Hotel.

Ruxton may have kept his powder dry for a couple of days, not confronting Isabella with his suspicions of a dalliance with Bobby Edmondson.

But on Friday, 13 September, his cleaner Agnes Oxley overheard the doctor and Isabella quarrelling. She distinctly heard Ruxton call Isabella a prostitute. The doctor sent Mrs Oxley out to dust his car in the alley behind the house. He soon came out to speak to her. He said, 'Oh, Mrs Oxley, she is breaking my heart; talk to her; talk to her, and ask her not to go but stop with her children.' Mrs Oxley said she would. Then Ruxton got in his car and drove off.

The final day in the lives of Isabella Kerr Ruxton and Mary Jane Rogerson dawned on Saturday, 14 September.

Mrs Oxley was engaged in her duties as usual at Dalton Square. Mary worked alongside her in the kitchen.

Ruxton came in and explained that Isabella was going to Blackpool that evening to meet her sisters and see the illuminations. The doctor asked Mary if she would mind staying that night to look after the children. She hesitated. Normally, she would have gone home to Morecambe to see her parents. But, keen to please, she agreed to help the doctor out.

Mrs Oxley finished her work and left at twenty minutes past twelve. She said goodbye to Mary. The young nanny looked well and happy. She would always remember Mary that way.

It would be the last time Mrs Oxley saw her.

At 10.15 that morning, Isabella went to have her hair done by her hairdresser Clara Maureen Grosse, who worked in a salon at Cheapside, a five-minute walk from Dalton Square. For the past two and a half years, she had enjoyed having her hair done two or three times each week. Clara would later note that Isabella had worn her hair long and in a bun until late 1933, after which she wore it in a long bob that curled at the bottom.

Perhaps Mary had been keen to go to her parents' that day because the annual Morecambe carnival was due to take place. As a child she would no doubt have participated in the celebrations. It was a popular event, attracting thousands of visitors, and coverage would feature in the following morning's newspapers, a number of which would be delivered to the Ruxton home. But on this occasion, Mary had agreed to look after the Ruxton children while Isabella was out.

Isabella had made arrangements to visit Blackpool with two of her sisters, Jeanie Nelson and Eleen Madden, and the latter's husband, who were visiting the Lancashire resort from Edinburgh. They had travelled by charabanc.

The trip was something of an annual tradition for the sisters. Blackpool is a seaside resort, 25 miles south-west of Lancaster, on the Fylde coast, and famed for its illuminations, sticks of rock with the name 'Blackpool' running through the middle, and an Eiffel-style tower on the seafront. By 1935, Blackpool had become the most popular Lancashire resort, elbowing aside Morecambe. Its illuminations attracted hundreds of thousands of visitors each autumn. A well-known personality would flick the switch to spark into life the lights, strung like pearls along the promenade. In 1935, they would be turned on by Audrey Mossom, a teen beauty queen from nearby Preston, who would later become a well-known dancer and would meet Joseph Stalin during a peace trip to Russia.

Isabella said goodbye to Ruxton, Mary and the children. Little Elizabeth was playing with the two Jackson children from 13 Dalton Square.

Isabella started the engine of Ruxton's Hillman Minx and drove to Blackpool. She enjoyed a light meal with her family before they went to see the lights on the seafront.

Meanwhile, in Lancaster, at ten past seven Mrs Jackson called at Ruxton's to collect her children. Ruxton opened the door and asked her inside. He called up the stairs to Mary, asking her to bring the children down. Mrs Jackson chatted with the young nanny before taking her children home to 13 Dalton Square.

At 11.30 p.m. after an enjoyable evening, Isabella said goodbye to Jeanie, Eleen and Mr Madden. She told them she would see them the following day, as they had made further arrangements to spend time together. The sisters later recalled that Isabella had been in 'very good spirits'.

Ruxton waited for Isabella to return. Elizabeth, Diana and Billy-Boy, his 'wee mites', had been asleep in the room they shared with Isabella on the top floor of the house for hours. Mary had got them off to bed. She too was in her room on the top floor, no doubt asleep.

It was after midnight on Sunday, 15 September, when Isabella parked the Hillman Minx outside 2 Dalton Square. The Town Hall towered watchfully over the square, twinkling in the lamplight.

Isabella locked the car and walked up to the house.

Nobody saw her. Not even the Queen Victoria statue, which was turned away from the Ruxton home.

Isabella Kerr Ruxton went inside to die.

AFTERWARDS

Isabella and Mary were dead.

Ruxton was at a crossroads. He could tell the police what had happened and admit his guilt. Or he could hide the truth. The former path would lead to the gallows; the latter to a tormented existence, a life spent looking over his shoulder.

The clock was ticking. Two o'clock, three o'clock, four o'clock, five o'clock. Soon it would be light on Dalton Square. Mrs Oxley would arrive to start her chores at ten past seven. Mrs Curwen, the general housekeeper, usually came on Sundays by ten o'clock, but two days earlier, on Friday, 13 September, Ruxton had told her she need not come again until Monday as there was nothing for her to do.

A third charwoman, Mrs Mabel Smith, who had been employed since August, worked at the house only on Mondays, Tuesdays, Wednesdays and Thursdays in the afternoons.

Mrs Oxley was the problem.

Ruxton left the children sleeping, alone in the house. He took the Hillman Minx, still parked where Isabella had left it, and drove to Mrs Oxley's home. It was almost 6.30 in the morning.

Mrs Oxley was in bed when there was a knock at the door. Her husband went downstairs to see who it was. Mrs Oxley, standing on the staircase, recognised the voice of the unexpected caller: it was Dr Ruxton. 'Tell Mrs Oxley not to trouble to come down this morning,' the doctor said. 'Mrs Ruxton and Mary have gone on a holiday to Edinburgh and I am taking the children to Morecambe, but come as usual tomorrow.'

Mrs Oxley had never missed a day's work at Dr Ruxton's; to receive a personal call from him at 6.30 in the morning struck her and her husband as strange.

✢

Miss Winifred Emma Roberts was a little later than usual that Sunday morning.

She worked for Graves's newsagents in Lancaster, delivering newspapers to local homes. It was a job she had done for around five months. Dr Ruxton was a regular customer, taking the *Daily Express* on weekdays and the *News of the World*, *The People* and *Sunday Pictorial* on Sundays. Miss Roberts would normally have delivered his papers at quarter past eight, but on the morning of Sunday, 15 September, Mr Graves had given her a slightly altered delivery route and consequently she arrived later.

The early morning rain had stopped and it was turning into a bright morning. As Miss Roberts approached Ruxton's front door, the Town Hall clock across Dalton Square struck nine o'clock. There was no answer when she rang the bell. She hovered around Dalton Square for ten minutes, within sight of Ruxton's front door, and did not see anybody come or go from the doctor's surgery. When she tried the doorbell again there was still no immediate reply, but eventually the front door was opened. She expected to see Mary Rogerson, Mrs Oxley or Mrs Curwen, as it would normally be one of them.

Dr Ruxton stood before her.

He was dressed in a pale cream shirt and light grey trousers, and had tucked his right hand in close to his body. Miss Roberts initially thought he was holding up his trousers but then she realised he was wearing braces. Something was not right; Ruxton seemed on edge and agitated.

She apologised for disturbing him and asked for payment for the past two weeks of newspapers. He told her that Mary the maid had gone to Scotland with Isabella.

At ten o'clock, Mrs Margaret Maria Hindson arrived with Ruxton's daily delivery of 4 pints of milk. She rang the doorbell and Ruxton answered, which was unusual though not unheard of as he had once or twice let her in if he happened to be in his surgery. The doctor seemed quite normal. He explained that Isabella and Mary had gone away. He also said the children had gone with them. He told Mrs Hindson that he had informed his charlady, Mrs Oxley, who would usually have answered the door, that she was not needed that morning.

The doctor had bandages around his right hand. He told her that he had 'jammed' it.

Mrs Hindson would normally take the milk through to the scullery at the back, but today Ruxton asked her to leave it on the table in the hall.

After Mrs Hindson left, Ruxton got into his stone-coloured Hillman Minx and drove to the Midland Station garage near the town centre railway station at Green Ayre. It was a garage he used from time to time. He was served by 15-year-old William Waite, the son of the garage owner, Herbert Waite. Ruxton paid for two tins of petrol, each holding 2 gallons, but rather than having young Waite put it into the car's petrol tank, he asked for the tins to be put on the front passenger seat of the car.

From there he drove to another garage owned by the similarly named but unrelated John Waites at Nelson Street, around the corner from Dalton Square, where he had a private lock-up to garage the Hillman. Here he paid for a further 4 gallons of petrol, asking the garage hand John Longton, whom he knew, to put the fuel directly into the tank.

Neither John Longton nor William Waite was aware that Ruxton had purchased petrol from the other. Had they known, they might have concluded the doctor was planning a long-distance journey or intended lighting a bonfire.

At quarter past ten, Thomas Partridge called at Ruxton's home. As usual, the front door was open but the inner vestibule door was closed. Partridge was a Lancaster labourer who delivered newspapers on Sundays for another newsagent in the town, Mr Capstick. For the past year Partridge had delivered one paper, the *Sunday Graphic*, to Ruxton's home. On Sundays, Partridge usually knocked for Ruxton's paper money, but as there was no reply, despite several loud knocks, he pushed the newspaper under the door.

At ten to eleven, a patient called Mrs Isabella Whiteside arrived at 2 Dalton Square accompanied by her young son, Ronald. She rang the bell. Ruxton answered, opening the door about a foot. He was wearing a grey suit and a collar and tie. They had an appointment for Dr Ruxton to circumcise Ronald.

'I am sorry, Mrs Whiteside,' Ruxton told her, 'but I cannot perform the operation to-day as my wife is away in Scotland and there is just myself and my little maid, and we are busy taking the carpets up ready for the decorators in the morning.'

He said to her: 'Look at my hands, how dirty they are.' Mrs Whiteside could see only his left hand. Ruxton told her to bring Ronald back the following morning at eleven o'clock when he would perform the medical procedure.

The next person to see Ruxton that morning was Ethel Anderson, wife of Morecambe dentist Herbert. At half past eleven, the doctor arrived at their home in Balmoral Road in the town's West End. He had Elizabeth, Diana and Billy with him. Could she and Mr Anderson do him a favour, he asked. Could they look after the children as Isabella had gone away for a few days with Mary, their maid and nanny? Of course, agreed Mrs Anderson, who explained that Herbert, her husband, was in bed feeling unwell. Ruxton explained that he had a number of medical cases to deal with and would return later in the day. She asked him what had happened to his right hand and he said that he had cut it using a tin-opener that morning as he prepared the children's breakfast.

Shortly afterwards, Alwyn Hampshire, a young patient of Ruxton's, was standing outside his terraced home at 73 Bulk Road in Lancaster when the doctor drove up in his car and called him over. Ruxton asked Alwyn if his mother was in. He told Alwyn he would like her to go to his house to do some cleaning; the doctor explained that he had injured his hand and he had decorators coming in the following day. Alwyn's mother, Mary Hampshire, came out and got into Ruxton's car and they headed off for Dalton Square.

On the journey, which took five minutes from Bulk Road, Mrs Hampshire asked Ruxton about Isabella. He told her she was in Blackpool. She also asked about Mary Rogerson and the doctor said she had gone on holiday. Ruxton parked the Hillman outside his house; he and Mrs Hampshire walked up and he let them both in.

Mrs Hampshire noticed that Ruxton's stairs in the hall were in a filthy state. Straw was strewn on the stairs from the hall to the top floor. The stair and landing carpets had been removed. Ruxton asked if she could scrub the staircase clean. He would pay her 7s 6d.

Mrs Hampshire went upstairs with Ruxton, who showed her briefly into Mary's room on the top floor and then the bathroom. Ruxton showed her how to get hot water from the geyser. She noticed that the bath was a dirty yellow colour up to around 6in from the top. Ruxton asked her to give the bath a good clean. He and Mrs Hampshire went down into the cellar to put a shilling in the meter to ensure she had plenty of hot water for her chores. She knocked something over with her foot in the cellar. It was a red-coloured tin of petrol. The cap was off and petrol leaked on to her foot. Ruxton said he had tried burning a shirt and towels stained with blood from his injured hand in the yard but had failed because they were so wet.

She asked the doctor if it might be all right if her husband, Herbert, came to help her with the cleaning. The doctor said that would be fine.

Ruxton left Mrs Hampshire alone in the house at around half past four that afternoon. She set to cleaning. She swept the staircase, brushing the straw to the bottom of the stairs, then putting it in a bucket under the sink. There was a packet of Lux washing powder at the bottom of the stairs. Some of the straw had collected under the bedroom doors on the top floor. She was able to clean the straw from Mary's room, but the other two bedrooms, Isabella's and Ruxton's, were locked and Mrs Hampshire couldn't find a key. None of the rooms on the lower floors were locked, she noticed.

She tried unsuccessfully to remove the stains from the bath using hot water and Vim cleaner.

Mrs Hampshire went into the doctor's family rooms on the middle floor of the house. The table in the lounge was laid for two with plates, cutlery, cups and saucers, bread and butter, cakes, stewed blackberries, a partially eaten fruit salad and a chocolate blancmange. She also discovered an uncooked joint of meat. She washed up the doctor's few dirty plates and crockery in his kitchen.

In Ruxton's waiting room on the ground floor, she saw some carpets that were rolled up, some stair pads and a blue suit. Out in the backyard were two carpets from the landings as well as stair carpets. These were stained; one in particular appeared to be heavily marked with blood.

She also saw a shirt and some large surgical towels. Both were blood-stained. The towels looked as if they had been burned. Evidently, these were the ones Ruxton had told her about in the cellar.

✣

It was around half past five that afternoon when Mrs Anderson let Dr Ruxton into her home on Balmoral Road. Elizabeth, Diana and Billy would no doubt have been pleased to see their father. Ruxton asked Mrs Anderson if she and Herbert would go for a drive with him. But Herbert was still feeling ill in bed and it was suggested Ruxton leave his children with them overnight due to the doctor's injured hand. Ruxton was appreciative and so Mrs Anderson went in the Hillman Minx with Ruxton and the children to collect their night clothes from Dalton Square.

Ruxton, however, drove first to the home of Mary Rogerson on Thornton Road, which was five minutes from Balmoral Road. Mrs Anderson sat in the car as Ruxton knocked at the Rogerson door. Mrs Anderson could not make out who answered, but she overheard a conversation about the doctor's maid Mary having gone away for the weekend.

At Dalton Square, Ruxton took Elizabeth into the house for the night clothes while Mrs Anderson sat in the back of the car with Diana and Billy. Inside, Ruxton explained to Mrs Hampshire that the children were staying with the Andersons. Ruxton took Elizabeth upstairs to collect the clothes.

It was around seven o'clock when Ruxton came down the stairs to answer a knock at the door. It was Mr Hampshire, who had come to help his wife with the cleaning. Ruxton took Mrs Hampshire into the waiting room and said she and Mr Hampshire were welcome to have the carpets that were in there, as well as the ones in the backyard. He also said they could have the blue suit. He explained he had been wearing it when he cut his hand but suggested the blood would easily come out if it were cleaned; it was a good suit, he explained. Likewise with the carpets, he said the stains could be removed with cleaning. He said the carpets in the yard were sodden from the morning's rain so not to take those at that time.

Ruxton gave the Hampshires the key to the house and asked them to turn off the lights and lock up when they left as he might not be back. Then Ruxton took Elizabeth and left. Mr Hampshire scrubbed the stairs while Mrs Hampshire scrubbed the black and white linoleum of the bathroom on the top floor: there were drips of blood that had not been cleaned up very well.

The Hampshires stayed at 2 Dalton Square cleaning until around half past nine that night. They switched off all the lights, locked the vestibule door and left with Ruxton's key.

‡

On the journey back to the Andersons', Ruxton pulled up outside Taylor's Drug Stores on Regent Road in Morecambe. It was just after seven o'clock. He asked Mrs Anderson if she would call in and get him 2lb of cotton wool, explaining that he was short of it in the surgery. She went into the shop with Elizabeth, whom Ruxton had asked to buy a bottle of Dettol, an antiseptic for wounds and cuts. Mrs Anderson wanted to buy some Aspros (aspirins).

They were soon back at Balmoral Road. Young Billy was tired and so they left him with Mr Anderson while Ruxton and Mrs Anderson walked with Elizabeth and Diana along the promenade. As it was turning dark, Ruxton wanted his daughters to enjoy the Morecambe illuminations, which were just beginning to blink into life.

It was half past nine that evening when Ruxton kissed his children goodnight and left the Anderson home. He told Mrs Anderson he would collect the children the following morning, at around half past nine or ten o'clock. He was going to perform his night calls and surgery at Dalton Square, he said.

The house was empty and in darkness when Ruxton arrived at Dalton Square late that night, Sunday, 15 September, exhausted and in pain from the deep wound to his right hand.

'DADDY'S GARDEN'

Mrs Oxley arrived at Dalton Square ready for work at ten past seven on Monday morning. It was a miserable day, with heavy rain pelting down on the square. She rang the doorbell: no answer. She kept pressing the button until twenty to eight. Postman John Varley called and, seeing Mrs Oxley's unsuccessful attempt to rouse the Ruxton household, pushed the doctor's mail through the letterbox. Mrs Oxley gave up and went home. She returned at quarter past nine and still got no reply when she rang the bell.

Shortly afterwards, Ruxton's car pulled up outside the surgery. The door opened and out stepped the doctor. Mrs Oxley was shocked by his appearance: he looked dreadful. He was unshaven and was wearing a light brown overcoat, but did not have on a shirt collar. This struck her as odd because the doctor was usually such a dapper dresser. She noticed that his right hand was bandaged. He told her he had cut it with a tin opener on a can of peaches the day before and had 'lost gallons and gallons of blood'.

Ruxton opened the front door and Mrs Oxley followed him in. The electric light was on in the hall and Mrs Oxley noticed there was no stair carpet. She went to make the doctor some coffee before helping him to re-bandage his hand in the surgery. The house was silent; there was not a soul there. Ruxton said he believed Isabella and Mary's holiday to Edinburgh had been a ruse with an ulterior motive as Mary had asked for her wages in advance. He said the children were in Morecambe.

Mrs Oxley began her work. Ruxton left the house at around 10.30 and she never saw him again that day. She discovered that the doctor's bedroom, the drawing room and the dining room were all locked and she could not find the keys. She had never, in all her time working for Ruxton, known any of the rooms to be locked. In the lounge there was an untouched meal, including stewed blackberries and a chocolate blancmange, cakes, a fruit salad and a plate of bread and butter. She cleared the meal away and put it on a table outside the lounge on the landing.

She did not find an empty peach tin.

Ruxton went to the Hampshires' house on Bulk Road at nine o'clock and walked straight in without knocking. Mrs Hampshire was shocked by his appearance: he was unshaven, was without a collar or tie and was wearing an old raincoat. He usually looked so smart. She told him he looked ill; he said he *was* ill as he had not slept due to the pain in his hand. He asked what she and Mr Hampshire had taken away with them and asked where the suit was. It was lying on the table, so he went to it and picked it up. He could not believe how filthy it was and said he would take it away and have it cleaned, but Mrs Hampshire said she would pay for the cleaning as he had been so good as to give it to them.

'Look inside the pocket,' he said to Mrs Hampshire, and pointed to the suit-maker's tab, 'Epstein', and his own name, 'B. Ruxton', written inside. He asked for a pair of scissors to cut out the tab. Mrs Hampshire offered to do it after he left because his hand was badly cut, but Ruxton insisted she did it there and then, in front of him, because, he said, it was undignified for a man to wear another man's suit and for other people to know about it. So she cut it out. 'Burn it; burn it now,' he urged her, and she threw the suit's tab on to the fire in the hearth.

He asked her if she would go to his house once more because he said his charlady was ill. He also asked if she might open the door to his patients as they arrived. Mrs Hampshire told him he should contact Isabella in Edinburgh and ask her to return as he was so ill; he said he didn't want to spoil her holiday.

After Ruxton left, Mrs Hampshire properly inspected the carpets she and her husband had taken from Dalton Square. Two were not so badly stained, but a third was soaked in blood. She lay them in her back yard and threw around thirty buckets of water over them in an attempt to flush out the blood. The water that sluiced across her yard was scarlet. She left the worst carpet in the open air to dry and decided to try again on washday. Even then she would not get all the congealed blood out.

She inspected Ruxton's blue suit. She kept the coat and trousers but decided the waistcoat was so badly stained with blood that it should be disposed of. She burned it.

*

Ruxton took the Hillman Minx to the County Garage on Lancaster Road in Morecambe to be serviced by Henry Hudson, who had sold the doctor the vehicle the previous month, on 3 August. Ruxton told Hudson about his bandaged hand, about the tin of peaches and how he had almost severed his little finger. He asked Hudson if he could borrow a car while the Hillman was being serviced, but did not like the small Ford the garage owner offered. So Hudson suggested they walk to the adjacent Grand Garage and Sporting Cars showroom to look at a different vehicle. Hudson let one of the salesmen, John Milner, look after Ruxton and the doctor was fixed up with a large four-seater Austin saloon, stone-coloured like the Hillman. The registration was: CP8 415. Ruxton signed the hire papers for a period of a day and a half and drove away in the Austin.

At half past twelve, Mrs Hampshire returned to Dalton Square as Ruxton had asked. She had the key he had given her and let herself in. She went up the stairs to the top of the house to see if there was anybody at home. She was alone. She tried the bedroom doors and they were still locked. Ruxton returned at one o'clock. She asked why he requested her help when there was nothing to do.

'I have sent for you because you give me courage,' he replied.

Mrs Hampshire sensed Ruxton was hiding something; he was a broken man. She asked if he had eaten any lunch. He had not, so she made him call Tymns Café on Church Street in town to have a meal sent over. They went upstairs to the lounge on the middle floor and Mrs Hampshire, feeling sorry and concerned for the doctor whom she had known for a long time, asked why he didn't get Isabella to come home. He told her she was in London. She now knew something was wrong as the previous day he had said she was in Edinburgh. She told him he was lying and he admitted he was. He said he was the 'most unhappy man in the world' and that Isabella had gone off with another man and left him with their three children.

Ruxton poured his heart out. No doubt referring to Bobby Edmondson, he told Mrs Hampshire: 'You make a friend of a man, you treat him as a friend, and he eats from your table, and he makes love to your wife behind your back. It is terrible.' Mrs Hampshire would later say Ruxton was 'terribly distressed'. The doctor lay his head down on the table and he began to cry.

After eating lunch from Tymns, Ruxton had his surgery to attend to. A stream of patients came and went.

At about three o'clock in the afternoon, the dustmen arrived to empty Ruxton's bins. They called at the front door as the gate to the yard was locked; Mrs Hampshire unlocked it for them. Ruxton came into the yard and told them to take away everything, the stained clothing and some rubbish, but to leave the carpets, which Mrs Hampshire was to have. Joseph Moffatt Gardiner, who was the driver of the dustcart, noticing the bloodstained articles, asked Ruxton if he had had an accident. The doctor said he had severed a finger opening a tin. Ruxton explained he was looking after his three children because his wife was 'away touring in the car'. He asked the dustmen also to dispose of scrapings of plaster in a pile in the yard. The plaster was from the wall of the cinema next door; one of the dustmen said they could not take the debris as it was not part of their remit, but Ruxton was insistent and they did as he asked.

During the afternoon, Ruxton was visited by Edwin Slinger, a solicitor from Accrington, and spoke on the telephone with his Lancaster solicitor, Fred Gardner, in relation to a loan on the surgery.

Ruxton was planning to borrow £3,000 from money-lenders in London. This was a vast sum of money.

In the coming days, Ruxton visited his medical colleague Dr Mather at his surgery on South Road to ask for a reference to support his loan application. Mather was concerned by his colleague's injured hand. Ruxton told him the tale of the tin of fruit and explained that he had considered visiting Mather to have it stitched.

Just before seven on Monday evening, one of Ruxton's patients, Ernest Hall, called at the doctor's home. Hall, who worked as a projectionist at the County Cinema next door, occasionally did odd-jobs for the doctor. He had only just recovered from a minor illness that had left him bed-bound over the weekend; Ruxton had signed him off work. That evening, Ruxton asked him to take a look at the lavatory in the bathroom as the plunger wasn't working. Inevitably, Hall asked Ruxton about his hand and was told the peach tin tale.

When Hall left, Ruxton's thoughts turned to the children.

He called at the Andersons' at half past nine to ask whether the children could stay another night. Herbert and Ethel agreed, and so Elizabeth, Diana and Billy bedded down at Balmoral Road once more. Anderson, who was feeling better, asked Ruxton about his injured hand; the dentist could see that it was gashed from the apex of the finger to its joint, and there was a gash running diagonally across three of his fingers. He told Ruxton he thought it must be a 'peculiar' tin opener and that he would like to see it, but the doctor told him he had thrown it away as he was sick of the sight of it.

Ruxton was back in Dalton Square by half past eleven and went to bed after midnight.

The following morning, he collected the children at ten o'clock.

In the coming days, Ruxton's servants and friends noticed a dramatic deterioration in the doctor.

It had all happened since Mrs Ruxton and their nanny Mary had gone away together.

The doctor was wrestling with an inner turmoil. He was also struggling to look after his children and run his surgery. He had become slovenly, rarely shaving, and had stopped dressing smartly in a collar and tie. The house was a mess, doors were locked mysteriously, and Ruxton had offered bloodstained carpets to a number of servants. The amount of blood was perplexing. Ruxton told Mrs Oxley, 'If I go along a road and I run over a rabbit and I get blood on my tyre, people will think I have committed a murder.' She and Mrs Curwen noticed blood at the bottom of the casement curtains on the top landing of the stairs. Ruxton told Mrs Curwen to take them down; he tore off the blood-soaked parts and burned them. He gave the remainder of the curtains to the two women for dusters.

At different times that week, Ruxton confided in some servants that Isabella had gone off with another man. He explained that tales of her holidaying in Edinburgh or London were a cover. In fact, Mrs Ruxton had walked out on him and their children, he said.

It was harder for the staff to understand why Mary Rogerson had gone.

When Mrs Oxley arrived early on Tuesday, 17 September, Ruxton was still in his pyjamas. She made him breakfast and helped pack clothes for the children before he collected them from the Andersons'. He took Elizabeth and Diana to school at Victoria Parade in Morecambe. Then he took Billy-Boy, too young for school, for a long drive in the stone-coloured Austin hire car.

He told his son they were going to see 'Daddy's garden'.

At about 12.35 that afternoon, a young man called Bernard Beattie was cycling along Finkle Street in Kendal in the Lake District, 20 miles north of Lancaster. This was the main route to Scotland. As Beattie pedalled, heading south, he was clipped by a car coming up behind him. He was knocked off his bicycle and sent sprawling onto the pavement. Beattie, shaken but uninjured, shouted at the driver to stop. The motorist simply waved a hand without a backward look and carried on, turning south at the junction with Highgate, the main road south to Lancaster. Beattie quickly made a note of the car's number: CP8 415. Then, after inspecting his bike and discovering it was badly smashed up, he went to find the police officer on point duty outside the Town Hall and reported the accident.

Twenty-five minutes later, at one o'clock, PC James Lowther, an officer with Cumberland and Westmorland Constabulary, was on duty at the main crossroads in the village of Milnthorpe, a few miles south of Kendal. He saw a car approaching on the A6 from the north. He had received a call from Kendal police about a hit-and-run incident and had a note of the offending vehicle's number. The approaching car, a stone-coloured Austin, had the matching plate: CP8 415.

PC Lowther stepped into the road and flagged the car down. He approached to speak to the driver, who was a foreign-looking gentleman. There was a small boy in the passenger seat. Lowther asked if the man had been involved in an accident in Kendal; the motorist said he had. The constable asked him to pull his car to the side of the road. Lowther cautioned him and asked if he wished to make a statement. The driver suddenly became highly excited and emotional, and Lowther had incredible difficulty writing down what he was saying. The motorist did not have either his driving licence or his insurance paperwork with him. He told the officer repeatedly that he had been to Carlisle on business. After some time Lowther handed the driver a form requiring him to produce the relevant paperwork at a police station in the coming days.

The driver had given his name and address as Dr Buck Ruxton of 2 Dalton Square, Lancaster.

36

THOUGHTS ARE THINGS

Later on Tuesday, Ruxton visited the home of painter and decorator Arthur Holmes, who had done work at 2 Dalton Square twice before in the past, most recently in July when he decorated the bathroom and waiting room. Ruxton was met by Holmes's daughter, Ethel. The doctor told her he had had an arrangement with Mr Holmes to visit 2 Dalton Square the previous day to redecorate the staircase, but he had not come. Ethel knew nothing about it but said she would pass the message on.

Mr Holmes would send his apologies to Ruxton, but still did not call at Dalton Square. Ruxton would return to Holmes' house the day after, Wednesday, 18 September, but Ethel explained her father was busy. Ruxton was extremely keen to have the staircase decorated, and when Mr Holmes failed yet again to call, he returned to Holmes's house on the Saturday and Sunday, finally asking Ethel to get her father to call at the surgery the following morning before work and to bring a wallpaper pattern book with him.

Ruxton called at Lancaster police station in Dalton Square late on Tuesday with the form he had been given by Constable Lowther in Milnthorpe. He was told he would need to produce his driving licence and certificate of insurance within five days.

He collected the children from the Andersons' as Elizabeth was being measured the following morning for a dress to wear to an event allied to Morecambe carnival, which had taken place the previous Saturday. Elizabeth was due to appear with a dancing troupe run by a Miss Rigby.

That night Ruxton went to bed as usual just after midnight. He said a prayer and then lay in bed reading *Thoughts Are Things*, a book in which New Thought author Prentice Mulford encouraged his readers to take great care in creating strong, positive thoughts in order to manifest the things in life they most desired.

The following day, Wednesday, 18 September, Ruxton got Elizabeth ready to meet Miss Rigby and the other children of the dancing troupe on the steps of the Town Hall across Dalton Square. The children were catching the one o'clock special bus to Morecambe to take part in that day's carnival. Mrs Anderson telephoned Ruxton's house and left a message with his cook and housekeeper Mrs Curwen inviting the doctor to take Diana and Billy to the carnival too to watch their sister dancing. He took up the offer and the children enjoyed the event.

Early in the evening, Ruxton took Elizabeth with him to return the hired Austin saloon to the Grand Garage in Morecambe once his Hillman was ready to collect following its service.

On the morning of Thursday, 19 September, Mrs Oxley arrived at Dalton Square. Ruxton was again still in his pyjamas. She made him some breakfast; he said he was going to see a specialist about his hand. As she cleaned up the breakfast things in the kitchen, he closed the door and she heard him going up and down the stairs a number of times and out to his car at the back door. He left at eight o'clock.

The locked doors upstairs were now unlocked, Mrs Oxley discovered. There was an awful, dirty smell in Ruxton's room, an odour that she had never noticed before. The bath had an unsightly yellow discoloration to it. Mrs Oxley knew Mary Rogerson had cleaned the bath every week and before Mrs Ruxton and Mary had gone away it had been pristine apart from a mark under the tap caused by drips from the hot water geyser.

Ruxton took the children to Balmoral Road. He told the Andersons he was driving to Blackburn to see a room Isabella had rented and furnished – she had plans to start a business related to the football pools, he said. The room was at 18 Newmarket Street in the Lancashire cotton mill town.

Ruxton would later tell his servants about the Blackburn trip. He claimed he had parked his car and walked up and down Newmarket Street in the hope of seeing Isabella. He explained to Mrs Oxley that when she heard him going up and down the stairs that morning, it was because he had been carrying a camera and a tripod to his car. He told her he had intended to photograph Bobby Edmondson's car, which he suspected might be parked outside Isabella's room in Blackburn.

Later in the day, Mrs Hampshire saw Ruxton at his surgery. He asked if the blue suit he had given her had been cleaned yet. She lied and said that it had.

On Friday, 20 September, as Mrs Curwen served lunch, Ruxton told her there was a horrible, pungent smell in the house and he asked her to buy a spray and a bottle of eau-de-Cologne. He explained that the smell was coming from the wet size – or paste – on the plaster in the hall after the wallpaper had been stripped in preparation for the decorators.

At five o'clock that afternoon, Ruxton went to see Bessie Philbrook, the patient and friend who occasionally took Elizabeth, Diana and Billy for walks. He asked if she would mind taking the children out as Mrs Curwen was shopping. She agreed and as Ruxton drove her back to Dalton Square he told her that Isabella and Mary had gone to Scotland. He asked Bessie if she knew Mary was pregnant.

37

A DEATH IN MORECAMBE

In the early hours of Friday, 20 September, the body of a wealthy Lancaster widow, Mrs Florence Smalley, was found in a stable yard behind Clark Street in Morecambe, not far from the promenade. She had terrible head injuries; her clothes and valuables had not been interfered with. Police assumed she had been in the seaside resort for the fireworks on Thursday night, part of the week-long Morecambe carnival. Ruxton had watched his daughter Elizabeth dance there on Wednesday, with Mrs Anderson, Diana and Billy. Reports of the previous Saturday's carnival had been published in newspapers on the day Ruxton said Isabella and Mary walked out on him.

Morecambe police investigating Mrs Smalley's death made an appeal for witnesses in local and regional newspapers. A number of people came forward. Police were able to pinpoint the last sighting of the widow, who was known to like a drink, at ten minutes to ten that night as she left the Elms Hotel. This was where Ruxton and Isabella had spent the previous New Year's Eve.

The police's questions would soon lead them to Dalton Square.

Each afternoon that week, Ruxton lit fires in his yard to burn blood-stained items. He told Mrs Oxley and Mrs Curwen the blood had come from his hand. He instructed them to keep the fires going as he tossed more and more items into the flames, including papers. Mrs Curwen swept the yard of the ashes several times that week. Ruxton's efforts were not always successful. Various pieces of clothing made of blue and red material remained merely singed. Mrs Curwen thought the blue one resembled a coat belonging to Mary Rogerson, while the red appeared to be a dressing gown that the young maid wore.

On Saturday, 21 September, Ernest Hall, the County Cinema projectionist, spoke to Ruxton outside the doctor's house. Ruxton asked him if he would be able to install some new lighting on the coming Monday. They had originally discussed the work in July. Hall agreed he could do it and arrangements were made.

Hall arrived at Ruxton's at eight o'clock on Monday morning and spent two days cutting out plaster in the hall to install the wiring. On Tuesday, as Hall worked, Ruxton stood on the stairs and asked the projectionist if he recalled when he had first asked him to do the work. Hall said that he did.

'Well, I do not want you to forget when it was that I asked you,' said Ruxton.

Hall said the original discussion had probably been in July.

'Oh, that is all right then,' said Ruxton. The doctor told Hall that people were talking about him, gossiping that he had things to cover up.

Ruxton's friend Thomas Harrison saw the doctor in Dalton Square at four o'clock on the afternoon of Sunday, 22 September. Ruxton told him about Isabella and Bobby Edmondson and asked him to tell Bobby not to interfere with his affairs and to keep away from Isabella.

Mary Rogerson's brother, Peter, called at 2 Dalton Square at quarter past six on the evening of Monday, 23 September. Ruxton opened the door to him and Peter asked if Mary had come back.

He and Mary's parents were very worried as they had not heard from her in over a week.

Ruxton asked him to come into the house and said he would explain things the best he could. He told Peter that Isabella and Mary had gone on a tour and were expected to be away between a week and a fortnight. He quizzed the young man on whether his sister had any problems at home, to which Peter replied she hadn't. Ruxton also asked if he knew anything of Mary's relationship with a laundry boy. Again, Peter said he and his parents knew nothing of this. Ruxton said Mary had asked for an advance on her wages the week before. Before Peter left, the doctor paid him Mary's wages for that week, fifteen shillings.

That evening, Ruxton went to the County Cinema, next door, to see *Clive of India*, starring Ronald Colman.

Dr Buck Ruxton in a portrait probably taken in the 1920s when Ruxton was in his twenties. (University of Glasgow)

Isabella Kerr pictured in her early twenties. (University of Glasgow)

Mary Rogerson standing at the gate to her parents' house on Thornton Road, Morecambe. This image was later used in the work to reconstruct the bodies. (University of Glasgow)

Dr Ruxton with his younger daughter Diana about to enter their home on Dalton Square. Note the County Cinema sign and white telephone box behind them. (Public domain)

2 Dalton Square pictured at the time of the police investigation into Isabella's and Mary's disappearance. Note the advertisement for the Laurel and Hardy film on the County Cinema. (University of Glasgow)

The view from Ruxton's house across Dalton Square to the Town Hall as it is today. (Author's photograph)

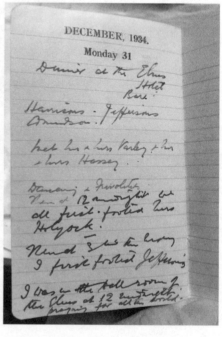

Diary entry for New Year's Eve 1934 in which Ruxton describes his prayer for 'all this world'. (Author's photograph of diary at Lancaster City Museum)

Police officers during the search for further human remains in the ravine at Gardenholme linn following the initial discovery by Susan Johnson on 29 September 1935. (University of Glasgow)

October 1935: Following Ruxton's arrest, Lancaster police seized the doctor's house. Pictured on the step of 2 Dalton Square are, from left, fingerprint expert Detective Lieutenant Bertie Hammond, Captain Henry Vann, Chief Constable of Lancaster Police, and Detective Inspector William Thompson. (Courtesy of Marilyn Wilson)

Professor S. Smith.   Professor John Glaister.   Professor J. C. Brash.

Three of the brilliant scientists: Professor Sydney Smith, Professor John Glaister and Professor James Couper Brash in a press cutting from the *Leeds Mercury*. (JPI Media)

Professor John Glaister and his assistant Dr Frank Martin captured by an Associated Press photographer in Dalton Square on 14 October 1935 at the start of their extensive search of Ruxton's house, which can be seen behind them. (Shutterstock)

The scrap of newsprint from *The Sunday Graphic* that was found wrapped around some of the remains. The page clearly shows the report of the crowning of Morecambe carnival queen. The event had taken place on the day that Isabella and Mary were killed. (University of Glasgow)

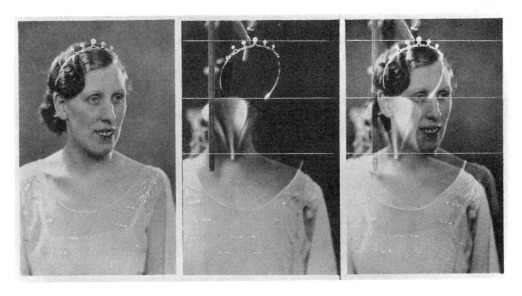

The portrait of Isabella taken by Cecil Thomas was used by Professor Brash and Detective Constable Stobie in providing the scale for the superimposition of photos of Isabella's skull. (University of Glasgow)

A police photograph of Ruxton's bathroom before the bath and fitments were removed and taken to Edinburgh for forensic examination. (University of Glasgow)

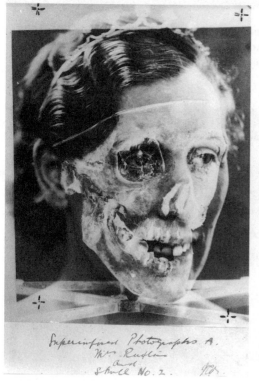

Superimposed Photographs A.
Mrs Ruxton
and
Skull No. 2.

One of the remarkable superimposed images produced by Brash and Stobie: Isabella Ruxton. (University of Glasgow)

The appetite for news stories about the Ruxton case around the world was intense. These are photographs possibly clipped from newspaper reports by Glaister or one of his team, and kept on file. Headshots of Ruxton, Isabella, Mary, Jeanie Nelson, Mrs Hampshire and Bobby Edmondson. (University of Glasgow)

Sergeant Frederick Harrison's scale model of 2 Dalton Square, which was used by Glaister and his team for reference during their investigation and, later, at Ruxton's trial at Manchester Assizes. (University of Glasgow)

The Ruxton children, Elizabeth, Diana and Billy, with Dorothy Neild, the housekeeper of Herbert and Ethel Anderson. This is a press photograph taken by Associated Newspapers in Morecambe on 17 October 1935 when the children were staying with the Andersons on Balmoral Road. (Shutterstock)

Crowds outside Strangeways Prison waiting for news of Ruxton's execution on 12 May 1936. (University of Glasgow)

The Parkside children's home in Lancaster, pictured in 2020. This is where Elizabeth, Diana and Billy Ruxton were cared for following their father's arrest. It is also where their aunts visited them from Edinburgh, bearing gifts of chocolate Easter eggs. (Author's photograph)

QUESTIONS

On Tuesday, 24 September, Detective Inspector John Moffat, of Lancashire County Constabulary based in Blackburn, visited Dalton Square police station. He was making inquiries into Mrs Smalley's death. She had lived at 21 Meadowside, a ten-minute walk from Dalton Square.

Earlier Moffat had routinely interviewed Elizabeth Curwen, Ruxton's housekeeper, as part of the inquiry. Now, Dr Ruxton had come into the police station in an agitated state, demanding to know why the police were questioning his staff.

Barely able to control himself, Ruxton told the detective:

Look here, Inspector Moffat, what the hell do the police want inquiring about my private affairs for?

I do not know Mrs Smalley. I have enough trouble on my mind. Come across and search my house and interview the whole damned lot of us. It is nothing but professional jealousy. I am the most progressive doctor in this town. I have over 2,000 patients on my panel and every doctor is jealous of me.

Moffat noted later that Ruxton had behaved oddly in his emotional state, grabbing his hair in both hands and shaking his head and blackguarding Isabella for leaving him with the three young children.

Ruxton's tirade lasted five minutes and Moffat struggled to take down everything he said; in truth the detective had found the doctor mostly unintelligible.

Before leaving the police station, Ruxton spoke to John Cook, a clerk in the municipal department of the Town Hall. Ruxton asked Cook if he would take a look at the wound on his hand, removing the bandage even after Cook asked him not to. The dressing was sticking to the wound, yet Cook could see the severity of the cut to the little finger and the third finger.

Ruxton explained that he had come to speak to detectives about Mrs Smalley. They were accusing him of killing her, he told Cook.

Ruxton went for a shave at Howson's hairdressing salon at 18 Dalton Square on the morning of Thursday, 26 September. He met his friend James Jefferson, the insurance man from Morecambe, who was also there. They fell into conversation and afterwards Jefferson went with Ruxton to the doctor's house. Ruxton told him of his suspicions of Isabella's affair with Bobby Edmondson. He said Isabella had left him, having gone away with his nanny Mary Rogerson. He said Mary's father, Mr Rogerson, had been to see him and was threatening to go to the police over her disappearance. 'Of course you know the type of man he is,' said Ruxton of Mr Rogerson. 'He is a man that would go to the police about anything.'

The same day, Morecambe detectives announced that they believed Mrs Smalley had died after being run over by a motorcar. Whoever was responsible had then taken her body and left it in the yard behind Clark Street. Detectives offered £50 for information that would help to trace the car.

39

DAY OF DISCOVERY

Sunday, 29 September began as a bright, fine day.

Ruxton decided he wanted to take the children out for the day. He had been feeling low and was in the mood for company. He invited a number of people, including the Andersons and Mrs Curwen, but none could go. He asked a patient, Miss Sarah Sharples, of 12 Daisy Bank, on the road out to the Forest of Bowland. She had a friend from Bishop Auckland staying with her, a Miss Robson, so Ruxton extended the invitation to them both.

And so Ruxton drove them and Elizabeth, Diana and Billy north, towards the Lake District. They stopped at a garage at Carnforth for petrol and then went on to Windermere. As they drove, Ruxton said, 'Sky is the limit, let us enjoy a run.' From Windermere they drove on through the spectacular scenery of the Lakes. In Keswick they stopped for tea at the Waverley Temperance Hotel. Ruxton was in the best spirits he had been for days. He joked with the waitress when each person in his party ordered something different, 'Please forgive the trouble but such is the lot of family life.'

The children visited the bathroom and on the way out Ruxton bought them chocolate. From there Ruxton drove north to Carlisle near the Scottish border. Miss Robson casually remarked she had never been to Gretna Green, where young lovers traditionally fled to get married. Ruxton made another joke: 'I say, it is rather tempting for me to go to Gretna with two single women.'

Ruxton bought a beret each for Elizabeth, Diana and Billy from a shop in Gretna, before they visited the famous blacksmith's. He signed his name in the visitor book and Elizabeth wrote MISS ELIZABETH in big letters. Miss Robson helped Diana to write her name.

It was quarter past six when they left the blacksmith's and Ruxton drove them a little further north, but he soon decided it was getting late, so he turned the car around and the party headed south for home.

They arrived in Lancaster just after nine o'clock.

Earlier in the day, not so very far from Gretna Green, Susan Johnson and her mother were walking near the Devil's Beef Tub and made their grisly discovery.

Dr Ruxton's happy mood would soon come to an end.

40

SCREAMING HEADLINES

The world first learned of the mutilated bodies found at Gardenholme linn through the headlines of local, national and then international newspapers. The discovery was described as 'Ravine Mystery' and 'The Bodies Under The Bridge' and then 'Ravine Murders' as more details emerged. Titles such as the *News of the World* boasted sales of well over 3 million copies each week and thrived on such gruesome stories.

In the coming days, further human remains were found. On 30 September, Charles Hunter came across three or four parcels of flesh under a bush not far from the stream on the embankment of Gardenholme linn bridge. On 2 October, George Lammie, a farmer who owned the property near the stream through the linn, found a piece of flesh in the water and took it to the police.

The final piece of the macabre jigsaw puzzle would be found on 4 November, when a maidservant from Moffat called Jen Gwendoline Halliday, out walking near Gardenholme linn, found a human hand and arm lying in grass a few yards from the main road. PC James Fairweather from Moffat police station removed the limb, which was wrapped in a scrap of the *Daily Herald* dated 2 September 1935.

Standing in the tiny mortuary in Moffat, confronted with the trestle tables of decomposing, maggot-infested flesh, Professor Glaister and Dr Gilbert Millar concluded a proper assessment could not be done there. Based on the recovery of two heads, they believed the remains constituted at least two bodies but could not rule out more. Both heads had had their ears, eyes, noses, lips and some skin removed. A number of teeth had also been extracted, which Glaister and Millar assumed at this stage had been removed after death. The less mutilated head was that of a young woman, they concluded, while the second appeared to be a man's. A pelvis recovered was also evidently a woman's.

The scientists were looking for early clues, anything that could aid iden-tification. There were four vaccination marks on the upper portion of a left arm, but many common features that would normally prove helpful had been carefully removed. These included the terminal joints of the fingers on two of the recovered hands. The scientists concluded that the perpetrator had been trying to hide the identity of the victim, who might have had some unusual quality about their nails or fingertips. It was also reasonable to assume that the bodies had been mutilated in such a manner to hide signs of violence or injury that might indicate how the victims were killed.

Glaister and Millar suspected very early on that whoever had dismembered the bodies was somebody who knew what they were doing – perhaps someone with medical training. Glaister later wrote, 'The bodies had been neatly dismembered into portions convenient for transport; and that had been done entirely by cutting through the joints with a knife. There were no signs of the use of a saw.'

That evening, they ordered the remains to be removed and transported to Professor Sydney Smith's Department of Forensic Medicine at Edinburgh University, rather than to Glaister's at Glasgow. Millar was acting for Professor Smith, who was abroad, at Edinburgh, and as Millar was in Moffat before Glaister, he had taken the lead. It was abundantly clear the body parts would need to be reassembled. This was a human jigsaw puzzle that would require the strongest of stomachs.

Glaister and Millar could not be certain which body portions belonged with which, but they made a very rough estimation. Then two boxes were labelled 'Body No 1' and 'Body No 2'. Into the first box were placed the head, pelvis and other remains, which they believed were from the body of a young woman. The second, more masculine head was placed in the second, along with other remains.

As the two scientists left Moffat they acknowledged the job of reassembly was far too big for them alone. It would require the expertise of many brilliant medical and scientific minds disciplined in various specialisms.

They drew up a list of those men – and in 1930s Scottish forensic science they were all men – who could come together quickly and work efficiently and effectively.

Glaister, with help from his assistant, Dr Frank Martin, would oversee all aspects of pathology and medico-legal matters.

Meanwhile, the police investigation fell under the jurisdiction of the Chief Constable of Dumfriesshire Constabulary, William Black. Given the logistical difficulties posed by the case, not least in conducting further searches of the Gardenholme linn area and the task of identifying the victims, Black realised he needed more resources. So he reached out to the much bigger police force, Glasgow Constabulary. The Chief Constable, Captain Percy Sillitoe, had a strong team of officers with expertise in police work that would prove invaluable in the coming days and weeks. These included David Warnock, Assistant Chief Constable, and Detective Superintendent Adam McLaren. They worked closely with Detective Inspector John Sheed, of the City of Edinburgh Police Force, who would be the liaison officer between the Glasgow officers and the Edinburgh-based medical experts.

But the two Glasgow officers who were about to find themselves at the heart of a landmark investigation were William Ewing and Bertie Hammond, both detective lieutenants.

Ewing was softly spoken and burly. His outward quietness and courteous manner belied a steely determination and a tough line in questioning when it was required. He was known universally as 'Willie' and would whistle tunelessly when turning a problem over in his mind. He had been with Glasgow Police for twenty-four years and had established a reputation for hard-nosed police work. He might have been a man who hated the spotlight, but he had not escaped the attention of newspaper reporters, who had once written that 'crooks feared him'.

Hammond was smaller, slim with black hair, piercing eyes and sharp cheekbones. He had been a sergeant serving in the Fingerprint Department at Sheffield City Police in England when Sillitoe was the Chief Constable of the Yorkshire city's force. When Sillitoe was appointed to the top rank in Glasgow in 1931, he invited Hammond to head north and modernise his new force's fingerprint operations. And so Detective Lieutenant Hammond took charge of Glasgow's Fingerprint Department and Photographic Department.

Hammond was in the thick of the investigation from that first day.

In his overcoat and trilby hat as protection against the autumnal weather, he meticulously photographed the bridge over Gardenholme linn from strategic points. Clutching his camera, he clambered down the steep embankment of the ravine to capture the view from below the bridge.

Hammond's photographs proved incredibly useful to the investigation. White crosses were etched on the prints marking the locations where bodily remains had been discovered. The drop of the ravine from the bridge's parapet to the bed of the gully was measured to be 37ft 8in.

Hammond's photographs allowed the police to draw certain conclusions. Most likely the body parts had been tossed over the parapet at night. Whoever had done so was sufficiently familiar with the local area to realise it would be a remote and difficult-to-reach place but not so familiar as to know there was a shallow stream below. This was significant because there had been heavy rainfall in recent days and the River Annan and the stream had flooded. This explained why the body parts were found strewn over a considerable distance, as the flood water had dislodged them.

Police consulted the records from a nearby weather rain gauge. The stream had been in spate overnight on 17 and 18 September with water levels likely still high on 19 September. There had then followed four or five days without rain. Based on this evidence and the state of the putrefying human remains, police believed the bodies had been thrown into the ravine immediately before or during the flood.

So, some time between 16 and 18 September.

There was no evidence to suggest where the crimes had been committed, so the police had no choice but to conduct inquiries over a wide area to probe reports of missing persons. It was most likely that the bodies had been taken to the ravine by motorcar. Detectives started to trace any unusual movements by motorists whose cars were registered in Dumfriesshire.

Willie Ewing inspected the scraps of newspaper found wrapped around parts of the bodies, turning them over to look for the slightest clue. A piece of the front page of the *Sunday Graphic* dated 15 September was particularly intriguing. There was a partial headline, '–AMBE'S CARNIVAL QUEEN –ROWNED'. Ewing deduced that this referred to Morecambe in Lancashire. Now, why would a national newspaper use such a provincial story as its front page 'splash' story? Surely there would be only limited interest in the carnival beyond Lancashire.

Perhaps Ewing whistled tunelessly, deep in thought. He had a brainwave. Newspaper reporters were milling around Moffat seeking titbits about the case. Ewing approached the pressmen and told them of the Morecambe puzzle. He soon had his answer. 'It might be a slip edition for that area only,' the newsmen told him. Ewing could see it now. The likelihood was the *Sunday Graphic* had printed a special edition featuring the carnival to circulate only in the Morecambe area.

It was a major breakthrough.

Chief Constable Black of Dumfriesshire Police issued a statement to the press at Moffat late on 1 October after Glaister and Millar had ordered the remains to be moved to Edinburgh. It ran: 'It is thought that the person or persons responsible for the mutilation of the bodies may have had some anatomical knowledge and that an obvious attempt has been made to efface any evidence which would lead to a ready identification ... Death is thought to have taken place about ten days ago and the mutilation shortly afterwards.'

The following morning the *Scotsman* newspaper reported: 'Evidence suggests crime was the work of a maniac.'

Police conjectured the remains had been taken to the ravine by motor-car. They were anxious for information, Black said, from garage proprietors and attendants 'as to suspicious car or cars from which offensive odours may have emanated'. He said he had sought the co-operation of Scotland Yard in London. He also said Central Police Office in Edinburgh had received a message from a man calling from a telephone kiosk in the city in relation to the remains. This line of inquiry, however, would later lead nowhere.

One of the reporters Ewing had consulted over the *Sunday Graphic* was the *News of the World*'s brilliant crime reporter Norman 'Jock' Rae, famed for his work on the most sensational murder cases of the era. Rae recognised the significance of the 'slip' edition of the paper before the police did and made his excuses to the rest of the press pack at Moffat, saying he had some personal problems to deal with. Another seasoned *News of the World* reporter, John Howie Milligan, took over from him covering developments in the Scottish town.

Having shaken off the competition, Norman Rae headed for Morecambe.

Late that night, Mr and Mrs Rogerson went to see Ruxton at Dalton Square. He was not expecting them, but he invited them in. They were worried about Mary as they had not heard from her in such a long time.

Ruxton said he did not know where she was, but he said Isabella and Mary had broken into his safe in the house and taken £30 from it. He believed the two of them were 'having a good time'. He showed them a letter he had written to Isabella's sister in Edinburgh, Mrs Jeanie Nelson, but it had been returned.

Don't worry, Ruxton told them, Isabella and Mary would return when the money ran out.

The Rogersons told the doctor they were going to tell Lancaster Police across Dalton Square.

HUMAN JIGSAW PUZZLE

At Edinburgh University's Anatomy Department at Teviot Place the following morning, Wednesday, 2 October, Dr Millar had the unpleasant task of unpacking the two boxes of their repulsive contents. He washed the remains in a bath to remove dirt and other matter obscuring them. Then he applied ether to the body parts and soft tissue with the aim of killing the maggots that were slowly but surely feasting on the flesh. Once complete, Millar placed the remains in weak formalin in tanks in order to preserve them. Then he locked the tanks, where they would stay for the next three days.

On Saturday, 5 October, he and Glaister would have the remains removed once more, this time to the Forensic Medicine Laboratory, the place where the scientists intended to carry out the laborious process of examining the dismembered body parts.

Once there, it would become apparent quite how thorough and extensive the work of dismemberment and mutilation had been by the perpetrator. In all, at that stage, Glaister and Millar had just under seventy separate pieces of body to contend with. In time a left foot and a right forearm would also be recovered from the Gardenholme vicinity, bringing the tally to precisely seventy.

Millar found a most unusual item among the remains. It had the appearance, Glaister later noted, of 'a piece of tough fungus scraped from the root of a tree'. Closer inspection revealed it to be a 'small, wrinkled mass of resistant tissue'. The two men concluded that it was a cyclops eye, a specimen – it was not clear if it were human or animal – of an unfortunate creature that has been born with two eyes very close together without any bone intervening.

Later, in Lancashire, Mrs Jessie Rogerson, Mary's stepmother, had had enough of Ruxton's excuses. She went to see the police in Dalton Square. She told officers that she and Mr Rogerson were worried about Mary. They had not seen her or heard from her since Thursday, 12 September, more than two weeks earlier. This was most unlike her, Mrs Rogerson told officers, as Mary would spend her free time at home in Morecambe with her sister or a friend. The only time she was not at home was when she was at the Ruxtons' home. Even during those two weeks in the summer she spent at Seatle near Grange-over-Sands, she had written home every day.

Mrs Rogerson said the last time they saw Mary, she had left at around six-thirty in the evening to look at the illuminations on the pier. Mary would normally have returned to Thornton Road to say goodbye, but on that occasion due to the long queue to see the lights she had caught her bus back to Lancaster.

In Mrs Rogerson's view, Mary was missing.

News of the World crime reporter Norman Rae arrived in Morecambe that Wednesday on the scent of a scoop. He knew he was ahead of the police. He now had to trust his reporter's instincts and see where they took him. He asked around in the resort. He soon turned up some gossip about a doctor from Lancaster whose wife had walked out on him and taken their maid with her. Rae learned that this was not unusual as the doctor and his wife were known to have a volatile relationship. What struck Rae as interesting, however, was the fact that his sources said it was out of character for the maid to vanish without a word to her parents.

Rae pressed his contacts for the name and address of the doctor: Dr Buck Ruxton of 2 Dalton Square. He thanked his tip, then headed off in the direction of Lancaster.

A decorator called Frank Eason called at Ruxton's home to ask for payment for some work he had done in the house earlier that year. While he was there, Ruxton asked Eason if he could quote a price and a start date for redecorating the staircase. The doctor was eager for the work to be done as quickly as possible. This was the first time Ruxton had asked Eason about this work; the decorator gave his price and began the work immediately that day, Wednesday; the stairs would be fresh and redecorated by the following Sunday, 6 October.

Later on Wednesday, Norman Rae knocked on Dr Ruxton's front door. As he awaited an answer, his reporter's eye took in the details of Dalton Square for later recall.

Ruxton must have been startled to see the esteemed crime reporter of the *News of the World* on his doorstep. Ruxton read the paper each week and no doubt recognised the journalist's name. Rae had built his reputation on being the newspaperman who could get the most sensational details from the most notorious murder cases. So renowned was he, that many years later the *News of the World* carried a mini-autobiography by Rae, under the headline 'My Front Page Murders', advertising a series of features Rae had written about his career. It was filled with sensationalist language, designed to crank up the melodrama to sell ever greater numbers of newspapers.

'I am a crime reporter. I am a face in the crowd which gathers round a death,' he wrote.

I am the man who lives, and listens, and writes in the shadow of the gallows. This is my job. I know that for every man who hangs there's more than one woman who weeps. I know to what heights of nobility a man can rise, and to what hideous depths he can fall. I have watched the nets of the Law close in and fasten tight – on devils, and fools, and madmen. I have heard the sound of fury on Execution Eve, and I have seen the eyes of women as the ones they loved were hanged. This too is my job.

I am Norman Rae, chief crime reporter of the *News of the World*. The man in whom murderers have so often chosen to confide.

Ruxton invited the pressman in and answered Rae's questions about Isabella and Mary.

The Moffat ravine mystery was big news, filling newspaper columns and being gossiped about in pubs and at railway stations. Perhaps Ruxton was aware of the whispers floating around Lancaster and Morecambe about Isabella and Mary. He was certainly anxious about gossip linking him to Mrs Smalley's death. Soon, however, rumour-mongers would speculate on a possible connection between Isabella and Mary's disappearance and the bodies under the bridge.

In the coming days, Rae would conduct a series of interviews with him. The doctor might have believed Rae was an ally; the reporter, however, was building a dossier about the doctor, suspecting he might have something to do with the bodies found in Scotland. Rae was nothing if not thorough. He interviewed more than forty of Ruxton's patients. His instincts kicked in when he discovered Ruxton had offered conflicting stories about why Isabella had gone away.

In the coming days as the case developed, *News of the World* reporter John Milligan took over from Rae, who moved on to other stories.

Already their sharp newspaper brains were forging possible angles they could follow with the story. Although they had no evidence, Rae and Milligan began to see the Indian doctor as a possible real-life Othello, the 'Moor' of Shakespeare's tragedy who murdered his wife Desdemona in a jealous rage.

On Friday, 4 October, Ruxton went to the police station across Dalton Square. He was seen by Detective Constable John Winstanley and told him that Isabella had taken Mary away on Sunday, 15 September. She had left Elizabeth, Diana and Billy at home. 'She can't have any love for the children,' Ruxton told Winstanley. 'Not even a postcard to Elizabeth.'

Ruxton took a letter from his pocket to show the detective. He said it was one he had sent to Isabella in Edinburgh, where he believed she had gone with Mary, and read Winstanley some extracts. The letter, he said, had been returned to him unopened. Winstanley listened to the doctor but was aware of the problems the couple had experienced and the occasions his colleagues had intervened. Ruxton was a notable local resident for many reasons, not least for being a nuisance to the police.

Ruxton told him he would take Isabella back, even after everything she had done. He was also troubled by the effect on his medical practice caused by his name being linked by gossip to the death of Mrs Smalley. These rumours, that Ruxton knew the widow and owed her money, would affect his business, he feared.

In a state of high agitation, he took a bunch of keys from his pocket and urged Winstanley to cross Dalton Square with him and search the house. Becoming increasingly emotional, the doctor then began blackguarding Bobby Edmondson, insinuating the young solicitor knew where Isabella was. He suggested to the detective that the police should intercept Bobby's letters to comb for references to his wife.

Winstanley, conscious that Ruxton was behaving irrationally, explained that the police did not have the authority for such a search.

Ruxton said that his telephone bills had been particularly excessive, and that after he asked the authorities to keep a record of calls made from 2 Dalton Square, he had been told that many calls had been made to Lancaster Town Hall and that 'silly love talk' had been overheard.

His temper boiled over and Ruxton banged his fist on the table in the police station. He told Winstanley, 'The blighter, I could murder him.'

42

MORBID ANATOMY

With the bodies now properly preserved, Glaister and Millar began a proper assessment of the mammoth task ahead of them in Edinburgh on Saturday, 5 October.

The remains were an amorphous mass of putrefaction but here and there were recognisable shapes that reminded the scientists they had once been human: a hand here, a foot there. The two heads were so outrageously defiled that they resembled rotting pumpkins.

Glaister and Millar had made a rough estimate of the remains that belonged together, which they had labelled 'Body No 1' and 'Body No 2'. The head of 'Body No 1' had been severed just below the chin. A thorough attempt had been made at removing identifying features: the nose and both ears had been sliced off; the eyes had been gouged out. The butcher had not stopped there. A large flap of the scalp had been peeled away from the right side of the head, while most of the skin on the forehead and face had also been removed. The lips had been all but cut away. The two upper central incisor teeth had been drawn and the tongue protruded through the gap.

There was a small tuft of hair just in front of the stump of the left ear.

The hair was a fair colour.

The part of the scalp that remained had a Y-shaped laceration and there was some hair remaining. Parts of the scalp near the forehead appeared to have been shaved in a rough manner.

The limbs that appeared to be from 'Body No 1' had been rather expertly disarticulated at the joints: the right upper arm, left upper arm, right forearm and hand, left forearm and hand, right thigh, left thigh, right leg and foot, and left leg and foot. There was no trunk found for 'Body No 1'.

There was no disagreement between Glaister and Millar that 'Body No 1' was that of a young female. 'Body No 2' had been more puzzling and initially they believed it to be male. They had revised this view and it was now publicly known that the bodies were those of two women.

The head of 'Body No 2' had been cut off from the trunk at a lower level than in the case of 'Body No 1'. If it were possible, there was even more mutilation to this head. The nose, ears, eyes and much of the skin had been savagely removed. There were tiny patches of scalp remaining. Both lips had been removed and almost all of the teeth had been pulled out. The swollen tongue protruded between the jaws and the tip had been sliced off.

The trunk of 'Body No 2' had been separated into two portions and the spine had been severed in the upper lumbar region. The other limbs and body parts included the right and left upper arms, right and left forearms and hands, both thighs, both legs and the left foot.

Three breasts had been recovered, as had two pieces of human remains that were identified as the external parts of female genital organs with some pubic hair still in place.

Whoever had performed the brutal disarticulation and dismemberment had cut through the upper part of one victim's vagina to remove the uterus, which, complete with both uterine tubes and ovaries, was agreed by both Glaister and Millar to have come from 'Body No 2', that of the older, more masculine woman.

It was not unusual for police and forensic scientists to be confronted with murder cases in which the victims' bodies had been dismembered. In the previous decade there had been a number of landmark cases, chief among these the Norman Thorne case of 1925. Thorne had murdered and cut up the body of Miss Elsie Emily Cameron in Sussex in the south of England.

Glaister and Millar noted that it was relatively straightforward to reassemble a single body dismembered roughly with a knife and a saw, as had been the case with Thorne's victim. The bodies from the Scottish ravine were a wholly different matter and posed huge challenges because of the level of mutilation and the intermingling of body parts of the two victims.

It seemed likely that in this case dismemberment had been done with a knife and the person responsible had done an incredible job of covering his or her tracks.

Glaister knew the task of reassembly would require a brilliant anatomist. He knew just the man.

43

CONFRONTING BOBBY

Ruxton visited the Edmondsons' terraced home at 4 Ullswater Road that Saturday morning in the hope of speaking to Bobby. The young solicitor was not there, but staying with friends, ironically for Ruxton, in Edinburgh. When Bobby's father, Robert, told Ruxton this, the doctor asked what the address was in Scotland. Mr Edmondson felt Ruxton posed the question slyly and detected an agenda. He asked the doctor what his business with Bobby was about.

Ruxton began to cry. Mr Edmondson told him to pull himself together and asked what was troubling him.

Ruxton told him, 'I am sorry for you. I think a lot about your Bobby, but my wife was going to Edinburgh and Bobby is in Edinburgh, and I know there have been telephone messages.'

Suspecting something untoward and wanting to protect his son, Mr Edmondson said Bobby would be back later in the day and would be able to explain the telephone messages.

Ruxton said he knew about Isabella's trip to Edinburgh and the Adelphi Hotel with Bobby and Barbara. Mr Edmondson cut Ruxton short and put him straight on that matter, explaining that he and Mrs Edmondson had also stayed at the hotel.

Ruxton said that Isabella had told him she had stayed with her sister in Edinburgh, not at the Adelphi. Mr Edmondson said he did not know why Isabella would say such a thing. Ruxton said he would still like to speak to Bobby.

When Mrs Edmondson and Barbara came into the room, Ruxton stood up out of respect. He discreetly put his fingers to his lips, a sign to Mr Edmondson to stay silent about their conversation. Quite calm now, Ruxton was charming and friendly towards the two women. As Ruxton left, Mr Edmondson promised him that he and Bobby would visit him the following day to clear up any concerns the doctor had.

The following day was Sunday, 6 October, and Mr Edmondson and Bobby drove to Dalton Square. The doctor was courteous and Bobby explained that what his father had told him the day before was correct: he did not know where Isabella was. Ruxton became emotional, speaking quickly and at a high pitch, finding it difficult to control himself, as a torrent of complaints poured forth about his wife's dishonesty, extravagance and gambling habits.

Feeling Bobby was being unfairly scrutinised by Ruxton, Mr Edmondson asked the doctor directly: did he believe his son had anything to do with Mrs Ruxton going away? This was Ruxton's opportunity to air his thoughts and suspicions, but he did not take it. Instead he said, 'Oh, no, no.'

Mr Edmondson became stern now. He told Ruxton, 'Well, if I hear of you or anybody else mentioning his name in connection with Mrs Ruxton going away now, there will be trouble.'

The scene had been a remarkable one. Ruxton's tendency to flare up at the slightest thing and his lack of emotional control had jolted Mr Edmondson and Bobby. Nevertheless, once Ruxton calmed down, they shook hands and parted on good terms. Mr Edmondson and Bobby left the doctor, believing the matter at an end.

However, Ruxton's conviction of an affair between Isabella and Bobby, if anything, burned brighter than ever.

Later, Ruxton visited Thomas Harrison, whom Ruxton and Isabella had spent New Year's Eve with at the Elms Hotel in Morecambe nine months earlier. Ruxton quizzed his friend on whether he had seen Isabella. He also asked him to warn Bobby Edmondson to keep out of his affairs and to stay away from Isabella.

Ruxton went to the Grand Garage in Morecambe and spoke to one of the garage directors, Robert Yates. He was curious about the size of the petrol tank of the Austin saloon he hired on 18 September. He explained that allegations were being made against him relating to the newspaper story of the bodies found at Moffat and he wished to show that he could not have travelled north to that part of Scotland.

44

ENTER BRASH

Braced against the sharp Edinburgh autumn, Professor James Couper Brash walked through the Gothic archway of the university's medical school at Teviot Place, off the quadrangle and into the laboratories.

With his customary modesty, Brash shook the hand of Glaister, took off his overcoat and dressed in his snow-white lab coat. Brash was 49, a quiet, owlish man with thick, black hair and a quizzical look when he peered from behind his round spectacles. He was universally popular with colleagues and students for his sardonic – or in the Scottish vernacular, 'pawky' – humour. He was also uncommonly kind, yet would rather drift into the shadows than take credit for his generosity.

It was time to examine the badly decomposed bodies and attempt to piece them back together. Glaister later wrote, 'Our task required all the help available. For a start, I decided the services of a highly experienced anatomist were needed.'

No anatomist came more highly experienced than Professor Brash. He had succeeded the celebrated Arthur Robinson in the Chair of Anatomy at Edinburgh University in 1931, the pinnacle in a career distinguished by professional highs. Brash was a proud Scot, born in Helensburgh, a handsome resort popular among visitors on the River Clyde, west of Glasgow. The son of a bank manager, he was clever, dazzling teaching staff when he entered Edinburgh University in 1903. He threw himself not only into his studies but also into the social and intellectual life outside of the classroom. In essence, Brash was a team-player, a quality Glaister would come to cherish during work on the Moffat case.

After graduating, Brash had become a Demonstrator in Anatomy under Arthur Robinson. He served with the Royal Army Medical Corps in Belgium and France during the First World War. He rose to the rank of major and was decorated with the Military Cross for gallantry. After the war, he held posts at Leeds and Birmingham, before fate brought him back to Edinburgh, a seasoned anatomist with a keen eye for detail and a special expertise in the growth of the human jaw and the movement of teeth.

While Glaister would oversee the investigation, it was essentially Brash, the anatomist, who would do the grim work of handling the body parts and performing their rearticulation.

There were several intriguing historical cases of bodily dismemberment that would prove touchstones for Brash and Glaister.

The head, limbs and trunk of a woman were found scattered at separate locations across London in the 1837 Greenacre case. Identification was made after the startling discovery that the victim lacked a uterus. In Boston in the United States in 1849, anatomists were able to reconstruct a body from scant remains found in the laboratory of a professor of chemistry called Webster. The professor was eventually convicted of murder thanks to evidence given by the victim's dentist. In 1910, the conviction of Dr Crippen hinged on the evidence of Sir Bernard Spilsbury in relation to the leaf of skin with a scar resembling the one that Crippen's wife bore. In 1917, bloodstains in the London flat of French butcher Louis Voisin led to his downfall after he dismembered the body of his victim. The police's belief that the mutilator knew how to use a knife also proved crucial in Voisin's conviction.

Brash and Glaister were also mindful of three more recent murder cases involving dismemberment.

The first was the Mahon case of 1924, which had led to Spilsbury's evolution of the police crime scene bag. The second was the murder of Elsie Cameron in Sussex by Norman Thorne, although identification was not necessary as Thorne admitted killing her.

The Charing Cross trunk murder of 1927 foreshadowed the Mancini case in Brighton in 1934. Inside a trunk left at the London railway station was the body of a woman, minus her legs and arms, removed with a knife. A man called Robinson was eventually convicted on evidence relating to laundry marks on clothing found in the trunk, a bloodstained match and a hairpin found in his wastepaper basket.

These were all medico-legal precedents to which Brash and Glaister looked for honest inspiration. None of these cases, however, came close in complexity to the gory puzzle they faced. Unlike the previous cases, they were dealing not with one but two bodies, intermingled.

It truly was unprecedented.

The rearticulation would require new thinking and techniques if their work was to be translated into effective evidence at any future criminal trial.

The reconstruction work would prove slow and painstaking, a process of trial and error using a panoply of technical equipment including X-ray examinations. Key to its success was Brash's superior anatomical knowledge and ability to determine when he had correctly reassembled parts, which could then be proved beyond reasonable doubt. The accuracy of this reconstruction depended on such factors as the height, stature and age of the victims.

While it was now clear the bulk of the remains were from no more than two bodies, it was essential to sift the evidence forensically to rule out the presence of even a particle from other victims. They knew that asserting with certainty that the remains constituted two bodies and two bodies only was an evidential necessity. After some work, they were satisfied that this was the case.

When the bodies were recovered from Gardenholme linn, the most mutilated head had been put with the trunk of 'Body No 2' as they appeared to go together. But now Brash needed proof. He lifted each head in turn and placed them at the top of the trunk of 'Body No 2'. Key to his conclusions were comparisons using X-rays of the vertebrae remaining on each head and those on the trunk. 'The cumulative effect of all these pieces of evidence made it quite impossible to doubt that Head No 2 belonged to the same body as the reconstructed trunk,' Brash and Glaister later wrote. So Glaister and Millar's original assumption had been proved correct.

There were two sets of limbs found in the ravine. The next step for Brash was to establish which of the forearms and thighs and legs were from the body with the trunk as that would provide the most complete body of the two. He took the limb segments that matched each other in left and right segments according to measurements and rearticulated upper arms with forearms at the elbow joints, and thighs with legs at the knee joints. He and Glaister wrote: 'The opinion that not more than two bodies were represented was thus progressively confirmed.'

Now it was time to see which set of limbs would match the trunk from the remains designated as 'Body No 2'. Tests were carried out to confirm what was already suspected based on the difference in size between the sets of limbs: one of the victims had been taller than the other and it was the longer-boned limbs that articulated perfectly with the trunk. Both hands of the longer limbs had been badly mutilated, making identification difficult, with the terminal segment of each thumb and the two terminal segments of all the fingers cut off.

There were three significant pieces missing from the reassembled limbs. Fortune would bless Brash and Glaister in the coming weeks when the left foot of the longer limbs ('Body No 2'), cut off at the ankle bone, would be found on 28 October in the ravine area, while the right forearm and hand of the shorter set of limbs ('Body No 1') would be discovered on 4 November. Only the right foot of 'Body No 2' would remain unaccounted for.

'Body No 2' was the most complete; 'Body No 1' had many missing parts besides its trunk, including the shoulder blades.

When every piece had been rearticulated and assembled into the two separate corpses, Brash and Glaister set about preparing them for measurement and photographing. Each reconstructed body was suspended in correct anatomical proportions, like a medical student's instructional skeleton, and placed next to a measuring bar.

The police had told the press on 1 October that the likely perpetrator would have had anatomical knowledge. This assumption had not changed following Brash and Glaister's work. Dismemberment had been achieved without exception through bodily joints and had been done neatly and efficiently without damage to surrounding tissue. A complete amateur, lacking anatomical knowledge, was more likely to use a saw to cut through bone, a formidable task, the scientists concluded.

In the view of Brash and Glaister, the ravine butcher had used a knife throughout the dismemberment, knew precisely where the joints were located and made use of them in the morbid task. There were one or two fractures in bones in the remains that might have been caused when the bodies were being cut up, but they might also have been caused when the remains were flung into Gardenholme linn.

The fact that eyes, ears, lips, fingertips and teeth had been removed showed not only the perpetrator's desire to remove identifying features, but also an understanding that such features can reveal signs of asphyxia, another incriminating piece of evidence. While such absences in theory made identification more difficult, Brash and Glaister recognised the paradox that in removing them the person had unwittingly drawn attention to these features, which might prove useful in a 'photo-negative' way when trawling through descriptions of missing persons.

Glaister and Brash were required to state how long they thought it would have taken to butcher the two bodies. After careful consideration, they concluded it would have taken the person, using the proper, sharp instruments, five hours for 'Body No 2' and three hours for 'Body No 1', which was less mutilated.

That person would also have possessed a professional level of dexterity.

The trunk of 'Body No 1' would never be found. Brash's conclusions, after hours and hours of anatomical reconstruction, were as follows. The victim whose cadaver formed 'Body No 1' had been small in build, of between 4ft 10in and 4ft 11½in in height. She had weighed around 7½ stone. Bone development showed that she had been aged somewhere between 18 and 25. But Brash believed she was most probably 20 or 21.

The reassembled parts of 'Body No 2' showed that the woman had been 5ft 4½in tall, weighing between 9 and 10 stone and aged between 35 and 45 years of age.

Having watched him at work, Glaister had huge confidence in Brash and later described how his admiration had grown during those early days of October. But they both knew that the ultimate test of their work would be in any subsequent trial should the police succeed in unravelling the mystery.

Although it was not yet known, the bodily attributes established by Brash perfectly fitted descriptions soon to be circulated of Mary Rogerson ('Body No 1') and Isabella Ruxton ('Body No 2').

45

SUSPICION

On Monday, 7 October, Isabella's sister Jeanie Nelson was at her home in Bothwell Street in Edinburgh. The postman delivered a letter postmarked Lancaster and Morecambe. It was from Ruxton. It was an incredible, impassioned document, soaked in Ruxton's apparent distress over Isabella.

The letter began: 'My dear Sister, I am heart-broken and half-mad. Isabella has again left me. She has done this trick again after about ten months.'

Ruxton wrote that Isabella had been making plans to take on responsibility for promoting the football pools for the county of Lancashire. He said he had discovered she had planned to rent rooms in Blackburn for this purpose. She had furnished the rooms but had not yet begun using them, yet the rent was starting to mount up. He continued:

> I am sorry to have to tell you a tale, but ever since she has left there is no end of bills that I am getting. She has bought clothes and other things to the tune of over £100 from various shops in Lancaster. She has been evidently backing horses, and a prominent bookie in Lancaster is demanding £21 15s from her. The most important thing is that she is trying to help our maid who is in a certain condition. I hope she does not involve herself into any trouble with the law, because she will be liable for helping her for such affairs.

By 'certain condition' Ruxton meant Mary was pregnant.

His thoughts turned to Elizabeth, Diana and Billy: 'The children are asking for her daily and I really cannot sleep without her.'

He said Isabella had been telling him for months that she wanted to go into business on her own. He wrote: 'Do you think she needs to do all that? I am afraid I cannot knock sense in her. She is highly impulsive and thinks she can be a millionaire overnight.'

The mystery of Isabella's whereabouts hung heavily over the letter. He wrote: 'According to the latest information she is somewhere in

Birmingham, but I cannot keep on running after her. I have got a very bad hand and it is my right hand. It is all painful and swollen. I am intending to come over to Edinburgh on Wednesday [9 October] to talk things over with you.'

In the letter Ruxton asked Jeanie whether the Kerr family had relations in Canada, as Isabella had 'some time ago got into her head to go to Canada'.

> I really don't know one minute what next she is going to do. My life is impossible without her presence in my house. I do admit I have a temper, but your sister gives me strong cause of provocation now and again. In spite of all that I am terribly fond of my Belle. How could she be so heartless to leave me like that?

He asked a favour of his sister-in-law. Could she supply addresses of people he listed in various places in Scotland where Isabella might have gone? Ruxton's impulses and emotions cascaded down the page, with no breaks between thoughts. In his next breath he asked:

> Has she been to your place or not? I want you to tell me the honest truth. Please do not intentionally help Isabella to keep away from me. I want you to help me to keep my home together. I am simply distracted. I cannot even keep my mind on the practice. You must ask her on your own to come back to me. I am surely coming to see you on Wednesday afternoon at about four. Till then, yours affectionately, Bommie.

Disturbed and upset by the letter, Jeanie showed it to her son, Jim, who would not allow his mother to reply. Instead he wrote back to Ruxton on her behalf, to spare her any further distress. Jim Nelson informed the doctor that neither his mother nor any of the family could help him further and that he should not visit them in Edinburgh.

Jeanie received another letter from Ruxton on the morning of Wednesday, 9 October. Ruxton had written it the day before. He said:

> Dear Sister Jean, I have received word per Jim. You say you cannot help me and do not wish me to come to Bothwell Street. I never knew I was so unwelcome at yours. Perhaps Belle has told you something which might have put you against me. Moreover after all she is your sister and you must side with her. All I wanted you to do was to persuade Belle,

once more, as you did last year, to come back to me and the children. Anyway, I should be very much grateful to you if you would kindly see me at sister Lizzie's [Mrs Trench] to-morrow afternoon at about four o'clock. The train will reach Edinburgh at a quarter to four. I know Isabella a little better than any other person. She will never be happy anywhere the way she has left me and the children.

He repeated his belief that Isabella was seeking to go to Canada and had been in communication with somebody in Saskatchewan; Isabella had told him once she had an old aunt who lived there. She had taken her belongings when she left, he wrote, and had run up debts of £100 in shops in Lancaster for clothes she had bought. He continued:

Even this morning I have got a fresh bill from a dressmaker. You can imagine how I feel. I just want to see you at least once and I can assure you I will not take up much of your time. Please do not misunderstand me, but remember that you have got children of your own and one of them is already married happily. I request you to try your level best to help me to keep my home together. If you are intentionally helping your sister to keep away from me by listening to her one-sided story I want you to hear my story, which I can prove by documents. Then if you feel satisfied that there is just grievance on my part, you can ask your sister to go back to me.

Sure to goodness I am not such a terrible person that she cannot live with me. I do admit we have had rows, but Belle has given me lots of causes of provocation.

He repeated the claims about Isabella and her plans to run a football pools business from Blackburn, as well as her heavy gambling. He concluded:

If she does not turn up soon I will have to publish her photo in the newspapers. I do not want to do that if I can help it. Please if you know where she is I appeal to you to let me know. I will not even speak a wrong word to her if she would just come back. I can't understand her sudden change of attitude. Well, I am hoping to see you to-morrow. Till then, yours affectionately, B.

Jeanie relented. Ruxton arrived at Waverley railway station that Wednesday, having taken the train from Lancaster. He met with Jeanie at the home of her sister, Lizzie Trench, at 7 Heriot Mount, the tenement home where Isabella had been living when she married Van Ess, at half past four that afternoon.

Ruxton was again extremely excited and unable to control his emotions. He asked Jeanie if she was hiding Isabella.

'Don't you know where she is?' she asked him.

'What do you mean?'

She was direct with him: had he done anything to Isabella?

'I would not harm a hair on her head,' he replied. 'I would not hurt her. I love her too much. I do not stand to make a penny by her death.'

Neither of Isabella's sisters could get a word in as Ruxton raged about Isabella's extravagance. He believed Mary Rogerson had gone away with her and that Mary was pregnant. He knew this because he had heard his children saying that Mary had 'a sweetheart', who was a laundryman. He told the sisters he had told Isabella of this and that it could mean Mary would leave their employment and get married, leaving them without someone to care for Elizabeth, Diana and Billy.

He claimed to have asked Mary if she intended to get married. Mary had apparently replied, 'Ask no questions and you will be told no lies.' He claimed to have told Mary he could 'see her condition himself'.

Ruxton quizzed the sisters about Isabella's visit to see them in Blackpool on 14 September, asking whether she had been alone. Jeanie told him she had been. He also talked about Isabella's visit to Edinburgh with the Edmondsons the week previous. He admitted he had followed them in another car and it had been raining. He had placed a brown paper screen in the car windows so that he could not be seen but he could still watch them. He claimed to have seen the Adelphi Hotel's guest book and had seen a Mr and Mrs Ruxton or Dr and Mrs Ruxton registered. Isabella had been sleeping with Bobby, Ruxton claimed. He had seen his own car, the Hillman Minx, parked alongside the Edmondsons' car in the hotel garage. 'Imagine my feelings to see such a thing,' he told the sisters.

Jeanie told him he was being ridiculous as Bobby's parents and sister had been staying in the same hotel.

Ruxton said he had arrived back in Lancaster first following the 7 September trip. He described what happened when Isabella walked through the door in Dalton Square: he said he welcomed her and asked about her journey home, expressing concern that she must be tired. Isabella had told him she had stayed at Jeanie's home in Bothwell Street. He had called her a liar and accused her of sleeping with Bobby. He ranted again about the people in Edinburgh he wanted to trace to see if Isabella was with them.

Jeanie was tired of his tone. She questioned how Isabella could have cleared out all her possessions without his knowing; he said she had done so before. He repeated that he would have to publish Isabella's photograph in the newspapers.

Jeanie cut him dead: she said that was all right – the police would be looking for her. She told him she had had a letter from Mr Rogerson, Mary's father.

Ruxton said that Mrs Rogerson was a nice woman, but Mary's father was 'very unreasonable' and did not believe what Ruxton told him. He said he had visited the Rogersons and Mary's father was critical of him for sending her to Mrs Holme's farm at Seatle, near Grange-over-Sands, in the summer.

It was time for some home truths. Jeanie told Ruxton that Isabella had intended leaving him as soon as she could, planning to return to Edinburgh and take a flat there. Isabella had asked her if she would share the flat as she was a widow.

Ruxton's visit went on and on. The sun had set and curtains on the street had been pulled to. Jeanie Nelson and Lizzie Trench were exhausted. They were none the wiser about where their sister was; they were unimpressed with Ruxton and his account of what had happened. They knew Isabella was impulsive and headstrong. It might have been painful to admit it, but they knew Isabella loved Ruxton and he her, but they also knew things had gone wrong with their relationship; they knew of the emotional and physical abuse Isabella had suffered at Ruxton's hands.

Eventually Ruxton calmed down. Mrs Trench showed him to the door at around ten o'clock that night; Jeanie Nelson did not follow, but she heard Ruxton say to Lizzie as he left: 'If anybody comes asking questions, do not answer them.'

A seed of doubt about Ruxton's claims had been planted in the minds of Isabella Kerr Ruxton's sisters.

Meanwhile that afternoon, Detective Constable John Winstanley of Lancaster Police had called on Mr and Mrs Rogerson at Morecambe over their concern about Mary. He wrote down a description of her and sent it to Lancashire Police's headquarters at five o'clock. It was circulated to all police forces across the north-west of England.

And because Ruxton had told Mrs Rogerson that Mary had gone with Isabella to Edinburgh, it was circulated to all Scottish forces too.

Mrs Rogerson, racked with worry, telephoned the Glasgow *Daily Record* personally to pass on Mary's description.

Ruxton's train from Edinburgh pulled in at Lancaster Castle railway station at ten to four on the morning of Thursday, 10 October. He was tired from the events of the previous afternoon. As he stepped down from the carriage, he was recognised by Inspector Thomas Clark of Lancaster Police. It was customary for an officer to meet all the trains in and out of Lancaster Castle station during the night. Standing on the platform, Ruxton told Clark he had been to Scotland in search of Isabella, but he had been unsuccessful after meeting with her sisters, who did not know of her whereabouts.

Clark said his car was outside; he would drive the doctor home to Dalton Square.

During the ten-minute journey, Ruxton recounted the saga of Isabella's trip to Edinburgh with Bobby Edmondson on 7 September. Ruxton said: 'Inspector, Edmondson knows where my wife and maid are. I will tell you something. A few weeks ago my wife asked me for a loan of my car. I allowed her to take it. I became suspicious. I hired a car unknown to my wife.'

He repeated the story of Isabella and Edmondson checking into the Adelphi as 'Mr and Mrs Ruxton', but did not mention Bobby's parents and sister being on the trip.

By the time Clark's car pulled up outside 2 Dalton Square, Ruxton had also told him about his accident in Kendal, explaining that he had been returning from Seatle.

As Ruxton got out of the inspector's car, he told Clark, 'You inquire of Mr Edmondson at the Town Hall, and he will be able to tell you where my wife and maid are.'

William Black, Chief Constable of Dumfriesshire Police, had called in expert help with the investigation. Inspector Jeremiah Lynch of Scotland Yard's famous Flying Squad, a formidable detective, brought his considerable talent and experience of missing persons to the case. Lynch was an Irishman, hailing from County Kerry, aged 46, strong and powerfully built, and known for his good humour. He bore a close resemblance to the Hollywood gangster movie star Edward G. Robinson. Lynch was also interested in the newspapers that had been found with the bodies. Officers had preserved the pieces of sodden newspaper by drying them with blotting paper and then placing them between sheets of celluloid.

Lynch and Detective Willie Ewing found that the scraps came from three different newspapers. There were pieces from *Daily Herald* issues dated between 5 August and 2 September, and the *Sunday Chronicle* of 8 September.

Two scraps torn from the most recent newspaper – and the one of most interest to detectives – came from the *Sunday Graphic and Sunday News* dated Sunday, 15 September. These were the ones that had caught Ewing's eye. One piece was from the front page with the *Sunday Graphic and Sunday News* masthead, a banner headline: 'Lady Londonderry's Frank Memoirs' and a teaser: 'LAUREL AND HARDY TO-DAY'. There was a serial number, 1,067. On the reverse was a photograph of two young girls, one wearing a crown.

Due to the way it had been torn, the second scrap from the *Sunday Graphic* had the incomplete headline: '–AMBE'S CARNIVAL QUEEN –ROWNED'.

Ewing's belief that this concerned Morecambe proved correct. The report was about the resort's carnival on Saturday, 14 September. He interviewed the *Sunday Graphic* circulation manager, Edwin Vaughan Morris, who confirmed what reporters told him in Moffat, that the page was from a limited souvenir 'slip' edition issued only in Morecambe, Lancaster and neighbouring towns. Police asked how many copies were printed and circulated. Morris replied: 3,700. He was able to help further. A total of 728 copies had been supplied to Albert Merrett, a wholesale newsagent based in George Street in Lancaster on Saturday, 15 September.

Detectives spoke to Merrett, who confirmed twenty-four copies had been supplied to newsagent and tobacconist George Capstick, who had a shop in Lancaster. Capstick provided detectives with a list of customers who took a copy of the *Sunday Graphic*.

Scotland Yard's Inspector Lynch set to work tracing every single one of the customers who had received a copy of the paper from Mr Capstick.

On that list was the name and address of Dr Buck Ruxton of Dalton Square.

The scrap of newspaper was fortuitous but it resulted in one young man being wrongly suspected of double murder and plunged into a nightmare worthy of Franz Kafka.

Richard Dugdale was 26, and newly arrived in Moffat at the time of the discovery at Gardenholme linn. He originated from the railway town of Carnforth, a few miles north of Lancaster, and worked primarily as a driver. In 1935 he answered an advert for a chauffeur with a Moffat doctor in general practice, who had temporarily lost his driving licence. Dugdale got the job and drove the doctor to remote properties around Moffat. While the GP saw patients, Dugdale would stretch his legs.

In late September, the doctor was seeing patients near the Devil's Beef Tub. Dugdale went for a stroll in the nearby countryside and found himself on the bridge spanning Gardenholme linn. A keen fisherman, he paused to peer into the stream below, no doubt picturing himself on the bank with a rod and tackle, whiling away a few pleasant hours. The bridge was a quiet and lonely one; traffic and walkers crossed it occasionally, but Dugdale was oblivious, lost in the reverie of his fishing fantasy. In time, he strolled back to the car. Finding the doctor ready, he drove him back to Moffat.

Dugdale was plunged into a nightmare after the bodies were discovered. A witness reported seeing him peering over the bridge into the ravine. In light of the newspaper linked to Morecambe, police became suspicious when they learned Dugdale was originally from that area and received a copy of the *Lancaster Guardian* each week from his parents.

He was pulled in for questioning on suspicion of double murder. It was the type of nightmare scenario film director Alfred Hitchcock specialised in. Only that summer, Hitchcock's version of *The Thirty-Nine Steps* about an innocent man who becomes a fugitive after being caught up in a murky espionage plot had played in cinemas, and he would go on to make further classics of Kafkaesque paranoia such as *The Wrong Man* and *North By Northwest*.

In later life, Richard Dugdale rarely talked about being wrongly suspected in the murders. He told his stepson, Sandy Crosthwaite, about it only once and completely out of the blue, prompted by a television documentary on the case.

'I had a devil of a time convincing them I hadn't done anything,' Dugdale told his stepson and then promptly dropped the subject.

In early October 1935, there would be a fresh turn of events that would put Richard Dugdale in the clear.

46

A CONNECTION IS MADE

As detectives interviewed Lancaster newsagents, on Wednesday, 9 October, the day Ruxton had gone to Edinburgh, Chief Constable Black read a report in the Glasgow *Daily Record* about the disappearance of a young maid from Lancashire. The story included Mary Rogerson's description circulated by Lancaster Police.

Given the *Sunday Graphic* development, Black's suspicions were aroused. He immediately contacted Henry Vann, the Chief Constable of Lancaster Police. He learned that Mary Rogerson was the maid of a Dr Buck Ruxton, whose wife had left him at the same time that Mary went missing.

Mid-morning on Thursday, 10 October, Ruxton visited Mrs Hampshire: he was concerned about his suit. It was upstairs, she told him. 'Do something about it,' he implored her. 'Get it out of the way. Burn it.'

He told her the police had been asking him about Mary Rogerson. Had she cleaned the carpets he had given her? She told him he was standing on one of them and said it had been a devil's job cleaning it. He told her to burn them also.

Ruxton was extremely agitated. He asked if she would stand by him. He said he did not have a single friend. She would later recall Ruxton had seemed quite desperate, and that he was convinced the net was closing around him.

As he left her home, he turned and said he intended giving the police a statement about Isabella. He made one last request: not to speak to the police before he had done so.

Ruxton next drove to the Rogersons' home on Thornton Road in Morecambe. He told Mrs Rogerson he had seen Isabella's sisters and had been trying to trace Mary.

At ten o'clock that night, Ruxton walked across Dalton Square to the police station. On duty was Detective Constable John Winstanley, whom Ruxton had spoke to on 4 October.

'Winstanley, all this damned nonsense is ruining my practice,' complained Ruxton about the gossip now prevalent, linking Isabella and Mary's disappearance to the bodies in the Scottish ravine. 'Can nothing be done to stop this talk?'

This would not be the last time Ruxton would make such complaints to the police. Winstanley told him what other officers would tell him: the police had no authority over what was reported in the newspapers. He said it might be prudent to put out a description of Isabella and report her as missing. So Ruxton dictated one to Winstanley and signed it.

The description read:

> Buck Ruxton says: I am a medical practitioner and I reside at 2 Dalton Square, Lancaster. The following is a description of my wife: Name, Isabella Ruxton, 35 years, about 5 ft 5 ins or 5 ft 6 ins. Well built, fair hair, bridge of nose uneven. Three false teeth left upper jaw, gold clip shows when smiling. Fair complexion. Dressed in cream silk blouse, light-brown small check coat and skirt, suede shoes dark brown colour, and had a V-shaped ring on forefinger of left hand. Speaks with strong Scots accent. I would like discreet inquiries made by the police with a view to finding my wife. She left home on Sunday the 15th of September, 1935, and I have not seen her since. Signed, 'B. Ruxton'.

Winstanley walked back across Dalton Square with Ruxton to collect a photograph of Isabella to accompany the description.

Later that night Isabella Ruxton's description and photograph were circulated to the newspapers.

The following day, Friday 11 October, Ruxton went to the police station again and spoke to Detective Inspector William Green, who was making inquiries into Mary Rogerson's disappearance. Green told Ruxton he had seen Mr and Mrs Rogerson. He asked the doctor how he knew Mary was pregnant. Ruxton said:

I have not examined her, but it does not require a doctor's examination to tell when a girl is pregnant. One day we had some friends for tea and she was passing me to serve at the other side of the table, and she was holding herself in such a position … [Ruxton showed Green the position he meant] that it suddenly flashed through my mind there is something wrong with that girl. I looked again and noticed that her face was pinched, but, of course, a woman can conceal her condition until she is six or eight months' pregnant. I just noticed a slight swelling. I should say she was two or three months pregnant.

Green turned the conversation to the last day Isabella and Mary were seen, 15 September. He asked Ruxton what time they had left the house. Ruxton replied:

Well, I will tell you. My wife was always changing her mind. We had all arranged to go away for the day and I got up early for that purpose, when my wife changed her mind and said she was going to Edinburgh and taking Mary with her. I was not surprised at this, as she was always changing her mind. About 9.15 that morning I was in the bathroom when she tapped at the door and said, 'I am going, dear.' I replied 'All right,' or something like that – I am not sure of the exact words.

Green inquired what luggage the women had taken and how they had travelled to Edinburgh. Ruxton said he did not know as he did not see them leave.

Frank Eason, who had decorated Ruxton's staircase at the start of October, called for payment for the work. Ruxton was full of questions for the decorator. He wanted to know whether Eason recalled doing work at the house in early May. Eason replied that he did. Ruxton was keen for Eason to remember being asked to decorate the staircase.

'No, you said interior decorating,' Eason corrected the increasingly agitated doctor.

Ruxton said, 'Do you not see they are saying I have got you to decorate my staircase to cover up the bloodstains, as I have done a murder?'

Eason was unaware the police were investigating the disappearance of Mary Rogerson.

✚

The evening's newspapers carried stories of Isabella and Mary being reported as missing. Juxtaposed with fresh reports of the Moffat investigation, they left Ruxton fearing local gossip would link the two. At 9.30 p.m., he strode across Dalton Square to the police station for a third time in twenty-four hours to speak to Chief Constable Vann. Inspector Green was also present.

Ruxton took the Chief Constable by the hand and said, 'My dear Vann, can't you do something about these newspaper reports?' Ruxton showed the two policemen a report in the *Daily Express*. The story made reference to the teeth of one of the bodies.

'Look at this. This newspaper says that this woman has a full set of teeth in the lower jaw, and I know, of my own knowledge, that Mary Rogerson has at least four teeth missing in this jaw,' Ruxton told Vann, suddenly becoming excited, waving his arms about. 'This publicity is ruining my practice; particularly at a time when I am negotiating for a loan on my practice,' he said.

Ruxton pulled a letter from his pocket. 'I did not want to show you this, but here it is. Read it and you will see.' Vann did not look at the letter, but recognised the name of the firm on the heading; it was most likely a letter related to the loan.

The doctor sat on Vann's table, put his feet on the chair and stamped his foot violently. He ran his fingers through his hair. Vann later said Ruxton was in an 'agitated state', while Green would describe the doctor as being in 'a great rage'.

'This damned Bobby Edmondson is ruining my home,' Ruxton continued. 'One day I tapped a telephone conversation when [Isabella] spoke to this man. The conversation was in lovers' terms,' he told Vann and said he had confirmed the number with the telephone company. 'Have you any authority to intercept letters in the post?' Ruxton asked.

Vann now took control. He told Ruxton he had no such authority. Tears streamed down the doctor's face and he was terribly distressed. Calming for a moment, Ruxton asked, 'Can't you publish it in the papers that there is no connection between the two [the Moffat bodies and Isabella and Mary] and stop all this trouble?'

Vann told Ruxton that he would do that only when he was satisfied there was no connection.

Ruxton left Vann's office and returned to his home on the other side of the square.

Ruxton did not know it, but Henry Vann and the Scottish police had him in their sights. They had been biding their time since Wednesday, maintaining continuous communication across the border between Scotland and England. Brash and Glaister had now established definitively that the remains were those of two females. They could say with certainty that 'Body No 1' was that of a young woman, and 'Body No 2' of an older woman.

It was time.

That evening, Friday, 11 October, Chief Constable Black, Inspector Henry Strath of Lockerbie Police, and Detective Lieutenants William Ewing and Bertie Hammond, of Glasgow Police, caught the train from Scotland to Lancaster.

Vann welcomed them to the police station in Dalton Square. He had called in extra officers from Morecambe and Lancashire County CID, including Inspector William Green, who had questioned Ruxton about Mary earlier in the week. Vann's office was packed tightly with keen-minded officers picking over the evidence, working out a plan of action.

Chief Constable Black was keen for positive identification of the garments recovered with the bodies. They were shown to Mary's stepmother, Jessie, who broke down when she recognised the blouse. She had bought it from a jumble sale in Morecambe and had repaired it by sewing a patch under one of the arms before giving it to Mary. She told police she did not recognise the rompers, but she knew Mary had been given some clothes for the Ruxton children by a lady who lived at a farm near Grange-over-Sands in the Lake District.

Mrs Edith Holme of Seatle immediately recognised the child's woollen garment when officers showed it to her.

Late on Friday, Dr Leonard Mather had been reading in his study at South Road, when his housekeeper had knocked on his door. She apologised for disturbing him, but said she had had a horrible thought. She had read the local newspaper report about the disappearance of Dr Ruxton's wife and maid. She shared her thoughts: could it be that the bodies found in the ravine at Moffat were Mrs Ruxton and Mary?

Mather later wrote, 'Then everything fitted into position. Ruxton coming to my surgery with his cut finger, wanting to borrow £3,000, the timing of his visit when my surgery was about to commence and likewise his, so that we would both be in a hurry.'

He believed this was of great significance, so on Saturday morning Mather went to see Henry Vann at Dalton Square. He knew the Chief Constable well. He told Vann about Ruxton's loan and how he had been named as a referee. 'I told him that I had received a written acknowledgement from a firm of money lenders,' Mather later wrote. He had torn up the letter, but believed it might still be in his wastepaper basket. '[Vann] told me to go home and look for the paper and to return to the police station at 9 p.m. that night.'

47

DAY OF RECKONING

Early on Saturday, 12 October, Ruxton visited Mrs Oxley. He wanted to prime her on what to say, should she be questioned, about the morning of 15 September.

'Oh, Mrs Oxley, about that Sunday morning, tell them I came for you at seven o'clock,' he instructed her. 'Tell them I came at seven o'clock and told you not to come, and that I came again at nine and you came down till eleven.'

Mrs Oxley told him that she could not say that to the police. It was not the truth.

Shortly after Ruxton had gone, Detective Inspector Green visited her. He collected bloodstained carpets that Ruxton had given her from 2 Dalton Square, around the time he gave some to Mrs Hampshire. Green handed these to Detective Sergeant Walter Stainton at the police station.

Around half past four that Saturday afternoon, Ernest Hall, the County Cinema projectionist and odd-job man, visited Ruxton's home after receiving a message from the doctor. Ruxton took him into his consulting room and asked Hall if he remembered visiting 2 Dalton Square at 10.30 on the night of Saturday, 14 September, to repair a fuse. He told Hall that Mary Rogerson had answered the door to him. Hall could not recall the visit.

Ruxton said, 'Surely you remember coming in on that particular night?' He was quite insistent and wanted Hall to swear in a court that he had visited that night. When Hall again said he did not remember, and suggested the doctor meant the Monday night of 16 September, Ruxton became argumentative and said he did not mean the 16th. Hall said he could not have gone to Ruxton's home on that night as he had been ill in bed and the doctor had signed him off work.

Ruxton became excited and Hall found him unintelligible. The doctor sat at his desk and began scribbling notes on a pad. He told Hall he was going to make a statement to the police and became emotional as he muttered something about his children.

Henry James Vann had served almost twenty years in the police. Aged 37, he was tall and muscular with a bulldog face, often punctuated by a pipe clasped between his teeth. He was softly spoken and considered. He wore a tan overcoat and favoured a bowler hat over the trilbies and fedoras popular with his colleagues.

He was originally from Nottingham in the East Midlands, the only son of a hosiery-manufacturing father and a dressmaker mother. He served for five years in the West Yorkshire Regiment during the First World War and was wounded on the Somme in July 1916. He saw out his Army service as a physical training instructor with three stripes on his arm, having reached the rank of sergeant. In 1919 when he was discharged, he joined Swansea Borough Police Force as a constable. Fit and active, Vann played football for Notts County and, at Swansea, for the police team, and won a number of swimming trophies. He was talented, hard-working and ambitious. Within two years he had been appointed to work in the Chief Constable's office. Five years later he was a police sergeant and chief clerk to Swansea Police. By 1928 he was a police inspector. His desire for promotion led him to apply for the post of Chief Constable in Lancaster and in 1934 he arrived bearing the rank of captain at the small police station in Dalton Square.

Vann's suspicion of Ruxton hardened following the doctor's behaviour in his office. With detectives from Scotland and Lancashire ready to pounce, Vann was conscious of their timing. He later wrote, 'as it was desirable that the doctor's mind should be set at rest until the police were ready to act, I arranged with the Press at the next conference of the Press representatives on the Saturday afternoon to publish' a statement dispelling links between the disappearance of Isabella and Mary and the Moffat bodies.

So the evening newspapers carried reports of Vann stating he had no evidence linking the two. Ruxton read his copy of the *Lancashire Daily Post* and immediately lifted the phone to tell Vann of his delight.

Vann's ploy worked but he and the officers across Dalton Square were playing a delicate game of strategy. They wanted Ruxton to believe he was in the clear. The last thing they needed was for him to panic and abscond.

That evening, Ruxton gave an interview in his library at Dalton Square to *News of the World* reporter John Milligan. The reporter found it arduous because Ruxton was in turmoil over the police's interest and the rumours in Lancaster. Milligan wrote:

> He paced rapidly up and down the library floor, nervously fingering an oriental knife, ran trembling fingers through tousled hair, and occasionally thumped his forehead with the palm of his hand. Now and again he stopped, swung round, and almost screamed: 'I did not kill my Belle; I tell you she had gone away; she will come back. Tell everybody I am not guilty.' He sobbed, 'Tell them I loved my Belle too much to harm her.'

At twenty-five past nine, Ruxton's telephone rang. He interrupted the interview as he did not want the noise to wake the children. He lifted the receiver and answered the call.

It was Vann – he had some information relating to Isabella and asked if the doctor could come across to the police station.

At nine o'clock, Dr Mather had arrived at the police station in Dalton Square, just as Captain Vann had instructed him. He had the torn-up letter of acknowledgement about Ruxton's loan with him. Mather was invited into Vann's office. He later wrote that there were around a dozen 'strange men' with Vann, who explained that they were detectives from Lancashire and Scotland.

At twenty-five past nine, Mather saw Vann speak to Ruxton on the telephone and invite the doctor across to the police station.

Ruxton left Elizabeth, Diana and Billy-Boy asleep in their beds and alone in the house. He did not expect to be long visiting Vann.

He opened the front door. Dalton Square was dark. He looked across the cobbles to the Queen Victoria statue, the gardens, and beyond to the tower of the Town Hall.

He pulled the door shut behind him and began walking the few hundred yards to Vann's office in the police station.

He would not see the inside of 2 Dalton Square or set eyes on his 'wee mites' ever again.

48

'MY MOVEMENTS'

They waited for Ruxton in Vann's office.

The minutes ticked by.

Vann did not want Ruxton to see Dr Mather.

Mather hid behind a door.

Ruxton was shown in.

An officer whispered to Mather: 'This could be the last time Ruxton is at large.'

Ruxton's blood ran cold.

Vann's office was full of serious-looking men. Vann told Ruxton they were all high-ranking police officers from Lancashire and Scotland. He introduced them, including Detective Lieutenant William Ewing and Detective Lieutenant Bertie Hammond, both from Glasgow Police.

Vann asked Ruxton to sit.

He told the doctor he was anxious to trace Isabella and Mary Rogerson. Ruxton, he said, should help them in trying to find them. Ruxton would be required to explain where he had been and what he had done between the night of 14 September and 29 September. Vann then cautioned Ruxton.

The doctor had composed himself. He appeared brighter.

'Go on; ask me anything you like; I will be only too pleased to tell you,' he told Vann.

The Chief Constable told Ruxton he would take down his statement, day by day, in writing, at the end of which he would ask him to sign it. What Ruxton did next startled the police officers. He reached into his pocket and produced an envelope. Written on it were the words: 'My Movements'. The typewritten document covered precisely the days Vann had asked Ruxton to account for: 14–29 September.

Vann was astounded.

The long, arduous process began at half past nine that night. Officers gave Ruxton bread, cheese and coffee to sustain him while Vann's pencil danced across the paper. Ruxton became emotional, thumping Vann's table when talk turned to Bobby Edmondson. At one point he stood on his chair and stamped his foot. Vann and his officers had great difficulty restraining him. Yet, like a firework, Ruxton's temper rapidly burned itself out. His Jekyll and Hyde nature was evident. He was mortified and apologised profusely for his lack of control.

After many hours, the document was taken to the room next door and typed up. The clock read ten to four in the morning when the typescript was brought into Vann's office for Ruxton to read. It comprised eighteen foolscap sheets. It took the doctor a further eighty minutes to review.

It was still dark on Dalton Square when Ruxton signed the document at five o'clock in the morning.

It was Sunday, 13 October.

Ruxton had been thorough in compiling 'My Movements'.

He said there had been a children's party at 2 Dalton Square on 14 September, with Mary looking after Elizabeth, Diana and Billy-Boy, as well as the Jackson children. He claimed Isabella returned from Blackpool 'a little after 12 at night'.

He said she had suggested they went for a drive on Sunday, 15 September, but after he collected his car, she had changed her mind and asked if he minded her going to Edinburgh.

Ruxton claimed that as Isabella left she said, 'I am taking Mary with me.'

In his account, Ruxton wrote, 'I felt rather glad at that because I said to myself if she goes with Mary, she is sure to come back, because Mrs R had been hinting that some day she will go away for good. It was about half past nine when they left. She shouted "There is a cup of tea on the hall table for you."'

He claimed that a little while after Isabella and Mary left he had tried to open a tin of peaches and had gashed his hand badly in the process.

In his statement taken down by Vann, Ruxton admitted that he and Isabella slept in separate rooms and had 'not had intercourse' since the previous Christmas.

Ruxton provided explanations for the inconsistencies the police were interested in. Of the motor accident in Kendal where Ruxton knocked Bernard Beattie off his bicycle, he said he had collected the children from the Andersons, had taken the girls to school and then, with Billy in the passenger seat, had driven to Seatle near Grange-over-Sands. He said he had lost his way and had come back via an unfamiliar route through the Lyth Valley and Kendal.

He painted a picture of the apparent domestic rhythm of 2 Dalton Square in the absence of his wife and maid. He spoke of the daily visits to and from the Andersons' home in Morecambe, of how he stayed for coffee to talk with his friends, often staying until one in the morning before leaving the children there and returning to Dalton Square. There were descriptions of how Ruxton would get Elizabeth off to school with the help of various servants, including Mrs Curwen.

The statement done, Vann asked Ruxton to account for bloodstains on carpets recovered from Dalton Square. Vann later wrote that Ruxton 'made various evasive replies, some ingenious but all obviously untrue'.

Ruxton was allowed to rest as Vann went into a conference with Ewing, Hammond and the other officers. They decided Ruxton should be charged with the murder of Mary Rogerson, based on evidence so far compiled by Scottish police and the forensic scientists. There was little or no evidence to identify the second body as that of Isabella Ruxton.

Vann, sombre and tired, went into his office.

Ruxton looked up.

Vann told him: 'You are charged that between 14 and 29 September 1935 you did feloniously and with malice aforethought kill and murder one, Mary Jane Rogerson.'

Ruxton flew into a rage, shouting: 'Most certainly not; the furthest thing from my mind; what motive and why? What are you talking about?'

At just after seven o'clock, Ruxton was taken to one of the police cells adjoining Vann's office. He was exhausted.

PART SIX
SEEK

49

A TOWN IN SHOCK

Early on Sunday, Vann made preparations for Ruxton to appear in the police court above the cells where he was held. He also had to arrange care for the doctor's three children, who had slept at home, with a police officer present, oblivious to their father's interrogation.

Word soon spread that the doctor had been arrested. Vann made an early morning statement to newspaper reporters who congregated in Dalton Square.

'A definite point of identification has been established,' he said, 'linking the body of the young female found in a ravine at Moffat with Mary Jane Rogerson, the missing Morecambe girl.' He added that police were still searching for Mrs Ruxton, and concluded by saying he had arrested Dr Ruxton at five o'clock that morning following a lengthy questioning.

There was disbelief among local people over Dr Ruxton's arrest. The *Morecambe Guardian* described it as 'a sensational sequel to the reported disappearance last week of Miss Rogerson who was a nursemaid to the Dr. and Mrs Ruxton'. Crowds filled Dalton Square – the *Morecambe Guardian* described them as 'morbid sightseers' – swarming around Ruxton's house, now in police hands.

At the doctor's request, Vann arranged for Elizabeth, Diana and Billy to be taken to the Andersons in Balmoral Road, Morecambe, where they had spent so much time since Isabella's disappearance.

Ruxton contacted his solicitor, Charles Frederick Gardner, whose office was tucked away in the quaintly named Sun Street, a narrow thoroughfare popular with the town's legal professionals. Fred Gardner was 62 and originally from Preston. He had lived in Lancaster for more than twenty years, steadily building up a respectable business, dealing in wills, probate and financial estates. He was married to Ellen, had a son, Raymond

Benedict, and was rock-steady. Just the man Ruxton could rely on. There was one problem. Gardner lacked the necessary experience in criminal cases, so he asked Edwin Slinger, a lawman better versed in criminal cases, from Accrington, near Blackburn, to take the reins. Ruxton knew Slinger and approved of Gardner's decision. Slinger was middle aged and jowly. Sporting round horn-rimmed spectacles, he looked like British film actor Edward Chapman, who appeared that year in H.G. Wells' *Things To Come* and would later find fame as Mr Grimsdale in the Norman Wisdom films. Slinger took pride in his appearance, often sporting a bowler hat and spats.

During Sunday, Vann's officers conducted a thorough search of 2 Dalton Square. There were no carpets on the staircase and landings, and the stair-rods had been removed. Officers noticed the smell of fresh paint and found that the staircase walls had been repapered and woodwork repainted very recently. Only the banisters had not been given a fresh lick of paint.

They took away Isabella's and Mary's clothes and shoes, including a leather motor coat of Isabella's. Officers removed a scalpel, dental forceps, Ruxton's revolver and his diaries spanning 1919 to 1927. A sheet was removed from Isabella's double bed and sent to Fred Barwick, an expert in textiles at the Testing House of Manchester Chamber of Commerce, for examination.

Glaister and Brash were of the opinion that whoever dismembered the bodies would most likely have used a number of knives for the task. No knives were found among the equipment in Ruxton's surgery.

Glasgow City Police Force's fingerprint and photographic expert Detective Lieutenant Bertie Hammond entered 2 Dalton Square that Sunday and began his dedicated, painstaking work that would last for the next eleven days.

With his trusty camera, he photographed the exterior of 2 Dalton Square. The cobbles in front were empty, Ruxton's car now in police possession. The County Cinema next door bore advertising for *Vanessa: Her Love Story*, starring Robert Montgomery and Helen Hayes, and *The Live Ghost*, the latest Laurel and Hardy two-reeler. Stan and Ollie's smiles beaming down belied the sombre atmosphere on the square.

Hammond meticulously photographed the house, inside and out, collecting a record of the property. He took pictures of the back yard, the entrance hall, the kitchen, the first stair landing. He took pictures of the bathroom. He took pictures of the stair leading to the second floor landing.

He photographed everything, his flash bulb popping like a pistol.

Then the monumental task of fingerprinting could begin.

Ruxton's court appearance was set for the following morning, Monday, 14 October. Vann kept the time of the hearing secret. He wanted to avoid a circus at all costs. He told reporters to assemble outside the police station at quarter past nine. Shortly after, he led the men of the press along the corridors of the Town Hall to the courtroom. He told them there would be no public allowed at this first hearing. The reporters sat at the press bench. And waited.

Despite Vann's discretion, a large crowd massed in the garden of remembrance outside the police station. Press photographers set up their cameras. There was a rumour Ruxton would be brought out in front of the crowd on the way to the court. Police officers had to restrain the surging mob just before the court was due to sit. The crowd was disappointed. Ruxton was in the police cells and at the allotted time would be brought up a few steps directly into the dock.

The prisoner was being held in one of the white-tiled cells below the Town Hall. Despite a high ceiling, it was cramped and oppressive, its furnishings consisting of a rudimentary wooden slat bed, a toilet, and a barred window 7ft from the ground. Ruxton could pull a lever to a bell to gain the attention of the duty officer at the end of the corridor.

The doctor's spirits had plummeted. He was worried about his 'wee mites' and his medical practice. He was allowed visitors but must have felt shame when they walked into his cell. They noticed his once thick, black mop of hair was now streaked with silver and white. One visitor later revealed Ruxton was so low he had asked for a supply of morphine. The police refused, assuming he was suicidal.

To one visitor Ruxton would later hand a sealed envelope with the instructions that it should be delivered, unopened, to the Editor of the *News of the World* in the event of his conviction and execution.

In the wood-panelled courtroom Vann called out: 'Buck Ruxton.'

Moments later the doctor stepped 'smartly' into the dock, the *Morecambe Guardian* reporter wrote. Ruxton was accompanied by a uniformed police constable. He looked around the courtroom in a bewildered state. His solicitor Fred Gardner was sitting nearby. Ruxton composed himself and followed the court proceedings with 'intense interest'. Chairman of the bench was the Mayor of Lancaster, who was accompanied by fourteen magistrates.

The charge of murdering Mary Rogerson was put to Ruxton. The court clerk read the charge: 'That you, between the 14th and 29th September last, in Lancaster, feloniously and wilfully, and with malice aforethought, did kill and murder one Mary Jane Rogerson. What do you say?'

Ruxton replied: 'Nothing.'

Vann said the purpose of the hearing was to hear evidence from Mary's father and evidence of Ruxton's arrest and to seek a remand in custody of the doctor.

Mary's father, Mr Rogerson, stepped into the witness box. He burst into tears after he swore the oath and began his evidence. He explained that the last time he had seen his daughter had been Thursday, 12 September.

Vann then outlined how Ruxton had been questioned at the police station and subsequently charged with murder. Ruxton's response to this was: 'Most emphatically not. No, of course not. Furthest from my mind. What motive, and why? What are you talking about?'

Vann asked the court for Ruxton to be remanded in custody; the clerk asked if the prisoner could be held in Lancaster. The remand was approved; Ruxton was told he would be in custody until the next hearing on 22 October.

The crowd milled around outside the Town Hall and police station after the hearing, but there was further disappointment as Ruxton was taken back to the cells directly from the dock.

Vann allowed Ruxton to write a notice to his patients. At 12.30 p.m., police stuck the typewritten message to the front door of 2 Dalton Square following the court hearing. A crowd craned and stretched to see what it said. This is what they read:

To all my patients.

I appeal to you most humbly to remain loyal to me in this hour of trouble. I am an innocent victim of circumstances. Please do not leave my panel list as well as private list. My deputy will conduct business as usual.

Thanking you in anticipation for loyal support.

Signed,

B RUXTON

14TH OCTOBER.

That afternoon, Vann issued two appeals. The first called for any dentists who had treated Isabella. The second was for assistance from any person who had given a white blouse to a jumble sale at Morecambe Memorial Hall to raise funds for Trinity Parish Church in the winter of 1934. 'The purchaser has been traced as a Mrs Rogerson, who gave it to Miss Mary Rogerson,' the statement said. 'The blouse which was found at Moffat is a ladies' plain white, or cream wool and cotton marocain, long-sleeved blouse.'

Next, Vann issued a statement in relation to Isabella's disappearance. It read:

Any person who has seen someone resembling the description of Mrs Ruxton, whether or not in the company of the nursemaid, should communicate with the nearest police station.

We want to exhaust every possible inquiry as to whether she is alive or in the country. She may have gone to London or Edinburgh. The same time, the police are still searching for the torso of body number two.

It was possible to infer that police believed Isabella was the second victim in the ravine.

Meanwhile, police officers collected a piece of Ruxton's carpet from Mrs Curwen's house. At five o'clock that afternoon, they took two petrol tins from a recess that was in the backyard at 2 Dalton Square. Later in the day, a police constable made inquiries at Lancaster's bus stands and its two railway stations, the Castle and the Midland, to see if anybody had witnessed Isabella Ruxton leaving the town. He found no such witness.

That night, Ruxton was transferred to Walton gaol in Liverpool. Ghoulish sightseers were still hanging around Dalton Square in the hope of a glimpse of the doctor, but were thwarted one last time as he was led secretly out of a side door on Thurnham Street and into a private car.

Ruxton's house on Dalton Square stood empty and cold, a police crime scene. His children were tucked up in bed at Balmoral Road in Morecambe, their heads full of questions Mr and Mrs Anderson could not answer.

THE HOUSE

Fascination with the case had become a national pastime as newspapers threw readers every morsel they could. Interest was not limited to British newspapers, either, as major titles in America and Australia daily ran stories about the handsome Indian doctor in the small town in the north of England suspected of murdering his wife and maid.

As a consequence, any figure associated with the case, be he police or scientist, found himself the subject of press scrutiny. Professor Glaister noted how he and his colleagues were 'accompanied by an escort of press-men, hungry for the smallest facts with which to feed a public fascinated by what had happened at the house at 2 Dalton Square'.

On Monday, 14 October, he found himself literally in Dalton Square ready to step into the house.

Chief Constable Vann had invited the Scottish scientists to Lancaster to deploy their investigative powers in the place it would be most useful at that point in the investigation. And so Glaister and colleagues would spend part of each week that month in the Lancashire town. Glaister later wrote, 'The train journeys were often interesting in their way as we sat listening to a crowded compartment exchanging views on the case, and where lines of investigation were "slipping up".'

Glaister and his assistant, Dr Frank Martin, posed for a photographer from Associated Newspapers in Dalton Square on their arrival that Monday. Over the scientists' shoulders were Ruxton's house, the public telephone box and the County Cinema. Both men wore bowler hats; Glaister looked dapper with his round horn-rimmed glasses, immaculately trimmed moustache, a black-and-white spotted tie, long, black overcoat and black leather gloves to stave off the autumn chill.

The first time Glaister stepped into the cold, unoccupied rooms of Ruxton's home, he was struck by the Oriental decor, the blue ceilings scattered with golden stars.

Then he saw the blood.

There were large stains on the stairs, small, petal-shaped ones on the banisters.

Vann showed him around the house, pointing out the key areas the police were focused on.

As the black of night descended on Dalton Square, enveloping the Victoria statue and plunging Ruxton's home into darkness, officers from Lancaster's fire brigade set up flares inside the property to provide Glaister with greater illumination to work. Storm lanterns were set up in the backyard, which was hidden from outside prying eyes by a high wall. Glaister directed police officers to lift up flagstones and dig the soil beneath.

Glaister later wrote about working at Ruxton's home, 'At Dalton Square the house blinds had to be kept drawn so that we could work in privacy. Each visit made to the house quickly gathered a crowd of spectators, though what they hoped to see we couldn't fathom.'

In the coming days, he would often be working there at the same time as Bertie Hammond, whom he had met at Moffat. Glaister could see that Hammond's task was immense, but the detective worked with a younger assistant to ease the workload. Part of the challenge was the sheer size of 2 Dalton Square. Glaister noted that Hammond had made a sketch of the house's layout to ensure every inch was searched.

On one occasion as Glaister examined the bloodstains, Hammond sent his assistant off to take prints on the first floor. Moments later the assistant came rushing down the dimly lit staircase, spooked.

'There's something funny up there,' the assistant said. 'It must be another body.'

With trepidation, Glaister and Hammond followed him up the stairs to the first floor. There were three public rooms, interconnected by doors, allowing them to walk from the dining room to an ante room and into a large, cluttered drawing room. The three men were tense as they entered. The tension was broken, however, when they realised what had happened. The assistant had been feeling his way through the room, which was in darkness. Trying to locate the light switch, his fingers had grazed the face of a cold, marble bust standing on a pedestal. The assistant was ribbed mercilessly about his mistake, but the incident provided a light-hearted break from the otherwise grim work in which they were engaged.

From day one Glaister and Hammond and their respective assistants were clear about the purpose of the work at 2 Dalton Square. 'From the moment Ruxton was in custody, strenuously denying his guilt,' Glaister wrote, 'the whole pivot of the case became identification, the building up of a circumstantial web of fact … that no effort on the part of the accused could break through.'

On the evening of Monday, 14 October, Elizabeth, Diana and Billy Ruxton prepared to spend the night with the Andersons at Balmoral Road in Morecambe. They had not ceased asking the couple where their 'Mummy' and 'Nanny' were. It was a question they had been asking since 14 September, the last day they saw Isabella and Mary.

Mrs Anderson told a reporter from the *Morecambe Guardian* that she hoped the children would settle down at her home as they knew her well. 'They have been here several times before and were delighted to stay with me,' she said. 'They call me Auntie.' She then explained:

> Of course they have not been told anything about what has happened. They think their mother and nurse are on holiday. I will see that they are not disturbed while they stay with us. They may go to relatives later on. They are three bright and cheerful children and they are enjoying themselves so far.

The *Northern Whig* newspaper reported:

> Up to last night there was no news of Mrs Ruxton, who has been missing for some time.
> The Chief Constable of Lancaster stated last night that the police were anxious to hear from anyone who had seen a stone-coloured Austin Twelve four-seater saloon car travelling on the road between Lancaster, Grange and Kendal on September 17. He reiterated his appeal for information from any dentist who may have treated Mrs Ruxton.

On Tuesday, 15 October, the police sought the assistance of farmers, gamekeepers and anybody who worked on land in the open countryside in the northern area above Lancaster. Vann asked them to look out for

parcels or garments, and if they did find any, they were to report them to
the police immediately.

Vann told reporters, 'We are trying to get all the people in this part of the
country interested in the search for the missing torso. Any ditches, water
courses and places which may offer concealment should be searched.'

The *Morecambe Guardian* reported a rumour that a 'blood-stained bundle
of cotton cloth had been found in a hedge between Milnthorpe and
Kendal', but said it had not been confirmed, despite police inquiries.

Vann told reporters the excavation of Ruxton's backyard had not yielded
anything significant. 'We want to find the torso and so far enquiries have
failed to produce it,' he said.

That evening an appeal was made on the wireless for information that
might help determine the 'movements of an Austin four-seater saloon
12-horse-power car in the area comprising Lancaster, Grange-over-
Sands, Kendal, Carlisle, and Dumfries, between September 14th and
28th', according to the *Morecambe Guardian*. The paper told readers 'a very
material date in the investigations is September 17th between the hours of
9 a.m. and 3 p.m., when a car answering the description is stated to have
been seen travelling in that area'.

During a search of Ruxton's house on Wednesday, 16 October, Detective
Inspector William Green discovered an attaché case in a locked bookcase
in the library on the first floor. He also found a snapshot photograph of
Isabella and more of Ruxton's diaries. He would return on numerous occasions to recover evidence including bed sheets, pieces of furniture and a
pair of shoes from a cupboard in the kitchen.

One of the officers stationed at Lancaster offered Captain Vann his
considerable woodwork skills in the service of the police investigation.

Vann listened to Sergeant Frederick Harrison's idea and then told the
officer to take up his saw, wood glue and paint. The industrious sergeant
set to work constructing a scale model of 2 Dalton Square, the backyard
and the County Cinema wall, exact in every detail, even down to the
exquisite reproductions of Ruxton's furniture. The ½in to 1ft scale model

was a remarkable piece of craftsmanship and could easily be dismantled to expose the interior.

Harrison based the model on 1in to 4ft scale plans made shortly after Ruxton's arrest by Lawrence Holiday, an assistant surveyor in the Town Hall. Holiday also produced a scale plan of the route from Lancaster to Edinburgh, complete with distances to key staging posts for reference: Kendal (21 miles), Penrith (47 miles), Carlisle (64.9 miles), Lockerbie (89.2 miles), Moffat (105 miles), Penicuik (146.5 miles) and Edinburgh (156.3 miles).

Sergeant Harrison's exquisite painted model, with its unerring attention to detail, was a thing of beauty, comparable with Sir Edwin Lutyens' celebrated Queen Mary doll's house produced for the British Royal family a decade earlier.

The tragic circumstances fated that it would only ever be displayed in a court of law.

The model proved an invaluable tool for Glaister and his team. It allowed them to get a clear picture in their minds of the house. But with the best will in the world, it was never going to be sufficient. Progress was slow, hampered by the distance between Dalton Square and the labs in Scotland. Having to make frequent rail journeys to Lancaster was costly and inconvenient.

Glaister realised there was only one solution. He broached the subject with Lancaster Police on a visit with Dr Gilbert Millar on 22 October.

He said, 'There's a lot of detailed examination work to be done. It's the type of work which can really only be completed in a laboratory.'

The officers blinked at him. 'You mean …'

Glaister replied, 'I'd like to move parts of the house en bloc to Glasgow if that's possible.'

Glaister later wrote, 'There were in the house so many stains that looked like blood, that it would have been impossible to test them all on the spot.' It posed a logistical problem for the police, but it was possible.

And so, delicately to preserve the evidence, much of the staircase and sections of walls, as well as most of the fixtures and fittings in the bathroom, including the bathroom door, all the linoleum, the woodwork and the bath were dismantled piece by piece and transported north to the forensic department laboratories at Glasgow University.

Once on home turf, like film-set designers, Glaister and his team set about reconstructing the rooms of 2 Dalton Square within the laboratory. The work done, Glaister and his team stared at an accurate reconstruction of the Ruxton home, including the bathroom and the doctor's bath.

'I'd been even wiser than I had realised,' he later wrote.

> The length of time we spent working in and around these reconstructed rooms not only allowed us to complete our tests and checks with accuracy, finding highly incriminating human bloodstains, but resulted in a developing familiarity with the minutest detail of layout, a familiarity which we were to require in full under cross-examination at the trial ahead.

Moving much of the house north of the border did not exempt Glaister from further visits to Lancaster, however. He and Millar returned to conduct examinations in a room on the top floor. Reaching the top of the house was challenging because the original staircase was, of course, now standing in a laboratory at Glasgow University.

Glaister and Millar climbed a dizzyingly tall and all-but-vertical ladder to reach the top floor. It must have been a vertigo-inducing trial for the scientists, particularly in such a badly lit, eerie setting. Once they reached the summit they caught their breath and began their work; Bertie Hammond and his detectives were fingerprinting the kitchen on the ground floor beneath their feet.

Glaister and Millar had barely begun their work when Hammond shouted up, 'Are you all right, Professor? We're going out for lunch – we'll be back in an hour.'

Glaister called back, 'Righto.' He heard the front door slam.

The scientists completed their work within the hour and returned to the top of the ladder to climb down. They realised doing so would be impossible. The ladder protruded barely an inch above the floor and stood at such a sharp angle that it would have been treacherous to step on to the top rung. One slip and they would have tumbled through the murk to their deaths three floors below.

'We're stranded,' Millar said. 'Still, Hammond shouldn't be long.'

They had no choice but to sit and wait in the cold and the gloom.

It was the day the detectives took an extended lunch. After a further hour and a half, the officers returned. The sound of Ruxton's front door opening was a welcome one to the two chilled scientists stranded at the top of the house. Hammond and his men had to guide Glaister's and Millar's feet in turn on to the ladder to enable them to descend safely.

Ruxton's staircase stood like a macabre theatre set in the lab in Glasgow. Glaister meticulously numbered each step and handrail, beginning with the top flight of six stairs that had led from the bedrooms to the sub-landing where the bathroom had been.

He examined everything, looking for bloodstains.

His discoveries were startling.

Of the fourteen rails and stair surfaces he inspected, Glaister found around eighty bloodstains or markings. His tests revealed that in eleven stains he found human blood.

Glaister examined the bathroom door. On the bathroom side was a panel at the bottom, measuring an area of 16in by 9in. Glaister found significant staining, which was directed from above and downwards, with a slight oblique from left to right as one would look at the door.

Glaister confirmed these stains were human blood.

His examination found traces of human blood on the toilet seat, the woodwork panelling of the hand basin, the bathroom cupboard door, boarding at the back of the bath, the linoleum and the floorboards beneath.

He took scrapings of the surfaces of the bath stop and plug. These, too, had traces of blood.

INNOVATION

Detective Bertie Hammond and his assistant lifted hundreds of prints from objects and surfaces at 2 Dalton Square that October. 'For eleven days this search went on,' Hammond later wrote. 'Every article in Ruxton's house from bedrooms to cellars was examined for impressions.'

It was a truly mammoth task. But Hammond was an experienced fingerprint expert, having built the department at Glasgow Police into one of the most respected in the country. He had first inspected the remains properly at Edinburgh University shortly after their removal from Moffat. The fingertips had been removed from the two forearms and hands of 'Body No 2', so were of no use to him. But the left forearm and hand of 'Body No 1' was a different matter. The limb had been severed at the elbow, its fingers long and tapering, clearly of a female. The skin was wrinkled, so the hand had been softened in hot water before impressions of the fingertips and palm were taken successfully.

Now at Dalton Square, if it were to be proved the body was that of Mary Rogerson, it was imperative Hammond find a matching print. Every impression was photographed and enlargements made for the detective to make comparisons. Prints were taken of nine people who had had access to the house, including Ruxton himself, so that they could be eliminated from the search.

In a few weeks' time, on 4 November, a right forearm and hand would be found by maidservant Jen Gwendoline Halliday a few hundred yards from the ravine at Gardenholme, lying in bracken near the roadside. It was wrapped in newspaper and was badly decomposed. Hammond inspected it the same day. The epidermis – the outer layer of skin – was missing from all the fingers as well as the palm of the hand. The tip of the little finger was missing, while the right ring finger had been so badly eaten by maggots that it was beyond use for identification. If a successful impression were to be taken, a new technique would need to be devised.

Hammond did not know it yet, but he was about to break new ground in the science of fingerprinting with the greatest innovation in the field for forty years.

Meanwhile, Glaister was considering the huge volume of bloodstained evidence. There were the stair carpets and pads; there was the blue suit Ruxton gave to Mrs Hampshire; there was the staggering amount of staining on the staircase and in the bathroom; and there were the garments, towels and curtains seen in Ruxton's yard. Articles with important areas of staining had been protected with cellophane sheets during their transportation from Lancaster.

The challenge Glaister and his assistants faced was to prove these bloodstains were human.

'Each article in turn was systematically scrutinised by ordinary and by powerful illumination,' Glaister wrote, 'and the location, the size, and the form of each stain or group of stains were recorded.'

The bathroom fittings were reassembled in Glaister's lab in their original relative positions to aid the scientists' work. Glaister also asked for a volunteer who was prepared to don Ruxton's soiled suit so that he might get a better idea of where the stains were in relation to parts of the wearer's body. The experience cannot have been a pleasant one for the volunteer, standing in front of Glaister as he made notes, conscious that the marks on the fabric could be the blood of the two Moffat victims.

Glaister's tests were laborious. Samples would be taken by scraping the stains, and these were put into labelled watch-glasses and arranged on trays, with each piece of evidence having its own tray. The samples were put in a saline solution before Glaister inspected them under microscope and a micro-spectroscope.

As well as establishing the type of blood, Glaister was concerned with its distribution and direction of travel as it ran down surfaces such as the stair banisters and in the bathroom. He considered the possibility that much of it could have come from the gash to Ruxton's hand. With regard to the blue suit, two dentists, including Herbert Anderson, told police that Ruxton had assisted in dozens of extraction operations as their anaesthetist and had never worn a white coat. Another consideration was Ruxton's claim that Isabella's miscarriage in 1932 accounted for the blood on the stairs and walls.

However, the other, more chilling hypothesis, Glaister later wrote, was
that the ravine bodies were those of Isabella and Mary and that 'both
women met with violent deaths at 2 Dalton Square, Mrs Ruxton first
and then Mary Rogerson, because she was the only witness of the murder
of her mistress'. Glaister now had the benefit of Brash's findings, which
suggested 'Body No 2' (thought to be Isabella) had died by asphyxia by
throttling, while 'Body No 1' (Mary) had received blows to the face while
she was still alive, although cause of death could not be ascertained because
the body's torso was missing. 'It was suggested further that both bodies
had been dismembered in the bathroom and drained of blood in the bath,'
Glaister wrote.

On Saturday, 26 October, Detective Inspector William Green took
Ruxton's Hillman Minx, plate number ATC272, which was an almost
brand-new vehicle, on a special journey. Accompanied by Detective Willie
Ewing of Glasgow CID, Green drove from Lancaster to Gardenholme linn,
setting off from outside 2 Dalton Square at eight o'clock in the morning.
The officers travelled north through Kendal, over the Shap Fells, via
Penrith, Carlisle, Lockerbie and Moffat. The trip took them two and three
quarter hours to the bridge over the stream in the ravine. Green noted the
distance on the speedometer: 110 miles.

The following day, Sunday, 27 October, Green, accompanied again by
Ewing, drove the same journey in the Hillman Minx but leaving this time
at half past eleven at night. It took them three hours and ten minutes. The
officers, no doubt feeling tired by the monotony of the task, set off for the
return trip at ten minutes to three in the morning of Monday, 28 October,
arriving finally in Lancaster three and a quarter hours later at five minutes after six. The run each time had been clear and, apart from fog over
Shap, uneventful.

Glaister looked at the shoes police had taken from 2 Dalton Square. There
was a black leather slip-on with a woven pattern on the instep that Isabella
had bought from the Banks Lyon shoe store on Church Street in Lancaster.
Mary's was an open shoe with a strap across the instep. It was unclear
how these could be of use until the left foot of 'Body No 2' was found on

28 October by a Dumfriesshire council road worker who was walking on the main Edinburgh road several miles south of Moffat. It gave the scientists an idea. What if the victims' feet were slipped into the shoes to see if they fitted?

'It is curious that the simple step, towards identification of an unknown body, of testing whether the foot fits the shoe of a missing person does not seem to have been employed previously,' Glaister and Brash later wrote. The scientists knew a perfect fit would not be accepted as conclusive proof of identity in a court of law. However, they noted that 'its positive value can only be that of one fact which is consonant with identification; and it may therefore take its place with other items as a piece of circumstantial evidence'.

So preliminary tests were done, using the left feet of each body. Each foot was dried and powdered and slipped into a silk stocking, also powdered.

And then in turn they were tried in Isabella's and Mary's shoes.

The results were striking. Encouraged, the scientists took casts of the feet that could be used for demonstration purposes at Ruxton's trial.

The police investigators and scientists had found themselves deep in a case the likes of which had never been seen before. Their expertise and brilliance was severely tested as wave after wave of new challenges hit the investigation. But it would be through solid teamwork, ingenuity and sheer bloody-mindedness that they imagined startling new means of recording evidence.

Necessity truly was the mother of invention.

RUXTON IN COURT

As the police and forensic investigation continued, Ruxton made weekly appearances at Lancaster police court, mainly for Captain Vann to apply for the doctor to be further remanded in custody. Ruxton had now been transferred from Liverpool to Manchester's Strangeways prison and would remain here until his trial. The red-brick, turreted building boasted a tall chimney visible for miles around, a sobering reminder to Mancunians. It was from his cell in this austere Victorian gaol that Ruxton was driven back to Lancaster for these preliminary court hearings.

On Tuesday, 5 November – Guy Fawkes' Night – Ruxton made his fourth appearance in the dock at Lancaster. He was brought up from the Edwardian police cells before the magistrates. Chairman of the bench was again the Mayor of Lancaster, William Simpson.

This was the first time members of the public had been allowed into one of Ruxton's hearings. The public gallery was packed. There was a real fascination with the handsome Indian doctor, the doting father of three beautiful children, accused of such terrible crimes. The disbelief that this kind man could be guilty was widespread in Lancaster, especially among his patients.

Newspaper reporters noted that a great number of the members of the public were women. Female fascination with Ruxton would grow as the case unfolded over the next few months.

A tired Ruxton got to his feet in the small, wooden dock rimmed with a metal handrail. A large clock hung on the wall behind his head. He faced the charges. He was accused of the murder of Mary Rogerson. And then he was further charged with the murder of Isabella. His Belle.

It was the first time the charge had been put to him.

Ruxton shouted and screamed; the torrent of words and sentences ran into one another. Reporters frantically tried to make sense of the outburst. Later they were able to establish Ruxton had shouted, 'It is a positive and damnable lie. It is all prejudice. I cannot bear the damned thing. Is there no justice? Who the hell is at the bottom of this? My home is broken up – my happy home.'

Ruxton's solicitor, the debonair Edwin Slinger, told Ruxton, 'Be quiet, and leave it to me.'

'The damn rascals,' Ruxton retorted.

Slinger told him once more to keep quiet.

Ruxton could not restrain himself. 'Do I look like a murderer? It is not my nature. It is not my religion. I observe the fasts. My blood is boiling now.'

Inspector Clarke of the borough police also tried to pacify Ruxton, but the doctor was raging and would not calm down.

He continued shouting: 'How can I be quiet? My blood is boiling now. One damn thing after another. Who the hell is doing this? You say, "Don't speak. Don't do this," but it is no damn good.'

Ruxton would not calm down, despite further efforts by the police officers. If anything, his outbursts intensified, as though his passion and anger were rising towards a volcanic explosion. He screamed, 'I have my children and my business to attend to.'

Inspector Clarke crossed the courtroom to the dock and pushed his arm through the two brass rails in an effort to pacify the doctor. Reporters noted that Clarke had meant the act to be compassionate and friendly, but Ruxton drew away from him and made an inaudible remark.

The courtroom was in discord; the public gallery electrified by the drama. Slinger made a request for a five-minute adjournment for Ruxton to calm himself. There were no objections from Mr G.R. Paling, the solicitor representing the Director of Public Prosecutions. The court rose.

During the adjournment, Inspector Clarke and Ruxton engaged in a quiet conversation; whatever the inspector said to the doctor, it had a pacifying effect.

For the remainder of the hearing, Ruxton sat meekly in the corner of the dock.

There was a legal discussion over who should take over 2 Dalton Square. Paling, for the prosecution, said arrangements had been made for the house to be handed over to Ruxton's legal representatives. This would be subject, of course, to allowing police full access to the property should the need arise, he told the justices.

On Tuesday, 12 November, Ruxton appeared at Lancaster a fifth time. It was the briefest of hearings, lasting no more than three minutes. Demand to sit in the public gallery was such that a crowd had begun assembling outside the Town Hall at seven o'clock in the morning. When the court opened a couple of hours later, the eager and expectant crowd had swollen to more than 200. Most were turned away.

Ruxton had again been driven to Lancaster from Strangeways. The driver was PC Norman Wilson, the Lancaster officer whose broken nose Ruxton had fixed a few years earlier. Wilson, one of only a few officers licensed to drive police vehicles, would stop for fish and chips for Dr Ruxton on the journeys from Manchester to Lancaster. It was an act of friendship by Wilson, who had always respected the doctor; Ruxton always had a passion for fish and chips.

The public gallery and packed press bench got their first glimpse of Ruxton that day when he emerged into the dock flanked by two police officers. He was dressed in the brown suit he had worn at previous hearings. He did not look at the public gallery, but instead bowed to the chairman of the bench, Mr D.S. Cross, and eight magistrates. His attention did not waver from the bench or the solicitors who sat before them, including Edwin Slinger and Fred Gardner.

Captain Vann told the court, 'In accordance with the arrangements made a week ago, I apply for a further remand of one week in this case.'

Slinger said:

First of all, in the case of Mary Jane Rogerson, the prosecution have failed to bring forward any identification as to those remains found at Moffat. Secondly, that so far as regards the charge made against the Doctor, in the case of Mary Jane Rogerson there is no evidence whatsoever before the Court at the present moment, to prove that the Doctor has committed the offence, if it should be Mary Jane Rogerson. Thirdly, that at two hearings of the Court, the public were not admitted, and I should like the learned Clerk to place my remarks on the depositions this morning.

Chairman of the magistrates bench, Mr Cross, said: 'The prisoner will be remanded in custody for seven days.'

Ruxton appeared to be about to say something, but thought better of it, perhaps under instruction from Slinger and Gardner following his emotional outbursts of previous hearings. He gave two respectful bows to the magistrates and then was led by the two officers down the steps to the cells.

As the crowd in the public gallery filed out into Dalton Square, perhaps with a sense of anticlimax, Ruxton remained in the cells. What unfolded next must have been a touching reminder for Ruxton of the esteem and affection with which he was held in Lancaster by many, many people.

He spent the next few hours with his solicitors, going over important legal points, no doubt asking about the welfare of his children and reflecting on his own mental state. As a compassionate touch, the police allowed him to send out for lunch while he was in conference with Slinger and Gardner. He chose to order food from a nearby café, possibly Tymns, where as a free man he had been a frequent visitor. When the food arrived on a tray with a knife and fork, Ruxton found a serviette with a message written on it. It said: 'Best wishes and good luck.'

Later, when the food tray was returned to the café, the staff found the serviette had also been returned. On it, Ruxton had written: 'Thanks for the wishes and luck. It is surely coming my way. B. Ruxton.'

A reporter from the *Morecambe Guardian* heard about this and reported, 'The writer of the message is treasuring the serviette as a souvenir.'

That evening, Ruxton was driven back to the cold and cheerless cell at Strangeways.

REVOLUTION

Professor Sydney Smith had spent a month in his native New Zealand before attending a meeting of the British Medical Association in Australia. He later wrote, 'Here I stumbled on one of the most extraordinary cases of my career.' Smith was called upon by police after a shark spat up a man's severed arm in the city of Sydney in Australia. He gave his view that the arm had been severed prior to the shark swallowing it, throwing suspicion on another man charged with murder. The trial collapsed, however, because of the lack of a body.

A tired Smith, ready for a quiet time back in Scotland, read about the Moffat bodies in newspapers on the return voyage. All thoughts of an empty in-tray were dispelled, however, when he read that the remains had been taken to his own department in Edinburgh.

Adjusting to the chill on his arrival on 7 November, Smith was keen to see what progress Glaister and Brash had made. Donning his lab coat, he inspected the human remains for himself. He was impressed with Brash's reconstructive work.

He agreed with their belief that the cause of death of 'Body No 2' – the older woman – was asphyxia. The victim had been strangled, most likely with bare hands. He agreed it was significant the nose, eyes, lips, ears and fingertips had been removed. Typically these were the parts of the body to betray signs of asphyxia. He agreed that whoever dismembered the bodies possessed competent anatomical knowledge and surgical skills.

Glaister and Brash showed Smith the work done with the feet and the shoes, all impressive work. They pointed to mutilation to the left foot of the older body, which corresponded with information that Mrs Ruxton had had a bunion on that foot.

But Smith was most impressed with a remarkable piece of detective work that Brash was doing with the help of Detective Constable Thomas Stobie of Edinburgh CID. As with so much of this case, the scientist and the detective pioneered a technique that would be written and spoken about for decades to come.

Detective Constable Stobie worked in the Fingerprint and Photographic Department of Edinburgh CID, the counterpart to Bertie Hammond's department in Glasgow. He had taken many of the photographs of the remains at the Forensic Medicine Department at Edinburgh University on 6 October. Once Brash's reconstructive work was complete, he photographed the two reassembled bodies on 8 November. Stobie's work was laborious, taking a long time to set up, and the young officer would from time to time need to step outside for fresh air as a break from the sights and smells before him.

Brash had an idea inspired by the portrait photographs of Isabella and Mary that had appeared on the front pages of newspapers. He later wrote that the photographs 'showed that the proportions of their features were not only unmistakably different but that they corresponded in a general way to the proportions of the respective heads from Moffat'. So distinct from each other were these proportions that 'it could have been asserted without fear of contradiction that Head No 1 could not be the head of Mrs Ruxton and Head No 2 could not be the head of Mary Rogerson'.

He wrote, 'The possibility of proving a negative in this way is, of course, in itself important in a problem of identity; but the making of a positive identification [is] quite another matter.'

Attempts had been made in history to authenticate the skulls of notable figures such as Dante, Bach and Robert the Bruce by comparing them to paintings and death masks. No such attempt had ever been made in a criminal case, nor had comparisons ever been done using photographs. Brash must have felt a tingle of excitement, but he knew its very novelty would make it vulnerable to exploitation by Ruxton's defence team.

Brash had a number of photographs of Isabella seized from 2 Dalton Square to work with. Three were small, amateur snaps where the definition was not great, but nevertheless showed different sides to her face. In one she was hatless and smiling; another showed her in profile, looking to her right and wearing a hat. Brash decided to use this latter image along with a fourth in his possession, the professional studio portrait of her wearing a tiara taken by Cecil Thomas in Lancaster on 26 February. 'The outlines of the head and face and the details of the features including teeth were clear; and the enlargements were made from the excellent negative without loss of detail,' Brash wrote.

In the case of Mary, there were only two photographs available, both taken by an amateur in July 1933 when she was 17. One was full face, the other a quarter-left profile. 'In both of them the outlines were partly obscured by the hair,' Brash later wrote, 'the nose and mouth were clear but not the teeth; and in each there was some doubt, especially after enlargement, about the upper limit of the hair and the exact position of the chin.'

Brash asked Cecil Thomas at his Lancaster studio to make life-size enlargements of all four images – two of Isabella, two of Mary. Then on 9 November he called in Stobie with his specialist Hunter-Penrose process camera and 16in lens. The detective photographed the skulls at their natural size in four positions as closely as possible to the position of the heads of the women in the pictures. Rather gruesomely, the heads had been cleaned and the remaining flesh removed to reveal the skulls below. They were then mounted in a special skull holder within a cubical metal frame, which allowed for each to be rotated into the various positions.

It was vital to determine the size of the two women's heads for comparison with the skulls. The scientists sought the help of photographer Cecil Thomas, as he had taken the studio portrait of Isabella. A novice in criminal investigations but a brilliant craftsman, he was about to pioneer a new and audacious forensic technique in his studio on Market Street in Lancaster.

Using the original negative, Thomas attempted a reproduction of the portrait in the same studio space with the original camera and the dress and tiara worn by Isabella mounted on a frame. The work was laborious, with frequent optical and geometrical checks and adjustments. Considering the original portrait's depth of focus, Thomas set up a three-piece target, with the sections set at different distances from the lens to allow experimentation with the quality of the focus. His goal was to produce a life-size image as close to the original as possible – but, heartbreakingly, without its sitter. By establishing the distance of Isabella's head from the lens in the original portrait, the investigators reasoned it should be possible to work out the size of her head. In the original, Isabella's right eye was nearest the camera and was clearly defined. Thomas fixed a pin vertically into a length of twine stretched horizontally on the frame holding the tiara and dress. He then manipulated it as closely as possible into the position where Isabella's eye had been in the original photograph.

He took his reconstructed portrait.

Satisfied, he gave an enlargement to Glaister and Brash, who intended superimposing life-size negatives of the skull of 'Body No 2' to see if they matched. They also now had a measurement for the size of Isabella's head.

There were greater challenges with the amateur shots of Mary Rogerson, which were no bigger than cigarette cards. The definition was not good enough in either. Glaister later wrote, 'Examining them, I noticed that one showed the girl posing beside an iron gate in a low brick wall.' He told Brash, 'If we find that gate and the camera which was used to take the picture, we may have a chance.'

In fact, it showed Mary standing in front of her parents' house in Thornton Road, Morecambe. Police found the original camera and Cecil Thomas visited the Rogerson home to set up a photograph using the same technique he deployed with the Isabella reconstruction. He carefully worked out where to stand for the same viewpoint, using certain landmarks for reference, such as the gate, stonework, a drainpipe and a window sill. A 5ft measuring stick was positioned as closely as possible in the place that Mary had stood when she had smiled for the camera in 1933. The resulting reconstructed photograph, again without the sunny disposition of its original subject, allowed the scientists to work out the size of Mary's head.

Next, Brash compared outlines of both skulls in each position with the outlines of the corresponding portrait photographs enlarged by Cecil Thomas. He made a careful note of the degree to which the outlines corresponded. Finally, the skulls were photographically superimposed on to the portraits of Isabella and Mary.

Brash and Stobie and Glaister and Smith were astonished by the results.

Equally as important to identification were the teeth of the victims.

Glaister asked Dr Arthur Hutchinson, the Dean of the Edinburgh Dental School, to examine the remains and to offer his considerable professional view. Hutchinson and his assistant, A. Johnstone Brown, inspected the two heads in turn, and took casts of the jaws to ascertain which teeth remained and which were missing. It was imperative they establish whether absent teeth had been extracted in a dental procedure during the victim's lifetime or drawn after death during mutilation.

Hutchinson was keen to see the effect of pulling a tooth after a person had died. This would assist him in establishing which gaps in the two heads were likely to have been caused by the mutilator. He conducted tests on dead sheep, extracting their teeth and observing the extent of blood clotting in the sockets and also the effects of putrefaction. In another test, he extracted teeth from a dying sheep whose heart was still beating to compare the results.

Turning to the human remains, Hutchinson found that 'Head No 1' (believed to be Mary's) had eight teeth missing, but judging by the complete healing of the bone and gums these were likely to have been extracted by a dentist sometime much earlier. Two, however, had open sockets, which suggested they had been removed recently. There was no evidence that the person had worn a denture.

'Head No 2' (thought to be Isabella's) was a different story. Twenty-nine of the head's thirty-two teeth were missing. Hutchinson could see fifteen were absent due to old extractions, while fourteen had been pulled recently.

However, lurking in the mouth was a tell-tale clue, which would prove significant to the investigation.

Hutchinson discovered that three of the old extractions left a continuous gap in the jaw. This would have been unsightly; it was likely the victim had worn a denture. The removal of neighbouring teeth, which might have revealed marks from a denture clasp, proved frustrating. And then Hutchinson noticed something else.

There was the stump of a tooth in the jaw, level with the gum, which appeared to have been ground by a revolving dental tool. The root canal was open but there was no filling inside. Hutchinson believed this tooth might have carried the clasp. He would need to remove it from the jaw and take microscopic photographs for closer inspection.

As Hutchinson worked, Glaister received dental records about Isabella and Mary from their dentists in Lancaster, who had responded to the appeal by Captain Vann.

When Ruxton had given the missing persons description of Isabella to Detective Constable Winstanley on 10 October, he had mentioned that she wore a denture with a gold clasp that was visible when she smiled.

Bertie Hammond had found right-handed fingerprints on various items including a washbasin in Mary Rogerson's bedroom at 2 Dalton Square that could not be identified. They could not be compared with 'Body No 2' as the fingertips had been cut off, but as the right hand of 'Body No 1' had now been recovered, Hammond wanted to test a theory he had. Although the epidermis of the fingertips had been lost to putrefaction, he believed the dermis, or underskin, might have the same characteristics as the outer layer. Such a notion had not been considered by the police before.

He took rather drastic steps to prove the point. He slid a cigarette from its cardboard carton, lit it and then proceeded to burn his own fingertip. Once the skin had blistered, Hammond sliced the surface layer off and then fingerprinted the raw dermal skin beneath.

It matched his original print perfectly.

Hammond and his boss, Glasgow's Chief Constable Percy Sillitoe were excited by this revelation. Would it work on the decaying fingers of the severed right arm?

As with Stobie's photographic work, this revolutionary fingerprinting technique would require a strong stomach and an absolute iron determination. Hammond was possessed of both. With Stobie's camera set up in a fixed position to take pictures of the flayed finger-ends, Hammond applied a special solution he had designed for the task to the fingertips every twenty minutes in the hope of producing a result. On one of the attempts, he spent as long as fourteen hours taking a print. The process would result in hundreds of sample prints before he was satisfied. These could then be compared with the prints found on the items from 2 Dalton Square.

Sillitoe later wrote, 'As this was the first time identification had been attempted on a dermal print in the British Isles, enlarged copies were forwarded to the Director of the Federal Bureau of Investigation at Washington with the request that these prints be examined by three experts and a decision given.'

The Director of the FBI in the United States was none other than J. Edgar Hoover and the decision in question was whether Hammond's findings were correct. Hoover would later give credit to Hammond, saying that his fingerprinting approach in the case was unique. Hoover had never heard of a law enforcement agency actively going looking for a deceased person's 'chance' prints as Hammond had done at Dalton Square. It was normal practice, Hoover said, for such identification to be made if corresponding prints already existed on police files. Fingerprint authority George W. Wilton QC would later describe Hammond's search for 'chance' prints at Ruxton's home as an 'absolutely new approach in fingerprint identification … a revolutionary development and the only one since 1900 in the use of fingerprints at [Scotland] Yard'.

EYEING BIRKETT

There was huge excitement in late November and early December as key witnesses spent two weeks giving depositions of their evidence for the first time at Lancaster Police Court before the case would be committed to a crown court for trial before a judge and jury. Sensational evidence including photographic enlargements and plaster casts of the victims' feet were paraded publicly, giving an inkling of the investigative work that had been taking place. Reporters scribbled down every word, ready to slip away to call their news desks. Ruxton listened throughout, making notes. Daily police dispersed a large crowd jostling outside the Town Hall disappointed at being denied access to the packed public gallery.

Inside there was a stir with each new witness. Most interest was reserved for Isabella's sister, Jeanie Kerr Nelson, and Mary's stepmother, Jessie Rogerson. Dr Leonard Mather later wrote, 'When I stepped out of the witness box a police sergeant asked me to sign on the dotted line and placed 30 shillings in my hand – all this in full view of Ruxton. It reminded me of Judas and his 30 pieces of silver.'

Ruxton began to weep when Mrs Nelson mentioned Elizabeth, Diana and Billy. At one point, he asked, through his solicitor Slinger, if the doors at the back of the court might be closed as there was a draught. Police officers dutifully pushed the door to.

The legal machinery was gaining momentum. The Lancaster hearings were merely the hors d'oeuvres before the main course: Ruxton's trial, which would most likely take place in Manchester after Christmas. Who would represent Ruxton? Norman Birkett was the most famous barrister in England, his stock riding high since the acquittal of Toni Mancini. He would not come cheaply. Fred Gardner put the wheels in motion to raise the funds.

Auctioneers and valuers Procter and Birkbeck, based at 32 Market Street, were invited to organise the sale of furnishings and effects at Ruxton's home. A large notice was stuck in Ruxton's window. It read: 'Sale by auction: Furniture now on view. Procter and Birkbeck'.

At ten o'clock on the morning of Saturday, 30 November, Dr Ruxton's home was opened to an eager line of visitors, who each paid two shillings for a copy of the sale catalogue, which was handed to them by a boy smartly dressed like a hotel bellboy in a suit and brimless pillbox hat. The *Morecambe Visitor* reported that the cover price was a measure to 'prevent any demonstration of morbidity'. Most of the visitors were women and even given the cost of entry no doubt some were drawn out of ghoulish curiosity rather than a desire to land a bargain.

There were fine examples of antiques in the house, a reflection of Ruxton and Isabella's eye for interesting pieces. Furniture in Ruxton's waiting room was not included in the sale, nor were his surgical instruments as he would require use of them should he be acquitted. Did prospective purchasers shiver when they saw included in the sales catalogue the imposing oil painting of Isabella, depicted in a pose mirroring Giorgione's *The Reading Madonna*?

Visitors thronged the rooms throughout the day, brandishing their catalogues, covers bent back as they checked items in each room against the list. The top floor of the house held particular interest. One interested purchaser, Mrs Edith Parish, from Rawtenstall, a Lancashire town in the Rossendale valley, scribbled 'Mrs Ruxton's room' and 'Mary Rogerson's room' in her catalogue next to sales items.

Included in the catalogue were carved oak bookcases, Louis XV-design cabinets, long-case and bracket clocks, Sheffield plates, as well as more intimate items such as the Ruxtons' bedroom furniture.

Dozens traipsed through the house that day and at five o'clock auctioneers' staff finally turned the key in the front door. It was open-house again on Monday, 2 December, with a long line of people waiting to enter.

On Wednesday, 4 December, the sale of Ruxton's possessions was held in the main upper room at the Alexandra Hall, a grand Victorian stone building, a moment's walk from Dalton Square on busy Penny Street. Winter sunlight streamed through high windows into the cavernous and ornate wood-panelled room, whose wooden floor was covered in a Persian-style rug. The room buzzed with activity. Eager bargain hunters sat in rows while dozens more stood along the walls. Auctioneer Thomas Edward Birkbeck of Procter and Birkbeck stood behind a table draped with a patterned cloth at the front of the hall, surrounded by the earthly possessions of the Ruxtons.

Every ledge and surface was covered with items – an expensive vase, say, or plaster bust – belonging to the Ruxtons. Birkbeck was a seasoned auctioneer. Over many years he had conducted such sales at Alexandra Hall, advertising them in the local newspapers such as the *Lancaster Guardian* and *Morecambe Visitor* as 'important sales of antique and modern furnishings'. He was a slim, tall man with a sharp jawline and a centre parting, and he wore a dark suit and tie. He had a habit of opening his jacket and resting his hand on his hip while he pointed with his other hand to acknowledge bids in the room. Birkbeck's assistants – burly men who might have been more at home as police officers – busied themselves lugging the lots as and when Birkbeck closed a sale and moved on to the next in the catalogue. A slight, owlish man in spectacles sat at a small desk in front of Birkbeck keeping a record of the sales.

Police cars were parked outside Lancaster Castle railway station on the evening of Monday, 9 December. Officers were awaiting the arrival of a train with the cream of Scotland's forensic scientists on board. The next day's newspapers would refer to them as 'the Big Six'. They were coming to give their depositions at Lancaster Police Court the following day. Emerging from steam on the platform were John Glaister, Sydney Smith, James Couper Brash, Dr Arthur Hutchinson, Dr Gilbert Millar and Dr Ernest Llewellyn Godfrey, who was a radiologist and assistant to the professor of anatomy at Edinburgh. The scientists were tired from their journey. Muffled against the winter chill in overcoats and hats, they climbed into the waiting vehicles and were driven to the police station in Dalton Square. Captain Henry Vann welcomed them, no doubt offered them refreshments and began a lengthy conference about the case in hand: Dr Buck Ruxton.

The following morning, Glaister was the first to give evidence at Lancaster Police Court at 10 a.m. It was a cold day, punctuated by rain showers. The public gallery was full with eager people drying off in the warmth of the courtroom.

Ruxton was brought up from the cells. He gave three bows – one for each of the magistrates – as he stepped into the dock.

Those in the court, including the packed public gallery, were given a glimpse of some items from the doctor's home. Among the bulky items were his bath, rolls of carpet and linoleum, banisters from the stairs, doors and pieces of wood.

But the real interest of the day's events was the appearance of Glaister, which created a stir in the public gallery.

During his evidence, Glaister handed a series of photographs, under discussion, to Ruxton's team. The doctor leaned across the rails of the dock to inspect the images, which were laid out on his solicitor's desk just below. A few moments later he sat back down on the wooden bench and started making notes.

During his evidence, which lasted five hours and forty minutes, Glaister stepped down from the stand to give a demonstration, using evidence in the courtroom to make his points. Items he discussed included linoleum from Ruxton's house; Glaister pointed to areas where he had found bloodstains. At one point, defence solicitor Slinger handed Glaister a tape-measure to aid explanation of his evidence; at another, it was necessary for two police officers to step down and join the professor in the well of the court to unroll the linoleum and show how it had lain in Ruxton's bathroom cupboard.

Ruxton looked on throughout.

On Wednesday, 11 December, Professor James Couper Brash took to the stand. He described the elaborate reconstruction of the bodies. His evidence – the first time it had been heard in open court – was intensely detailed, with gruesomely graphic flourishes too vivid for some.

A young woman in the public gallery fainted.

Professor Brash stopped speaking.

Attention swung to the wooden seats at the back of the courtroom.

The woman was carried out.

Glaister, who had been listening to his colleague, rose and went to perform first aid on the woman. She was soon feeling much better. But the harrowing nature of the crime had been underlined. Newspapers reporting that day's events led on the courtroom drama the following morning. The *Daily Independent*'s headline screamed: 'Woman Faints During Grim Ruxton Case Evidence'.

It was the first inkling the world had of the hideous crime of which the respected and charming Dr Ruxton was accused.

Families sat around the wireless on Christmas Day to listen to King George V's traditional festive address to the nation (it would be the king's last as he died the following month). The festivities were not shared by the Rogerson family in Morecambe, coming to terms with their first Christmas without Mary.

The Ruxton children were now in the care of the master and matron of the Parkside Institution, Lancaster's Public Assistance Hospital, which sat high above the town on Quernmore Road, close to Lancaster Grammar School. It was very close to Dalton Square, no more than fifteen minutes away. Parkside was the town's former workhouse and was an imposing stone building with tall, narrow windows peering across the town's skyline. Elizabeth, Diana and Billy had their own rooms and were looked after by a nurse; to shield them from gossip, they did not mix with the other children. By good fortune, Ruxton's colleague Dr Leonard Mather was the home's medical officer. To the three young children, torn from their home, perhaps his was a familiar, friendly face.

Ruxton sat in his cell at Strangeways, no doubt thinking about Elizabeth, Diana and Billy, heartbroken at their separation. Then came New Year's Eve. As revellers up and down the land raised their glasses to the dying moments of 1935, Ruxton may have cast his mind back exactly twelve months to the ballroom of the Elms Hotel in Morecambe where he had said a prayer for the world.

His prayer for 1936 must have been for Norman Birkett to save him from the gallows.

PART SEVEN
TRIAL

TRIAL OF THE CENTURY

The great Sir Bernard Spilsbury had not been invited to the party.

Although the purported victims were from Lancaster in England, the bodies had been found in Scotland, under the jurisdiction of scientists from Glasgow and Edinburgh. As he was the man who helped convict Crippen, the jigsaw murder case would have been ripe for the Spilsbury treatment. Yet there might still have been a role for the Home Office pathologist. On 8 February 1936, in an article above a report about Oswald Mosley's black-shirt British Fascists, the *Aberdeen Press and Journal* reported:

SIR BERNARD SPILSBURY FOR RUXTON TRIAL?
Negotiations in Progress
Famous as a Crown witness in many leading murder cases, Sir Bernard Spilsbury may appear in the Moffat ravine trial – for the defence.

It is learned that negotiations are in progress between the solicitors defending Dr Buck Ruxton and Sir Bernard Spilsbury with a view to the famous pathologist appearing for the defence when the case opens at Manchester Assizes at the end of this month or the beginning of March.

The Sheffield *Daily Independent* of the same day also carried the story. It added further details:

Although no official announcement has been made it is learnt that Sir Bernard Spilsbury was approached in connection with the case some weeks ago. The matter has been the subject of consideration ever since, for Sir Bernard was unable to give a definite decision at the outset. When approached yesterday, Sir Bernard said he had made no decision.

Later in the report, it was stated:

It has already been announced that Mr Norman Birkett will lead for the defence, and with the possible assistance of Sir Bernard Spilsbury on the pathological discoveries, the case should prove one of the most important legal battles in recent years.

As spring approached, Birkett was deep into studying the depositions of the Crown witnesses, whose words could put the doctor's neck in the hangman's noose. He later said, 'Nobody could read, as I read, all the facts the prosecution were going to prove without feeling that, well, this is a very difficult case. But it didn't make me any the less eager to do everything that I could for Dr Ruxton.'

In the end Spilsbury decided not to act for Ruxton. He did, however, offer advice to Birkett, drafting a list of questions to consider.

On Saturday, 29 February – 1936 was a leap year – *The Scotsman* reported that an official notice had been posted at Manchester Assize Court. It said the murder trial of Dr Buck Ruxton would begin that Monday.

Monday, 2 March was a cold, clear day. Britain was emerging from a mild winter but it was still overcoat-and-gloves weather in Manchester. There was a buzz of activity at the High Court of Justice on Great Ducie Street early that morning. This was where the Manchester Winter Assizes would sit. The imposing Venetian Gothic Revival building peered down in judgement on Manchester's scurrying citizens. The equally austere, smoke-grimed Strangeways prison stood guard over its shoulder. And sitting in one of the cells waiting to be led into court was Dr Buck Ruxton.

There was intense media interest. It was without doubt the most sensational murder case since Crippen twenty-five years earlier. Reporters clutched their press passes and notebooks and filed into the cavernous courtroom to take their seats on the press bench. Journalists from the nationals were packed cheek by jowl with Press Association reporters who would syndicate copy to the provinces and the rest of the world.

Photographers scurried along the pavements of Great Ducie Street, hungry for shots of witnesses arriving at court. On that first morning, the Associated Newspapers photographer snapped Susie Johnson, the young Scottish woman who discovered the bodies. She was dressed smartly in a thick fur coat and a black cloche hat. She wore black leather gloves and clutched a compact handbag under her arm. At her side was her brother, Alfred, in overcoat and trilby. Walking into court with them was Detective

Lieutenant Bertie Hammond, wearing a double-breasted overcoat and trilby hat. In the coming days, the Associated Press photographers caught the parade of key figures who were to give evidence at Ruxton's trial, preserving their images for posterity.

Captain Henry Vann arrived hatless, sporting a dark suit and striped tie, carrying a thick Manila folder under his arm. A cigarette smouldered between the first two fingers of his right hand.

Isabella's sister, Jean Kerr Nelson, strode into court stiff-backed and with a severe countenance, understandable given the circumstances. She was dressed in a long, heavy, fur-lined coat, a black felt-brimmed hat and round black-rimmed spectacles: she looked like she had stepped out of a Salvation Army band.

Key police witnesses Inspector Henry Strath and Sergeant Robert Sloan arrived in full uniform and peaked caps, having travelled down from Scotland.

A crowd had lined up in the hope of a seat in the public gallery. By eight o'clock in the morning there were already thirty people waiting – a dozen women and eighteen men. Police officers organised them into two lines either side of the huge door into the court, women on one side, men the other.

A middle-aged Manchester woman, Miss Mary Phillips, was the first in line, having queued since 10.30 the night before. 'I was determined to be first,' she told a journalist from the Press Association. 'I have taken a deep interest in the case. It was not until four o'clock in the morning that anyone else joined me. Then three men came along.'

The names of the legal teams for the Crown and defence were already known to the public because newspapers had run stories in anticipation of the huge interest in the case. The trial would be heard before Mr Justice Singleton; the Crown prosecutors were Joseph Cooksey Jackson KC, David Maxwell Fyfe KC and Hartley Shawcross; while Ruxton's defence was led by Birkett, assisted by Philip Kershaw KC, with instructions from Ruxton's solicitor Edwin Slinger. By a strange coincidence, a number of these illustrious men had links to Lancaster. Both John Singleton and Joseph Cooksey Jackson had been pupils, albeit at different times, at Lancaster Royal Grammar School, whose grounds neighboured Williamson Park on the road out to the remote community of Wyresdale. Singleton had also been Lancaster's Conservative Member of Parliament following the 1922 general election, but had lost his seat the following year. Meanwhile, Norman Birkett's mother Agnes came from a Wyresdale farming family.

On the first morning of the trial, the *Daily Mirror* reported:

> Three young children will be playing with their toys at the Parkside
> Home, Lancaster, today, blissfully unaware that their father will be facing
> the ordeal of a trial for his life in the dock at Manchester Assizes.
>
> They are the children of Dr Buck Ruxton, the Lancaster medical prac-
> titioner, who is charged with the murder of his 35-year-old wife, Isabella,
> and Mary Jane Rogerson, their 20-year-old nursemaid.
>
> For more than two months Diana, Elizabeth and Billy Ruxton have
> been cared for in the home that is controlled by the Lancaster Public
> Assistance Committee.
>
> They think their father has gone away for a holiday and have their own
> nurse and rooms apart from the other children in the home.

One hundred and fifteen witnesses for the Crown were expected to give
evidence at the trial; more than a hundred exhibits would be produced –
these had been kept in a locked room at the assize court over the weekend
in readiness for Monday morning.

Central to the case was the issue of identification: were the bodies those of
Isabella and Mary? The Crown's case was built on powerful circumstantial
evidence against Ruxton and the revolutionary police and forensic science
investigations. Birkett had scrutinised the evidence in fine-grain detail and
realised his best hope of getting Ruxton off was in persuading the jury that,
even if the evidence showed the bodies were those of the two women, it
did not prove the doctor was responsible for their deaths.

The courtroom was all set for an explosive battle of wits, a crucible in
which the Ruxton marriage and domestic home life would be dissected.
Reporters were keen to share details of the alleged crimes with their
millions of readers. They wanted to know exactly what Dr Ruxton
was accused of doing to his wife and children's nanny. They would not
have to wait long. The allegations would be outlined in graphic terms
that morning.

'Put up Buck Ruxton,' went the cry from the Clerk of Assize.

Ruxton was brought up into the dock and he glanced around at the
packed room, the judge, the barristers, the public gallery, the press bench.
He was wearing a dark blue suit, black overcoat and a black-and-white

check tie. A newspaper reporter later wrote, 'His dark curling hair had been carefully groomed.'

The Clerk of Assize addressed Ruxton directly: 'Buck Ruxton, you are indicted and the charge against you is murder in that on a day between the 14th and 29th days of September, 1935, at Lancaster, you murdered Isabella Ruxton. How say you, Buck Ruxton, are you guilty or not guilty?'

The words hung in the air; the room silent.

'I plead not guilty,' Ruxton replied.

The charge of murdering Mary Rogerson was included on the indictment but Ruxton would be tried only on the murder of Isabella.

The twelve members of the jury, all male, entered the court and were sworn in.

The Clerk now addressed the jurors. He repeated the details of the charge against Ruxton and also the doctor's plea of not guilty. He said, 'Upon his arraignment he has pleaded that he is not guilty and has put himself upon his country, which country you are. It is for you to inquire whether he be guilty or not and to hearken to the evidence.'

Joseph Cooksey Jackson rose from his seat, 57 years old, a formidable barrister who had defended the famous boxer Jackie Brown in 1934 against an assault charge. He began his opening speech for the Crown. Ruxton listened.

Jackson gave a précis of the case, painting a picture of Ruxton's early life, his education and time in Edinburgh, his meeting with Isabella, their volatile relationship, the 'discord' in their home and Ruxton's suspicions about Isabella's fidelity. Jackson quoted from Shakespeare's *Othello* to sum up Ruxton eloquently: 'Trifles light as air which to the jealous mind, are confirmed true as Holy Writ.'

'Various witnesses will be called to prove that the prisoner was a man of violent temper and that he inflicted violence on Mrs Ruxton on several occasions,' he told the jury. He described Ruxton's suspicions about Isabella and Bobby Edmondson, 'without, I submit, any justification whatever'.

'It is suggested that both women died a violent death,' the prosecutor said, 'and that the dismemberment was carried out by somebody with medical knowledge and surgical skill. I would remind you that the prisoner is a Bachelor of both Medicine and Surgery.'

And then the reporter's pens quickened as Jackson revealed the Crown's view of how the women had died at Ruxton's hands:

Now, it does not need much imagination to suggest what probably happened in that house. It is very probable that Mary Rogerson was a witness to the murder of Mrs Ruxton, and that is why she met her death. In that house the bedrooms are on the top floor; the back bedroom was occupied by Mary Rogerson, in one of the front slept Mrs Ruxton with her three children, and on the same floor was also the doctor's room. You will hear that Mrs Ruxton had received before her death violent blows in the face and that she was strangled. The suggestion of the prosecution is that her death and that of the girl Mary took place outside these rooms on the landing at the top of the staircase, outside the maid's bedroom, because from that point down the staircase right into the bathroom there are trails of enormous quantities of blood. I suggest that when she went up to bed a violent quarrel took place; that he strangled his wife, and that Mary Rogerson caught him in the act and so had to die also. Mary's skull was fractured: she had some blows on the top of the head which would render her unconscious, and then was killed by some other means, probably a knife, because of all the blood that was found down these stairs.

The statement was stark; the public gallery was transfixed. Ruxton sat in silence.

Jackson continued:

What is his [Ruxton's] position? He has on his hands two bodies that must be got rid of, and they must be got rid of so that they cannot be traced to Lancaster, and if possible be unrecognisable and unidentifiable; he has to get rid of the bloodstains in that house; he has to allay the suspicions of the relatives of both victims; and he has to cut up and dismember the bodies so that they may be carried the more easily and run less risk of identification.

He pointed to the circumstantial evidence suggesting Ruxton's guilt: the ripping up of carpets, the giving away of the blue suit, the purchasing of the cotton wool at Morecambe on the Sunday night.

If he had murdered two women, and was cutting up these two women, then cotton wool would be extremely useful in cleaning up the blood that would be splashed about the place, and, as you will hear, when those bodies were found at Moffat amongst the packing in which they had been carried was cotton wool.

Isabella and Mary's bodies were lying, parcelled up, at Dalton Square on the night of Sunday, 15 September, Jackson contended. The likelihood was that he had left his children with the Andersons in Morecambe at 9.30 and then had driven the remains to Moffat, a journey that could be done in around three and a quarter hours at night. If he had dumped the bodies and returned, then that would probably explain why he was not back home when Mrs Oxley arrived for work at 7.10 the next morning. It would also explain why Ruxton had looked unshaven and was dressed in such an unkempt manner when he saw Mrs Hampshire at 9 a.m. on the Monday.

Jackson touched on the matter of Ruxton hiring a car from the garage in Morecambe, bigger than his Hillman Minx, which he booked in for a service even though it did not require one. 'If he had parcels to carry away, no doubt he wanted a car with more room,' he said.

Ruxton had been returning from a trip to Moffat to dump remains when he was involved in the accident in Kendal, Jackson suggested. 'You do not go through Kendal to go to Seatle,' he said with regard to Ruxton's claim to have been visiting the village near Grange-over-Sands that day. He also told the jury of Ruxton's efforts to persuade acquaintances to cover for him by lying.

Jackson stood before the jury and concluded his opening remarks: 'You are only trying him for the murder of Mrs Ruxton, but the incidents connected with the death of the girl Mary Rogerson may help you considerably in deciding whether the prisoner is guilty of the charge that is brought against him.'

Jackson's opening speech had lasted some time. Once he sat down there was long enough to hear evidence briefly from the first witnesses for the prosecution. First was Lawrence Joseph Holiday, the Lancaster Corporation assistant surveyor who created scale plans of 2 Dalton Square and the route from Lancaster to Edinburgh. He was followed by Sergeant Frederick Charles Harrison who had constructed the scale model of Ruxton's home. Their work was presented to the court and would be used during the trial to provide context for the jurors. Ruxton eagerly leaned forward, craning his neck, to see the model of his home. He had not seen the building in reality in almost five months.

Next, Detective Lieutenant Bertie Hammond stepped into the witness box and outlined his initial involvement in the case and the photographs he had taken of Ruxton's home. His revolutionary fingerprint investigations would wait until later in the trial.

There was a stir in court when the final witness of the day was called: Mrs Jeanie Nelson, Isabella's sister. She gave her observations on Ruxton and Isabella's relationship and spoke at length about her sister's suicide attempts and Ruxton's efforts to be reconciled with her. She described the events of Saturday, 14 September and Isabella's visit to their hotel in Blackpool. She said that after a light lunch, Isabella, who had seemed in good spirits, had left around 11.30. The following day, Mrs Nelson had waited for Isabella, but she had not come. 'We went back to Edinburgh on Monday, 16 September, by motor bus. I have never seen my sister again from half-past eleven on the Saturday night,' she said.

The trial adjourned. Ruxton was taken back to Strangeways. The first day was concluded.

56

BOBBY'S EVIDENCE

The following morning, day two of the trial, began with Mrs Kerr continuing her evidence. Maxwell Fyfe for the Crown led her through her testimony, which included a discussion of the letters Ruxton had sent her prior to his visit in early October. Birkett cross-examined her before Jackson stood to re-examine her evidence a final time.

The hearing began to pick up pace now and the court heard from William Thompson, who had been a detective inspector at Lancaster at the time of the investigation but was now Chief Constable of Clitheroe in Lancashire, and PC Norman Wilson. Both related stories of domestic disturbances at the Ruxton home and the doctor's threats to Isabella. There followed evidence from three of the Ruxtons' domestic servants, before there was a ripple of excitement in the court at the next witness.

Bobby Edmondson stepped into the witness box.

The 24-year-old solicitor looked smart in his suit, hair slicked back. He was questioned by Mr Jackson.

'I am an assistant solicitor in the town-clerk's department of the Lancaster Corporation,' he began. 'I have known the Ruxtons socially and have frequently visited their house since March, 1934.'

Jackson asked if Ruxton had ever accused him of 'being intimate with his wife'.

'He has never suggested anything of the kind,' replied Bobby.

'Has there been the slightest intimacy of any description between you and Mrs Ruxton?'

'Most certainly not.'

Bobby described the events of the trip to Edinburgh on Saturday, 7 September, the room arrangements at the Adelphi Hotel in Leith and the return to Lancaster on the Sunday.

He said, 'On the following Monday [9 September] I met Dr Ruxton and he asked me whether Mrs Ruxton had taken my sister and who else had gone on the trip to Edinburgh. He was perfectly friendly with me.'

Jackson asked Bobby about the following weekend's events, the weekend of the 14 and 15 September. Bobby had gone to Blackpool that Sunday (15 September), the day Isabella had arranged to meet her sisters in the seaside resort.

'Did you see Mrs Ruxton at all?' asked Jackson.

'No, I have never seen her again since 14 September,' Bobby told the court. 'On that day I saw her about three in the afternoon. She was driving along Scale Hall Lane in the Morecambe direction; I was coming from Lancaster. She did not appear to see me and I did not stop and speak with her.'

The judge, Mr Justice Singleton, asked: 'That was the last time you saw her?'

'Yes,' replied Bobby.

'Were you always quite friendly with her?' asked the judge.

'Yes.'

'You knew her quite well and your mother and sister also knew her?'

'Yes.'

Bobby explained that he saw Ruxton on Thursday, 19 September. He said Ruxton had explained that Isabella had gone with her sister to visit an aunt in London. 'His right hand was heavily bandaged, and he told me he had cut it and that it was poisoned. I next saw him on Sunday, 6 October,' he told the court.

Jackson gave context for the jury: 'That is after the discovery of the bodies?'

Bobby continued:

Yes. I saw him at his house where I went with my father. I said that I had called to corroborate what my father had said, that I had no knowledge of Mrs Ruxton's whereabouts – he had seen my father the night before. He commenced by saying that Mrs Ruxton had a number of faults and the chief was a fondness for gambling; that she had lied and was extravagant; that he had been very cute, always giving her money by cheque, and he had found that these cheques were being endorsed over to some bookmaker.

He said that there were twelve pounds on the table every Monday morning, but that lately he had given her only a pound, which she spent as she wished, and he was settling the housekeeping accounts himself. He said he knew he had lost his temper with her on occasions and had slapped her.

He pulled a large number of documents from his pocket, and said he had learned from the letters that she had taken an office in Blackburn and that she had even taken a chair and a desk from his surgery to furnish it. He also produced another letter which he said he had sent to Mrs Ruxton in Edinburgh, but it had been returned unopened. I did not see the letter, but saw him reading it.

My father said that he, my father, was only concerned to remove any doubt at all that I knew where Mrs Ruxton was.

Bobby said Ruxton had told them he knew Isabella had been telephoning Bobby and that they had seen each other at the town swimming baths. He also told them that the previous week Isabella had been in Edinburgh staying with her sister.

'He then said that he really did want Mrs Ruxton back,' Bobby told the court, 'and he felt sure that she would be returning some day, and that if ever I heard from her, or even of her, would I try to do what I could to get her to come back.'

Jackson asked if Ruxton had ever suggested Bobby had been responsible for Isabella's disappearance.

'No,' replied Bobby, firmly.

'Did you part on friendly terms?' asked Jackson.

'Yes. It was perfectly friendly throughout. He shook hands with both my father and myself as we left.'

Jackson's examination was complete. Now it was Norman Birkett's turn to cross-examine the young man. He rose to his feet. He said, 'Mr Edmondson, you were friendly with Mrs Ruxton in the ordinary social way?'

'Yes,' replied Bobby, 'that is quite correct.'

'Did you occasionally, as an act of courtesy, drive her and, I think, Mrs Anderson sometimes, home from the swimming bath?'

'Yes, if Mrs Anderson was there, she came as well.'

Birkett asked Bobby about the trip to Edinburgh and the Adelphi Hotel on Saturday, 7 September, and the events leading up to it. Bobby explained how Isabella had originally planned to go in August and had invited Bobby's sister, Barbara, but this had fallen through. The visit in September was a new arrangement and Bobby and his parents were to go as well.

'It is quite clear, is it not, that what Mrs Ruxton said, if anything, to her husband, you do not know?' asked Birkett.

'I do not know,' replied Bobby.

'On 15 September, you said you were in the neighbourhood of Dalton Square at 10.15. Have you any particular reason for fixing the time?

'Yes. I go to church most Sundays; the service commences at 10.30, but I have to be there by 10.15 at the latest. The church is about 50yds from Dalton Square.'

'On that morning you say you saw Dr Ruxton's car in Friar's Passage, the passage behind his surgery. There was nothing very unusual in it being there?'

'No, certainly not. I often saw it there. I thought from the blinds that Mrs Ruxton must have come back after dark.'

'The next matter is about Monday, 16 September. You saw Dr Ruxton upon that day when he told you that his wife, Mrs Ruxton, had taken Mary and the children to Scotland?'

'Yes, he definitely said Mary and the children.'

Birkett said, 'I must suggest to you that you are mistaken about that, and that what he said was that Mary had gone with Mrs Ruxton to Scotland, but never said "and the children"?'

Bobby thought, then replied, 'Well, it was firmly fixed in my mind at the time that he put in the words "and the children".'

Birkett asked Bobby about his visit with his father to see Ruxton on 6 October. Bobby told the court that Ruxton was 'tremendously excited and he was very upset, you could tell. He was definitely overwrought', and added that 'you could not stop him when he got going'.

Birkett said, 'I want to get that fact before the Court, and that vivid phrase will do. You could not stop him; it poured out of him?'

'Yes, quite correct.'

'Throughout, from start to finish, he did not appear to be in control of himself?'

'With just odd intervals he was, but mainly he was very upset.'

Birkett had no further questions for Bobby Edmondson. The young solicitor stepped down from the witness box. The tension in the court dissipated.

Next it was the turn of Bobby's father, Robert Edmondson, who introduced himself as a cabinetmaker. Led by Jackson's questions, Mr Edmondson told the court Ruxton had visited him on 5 October to ask where Bobby was. He had told Ruxton that his son was in Edinburgh staying with friends at that time.

Mr Edmondson said:

The attitude that the doctor took up and the sly way he asked the question of their address naturally made me think there was something behind this and I asked him why he wanted to know. He burst out crying and I told him to pull himself together and tell me what was the trouble. He said, 'I am sorry for you. I think a lot about your Bobby, but my wife was going to Edinburgh and Bobby is in Edinburgh, and I know there have been telephone messages.'

I said that as regarding telephone messages these could easily be explained as Bobby would be back that day. He went on to say that he knew Bobby and Barbara went to Edinburgh, and also Mrs Ruxton, and stayed at the Adelphi Hotel. I told him that I could explain that trip and rather than let him go on talking I explained the trip to Edinburgh to him.

Mr Edmondson said he had explained he and his wife had also been on the trip and stayed at the Adelphi. Ruxton had said Isabella told him she had stayed with her sister, not at the hotel.

'I told him that I did not know why she had said this, and he replied that he would like to see Bobby,' said Mr Edmondson, and described how his wife and daughter had then arrived. Ruxton had stood up and placed his fingers on his lips, indicating to him not to say a word about their conversation.

He told the court that the following day he had asked Ruxton if he believed Bobby responsible for Isabella's leaving. 'Oh, no, no,' Ruxton had replied. Mr Edmondson had warned Ruxton that if there was any gossip connecting Bobby with Isabella, there would be trouble.

During Mr Edmondson's evidence, the Adelphi Hotel's guest register was produced in court, as Exhibit 198, with the entries for 7 September 1935 showing the names of the party, starting with Isabella's signature. It showed that Mr and Mrs Edmondson stayed in room 28, Bobby in 44, Barbara in 50 and Isabella in 49. Mr Edmondson explained that he had paid the hotel bill for the party, which had been made out in Isabella's name.

The scene had been electrifying in the courtroom, the public gallery transfixed. Ruxton had watched, listening carefully to the evidence of Bobby and his father. It was a sensation in the newspapers the next morning. Even though there was no evidence of an affair, the newspapers made the most of linking their names in headlines. Papers carried a photograph of Bobby looking handsome in a black fedora hat and Isabella in the now infamous studio portrait taken in Lancaster in February 1935.

The day's proceedings continued with a short testimony from another of Isabella's sisters, Mrs Eleen Madden, who had been at Blackpool on the last weekend Isabella was seen alive. Next was Mrs Ethel Jackson, of 13 Dalton Square, whose two children were friends of Elizabeth Ruxton and who had been playing at the Ruxton home that night in September. She recalled that Mary Rogerson, who had looked after the playing children, had a 'glide in her eye'.

Later in the day it was the turn of Mrs Ethel Anderson, wife of dentist Herbert, who had to all intents and purposes acted as the Ruxton children's mother during September and early October. She recounted the comings and goings of Ruxton with Elizabeth, Diana and Billy and the arrangements of their staying at the Anderson home in Morecambe.

She described the night of Wednesday, 18 September, when Ruxton had stayed at their home until almost one in the morning because he had fallen asleep exhausted in an armchair. Ruxton had said Isabella was going on holiday but had not mentioned Mary.

The hearing was adjourned. Day two was over.

57

RUXTON'S HAND

The trial fell into a rhythm as a stream of witnesses recounted the events of September and October. There was Mrs Hampshire, Mrs Oxley, Mrs Curwen. There was Bessie Philbrook, who took the children for walks. There was Dorothy Neild, the Andersons' housemaid. There were the various painters and decorators and odd-job men, many of whom Ruxton had tried to persuade to cover for him. Bernard Beattie, the motorcyclist knocked over in Kendal, spoke, as did PC James Lowther, who stopped Ruxton in Milnthorpe. There was Peter Rogerson, Mary's brother.

There was evidence from Ruxton's friends. Herbert Anderson said Ruxton had told him Mary Rogerson was pregnant and also identified Ruxton's handwriting in the diaries that were produced in court. He said Ruxton was not in the habit of wearing a white coat when he administered general anaesthetics at dental extractions but had worn his blue suit. He confirmed there was often much blood during such procedures. James Jefferson described journeys he had made with Ruxton to Seatle and the holiday their children enjoyed with Mrs Holme.

On the fourth day, the court heard from Dr Stanley Shannon, the medical officer at Strangeways prison. Giving evidence, he said:

The prisoner has been under my care since being taken into custody. On 22 October I examined his hand and found healed scars of wounds, but no actual wound on the right hand … in my opinion the cut across the hand started at the bottom, and was certainly caused by some very sharp instrument with a cutting edge. I think these cuts were caused by a knife or similar instrument passing through the hand when it was clasped from below, and that the severity of the two lower cuts probably caused the release of the grip, and that is why the two cuts on the first finger are superficial.

Jackson said to Dr Shannon, 'You know a surgeon's cutting knife. If anyone is cutting up a body with blood in it, are there any difficulties at all in regard to the knife?'

'Oh yes, there are several difficulties,' Shannon replied. 'It makes it slippery.'

Jackson asked if the tin opener could have caused the wounds to Ruxton's hand.

'Certainly not,' Shannon replied.

Two sisters, Dorothy Elizabeth and Catherine Annie Mather, who lived in a house overlooking the rear of Ruxton's house, recalled seeing a fire burning in the doctor's yard on the night of Tuesday, 17 September. Alfred Turner, the commissionaire at the County Cinema, described seeing Dr Ruxton poking a fire in his yard on Thursday, 19 September.

On the fifth day the evidence of Mary's father and stepmother was heard. Mrs Jessie Rogerson identified the blouse recovered with the remains at Moffat. She had bought it at a Morecambe jumble sale and given it to Mary. Mr James Rogerson confirmed his daughter had had some teeth drawn during her life. On the day of his arrest, Ruxton had visited him to inquire how many of Mary's teeth had been extracted.

The discovery of the remains at Gardenholme linn was revisited later on the fifth day when Susan Johnson and her brother Alfred gave evidence. The events were very well known already through the extensive newspaper coverage. But it was still fascinating for onlookers to hear Miss Johnson recount the chilling moment she saw the severed arm below the bridge.

On the sixth day, Mrs Edith Holme, of the Cottage at Seatle, gave evidence about the two visits the Ruxtons made to her farm in June 1935 and the two weeks Mary and the children spent there. She recognised the rompers produced as evidence by the Crown. The garment had been wrapped around the head of 'Body No 1', believed to be that of Mary Rogerson.

'This pair of rompers were mine,' she said. 'I got them for my little boy from a Mrs Perry, and gave them to Mary Rogerson. I recognise them in every way, and especially by the knot which I made when I put the elastic in, the old elastic being worn.' She explained the idiosyncratic way that she tied knots. 'It is the way I have always done it,' she said.

Fred Barwick, the director of Manchester Chamber of Commerce's testing house and laboratory, said he had made comparisons between cotton sheeting found with the remains and bedding from Isabella's bed at Dalton Square. He said he could discern no difference between the two. Indeed there was a microscopic fault in the weave of both that matched, which meant that they had come from the same loom. 'A fault like this would not be noticeable except under a microscope,' he said.

During these exhaustive rounds of evidence, Ruxton sat and listened. From time to time his agitation was visible to those who cared to look at him. There was little he could do besides scribble notes to Birkett or simply sit passively.

On day seven, memories of Isabella's traumatic miscarriage in April 1932 were recalled when evidence was given by nursemaid Jane Grierson, Mary's predecessor, and doctors Leonard Mather and Frederick Bury, who described the state of the house when they attended to her. All said there had been bloodstains – and quite a lot of blood – in Isabella's bed in the nursery, but that there had been none on the stairs. Mather was clear on this: the early morning sunlight was already filtering into Ruxton's home and he had a clear view of the stairs. He stood his ground when challenged by Birkett under cross-examination.

Birkett said, 'Do you remember that when the doctor met you in the hall and escorted you upstairs he told you that Mrs Ruxton had been running upstairs to the children and had fallen?'

Mather shot back, 'I do not think he said that at all.'

There followed a procession of police witnesses from Lancaster Police and the various Scottish forces, chief among them Captain Henry Vann, who gave testimony to Ruxton's excitable and suspicious behaviour in the days leading to his arrest. Photographer Cecil Thomas and Detective Constable Thomas Stobie spoke about the specialist photographic work they had done with the Scottish scientists.

The remainder of the seventh day was reserved for one of the highlights of the trial. The press and public had been waiting for the forensic evidence to be presented. It was here that the gruesome details and their significance would be revealed.

Into the witness box stepped Professor John Glaister. He would be the first of the science and police expert witnesses who would be on the stand for the next three days.

58

GLAISTER'S MOMENT

Glaister was due to give evidence on Monday, 9 March, the seventh day of the trial. He had travelled down to Manchester from Glasgow the day before and checked into his hotel. He had brought with him some important new evidence.

Once he had unpacked and freshened up, Glaister went to meet with the Crown Prosecution team and Assistant Director of Public Prosecutions, Gerald Paling, who had represented the Crown at Ruxton's hearings in Lancaster. They wanted to go through Glaister's evidence in preparation for the following day's hearing. Glaister was worried about cross-examination on the stand. 'In Norman Birkett,' he later wrote, 'Ruxton was represented by one of the ablest legal brains in Britain, and no detail was likely to escape his probing attention.' Glaister was concerned his opinion on how long the women had been dead 'might be open to challenge, [and] might be worn down to where it could cease to have value'.

A means of proving it had eluded him for some time until the solution came into his mind one morning as he lay in bed. He realised the maggots found on the remains could hold the key. He had always collected samples of extraneous materials from crime scenes as they might prove useful. And he still had sample maggots taken from Moffat in test tubes.

Glaister was probably inspired by a historic case. In Paris in 1850, workmen restoring an old property discovered the desiccated corpse of a young child. To determine the year in which the child died, a doctor examined the body and the hardened larval skin of flies. It was one of the earliest examples of forensic entomology.

Glaister took his test tubes to an expert entomologist – or insect specialist – in a neighbouring department at Glasgow University. Dr Alexander Gow Mearns was not only an expert in insects but also a physician and lecturer in public health. He very quickly identified the maggots as those of the common bluebottle.

Glaister did not tell Mearns his theory; he wanted to see what he would say without influence. Mearns inspected the specimens and gave his view on the stage of their development. What he told Glaister matched his estimate of between ten and fourteen days. Glaister wrote: 'I was heartened by his matching conclusion.' It corroborated Glaister's and the prosecution's view that the bodies had been dumped in Gardenholme linn probably during the early hours of the morning of Monday, 16 September 1935.

Now in Manchester, the day before he was due to give evidence, Glaister told the Crown Prosecution team he had this additional evidence and slides and microphotographs to back it up. He received a frosty reaction.

'No, not under any circumstances,' he was told. 'You mustn't put that forward, Professor Glaister.'

He was confused and told them so. Of the evidence, he said: 'But it is definite, positive –.' What concerned the prosecutors was the reaction the jurors might have to the evidence.

Joseph Jackson told Glaister, 'The jury are laymen. For a week now they've been exposed to evidence and exhibits which, to them, constitute horror and strain. So far they've stood up to it remarkably well.' At that time, under English law, if a member of a jury became ill then a trial could not continue with fewer than the required twelve. The prosecution team could not risk the Ruxton case going to a full retrial and it was their opinion the maggots could be the details to push a queasy juror over the edge.

Grudgingly, Glaister agreed. 'I won't volunteer this evidence,' he told them. 'But I must reserve the right to use it if it is necessary to protect my professional opinion and that of my colleagues. If my first opinion on the time of death is destructively challenged, then you must accept my judgement of the circumstances … and if necessary I'll use the maggot evidence.'

Glaister took the stand the following morning, after only a few hours' sleep. He peered out at the massed ranks of the press, the assembled medico–legal experts for both the Crown and Ruxton's defence in the seats in front of him, and in the distance the packed public gallery. He would be in the witness box for the best part of two days.

He told the court, 'I am a registered medical practitioner, hold various degrees and qualifications, and am Regius Professor of Forensic Medicine at the University of Glasgow.'

And so began the public account of the incredible work that Glaister and Smith and the rest of the scientists had done. David Maxwell Fyfe for the prosecution led the examination of the evidence.

Glaister talked about his arrival at Moffat and inspection of the bodies in the mortuary with Dr Millar. He outlined the dismemberment to the bodies and the efforts to conceal identifying features. With frequent reference to photographic exhibits, Glaister explained how the bodies had been dismembered and cut up. He also explained the injuries that the two women had suffered.

He said that a Y-shaped wound had been inflicted on the crown of the skull of 'Body No 1', believed to be Mary. Efforts to conceal the wound had been made by removing much of the skin. There were two small fractures of the skull below the wound. Neither he nor the other experts could state whether these had occurred before or after death, he told the court. The fractures had been caused by two separate blows. Had they been inflicted when the victim was still alive, it was unlikely she would have died, but she would no doubt have lost consciousness. This threw up the likelihood of some further injury to have caused death.

There were bruises on the arms, most of which were thought to have been caused while the victim was still alive. Because the trunk of 'Body No 1' was not present, it was impossible to assign the cause of death.

Glaister explained that the whole of the scalp of 'Body No 2' had been removed as well as all the skin of the face, apart from a few tags in certain places. There were a few medium-brown coloured hairs still present. He said there were five stab wounds on the left side of the body, the blade having penetrated the heart, aorta and the left lung. However, as there had been an absence of bleeding, he considered these to have been caused after death during the dismemberment of the body. He explained that the blood vessels in both bodies were empty and that the bodies had been drained of blood shortly after death.

He described the significance of the bloodstains he and his assistants discovered in Ruxton's bathroom. He told the court:

The majority indicate that the fluid flowed for a considerable distance from above downwards and subsequent tests showed it was human blood.

On the woodwork situated at the back of the w.c., near the tap end of the bath, I found eighty discrete spots of human blood, and from the shape and distribution of the stains I formed the impression that the material composing them had either been forcibly ejected or splashed on to the surface; for example, it might have been deposited there by the spurting of a small artery, or the hitting of an already moist surface might spread it by that means.

Glaister confirmed his view that the bodies must have been drained of blood and disarticulated within a few hours of death. Maxwell-Fyfe asked Glaister's view of how long it might take a person skilled in such matters to dismember 'Body No 2'. Glaister said a minimum of five hours. 'I think the draining of the blood would be accomplished as the disarticulation proceeded,' he said.

It was a tour-de-force performance, but exhausting for all concerned. The hearing was adjourned. The following morning, Glaister would be cross-examined by Norman Birkett. Glaister later wrote, 'This was our first encounter, and coming under his verbal scrutiny was an experience I'll always remember, an experience with a master in the art of cross examination, a man who could combine skilled probing with courtesy and scrupulous fairness.'

The next morning, Tuesday, 10 March, Birkett spent some time going over Glaister's evidence in relation to the bloodstains found throughout Ruxton's home, on the stairs, banisters, carpets and in the bathroom, as well as on Ruxton's suit. Glaister batted away suggestions such stains might have been present due to previous medical work and operations Ruxton had conducted, as well as from the doctor's injured hand. In each case of bloodstaining, Glaister said there had been a substantial amount of blood, which was consistent with Ruxton having committed murder.

Birkett picked over Glaister's theory that mutilation had been committed by someone with knowledge of anatomy, trying to trip Glaister up with the phrase 'expert anatomist'. Glaister was firm: 'I did not use the word "expert" … I think when you come to describe "expert" you are dealing with very fine terms, and I do not feel disposed to use that term. I think the expression I have used, "some definite anatomical knowledge", covers it.'

Throughout his cross-examination, Glaister wondered whether he would be challenged on the time of death. He had the maggots evidence with him and was ready to deliver it. As it turned out, he never had to call upon Dr Mearns's opinion. But it had been crucial evidence in providing

Glaister with the confidence to stand and present his view on the timeline of the dead women. It was the first time in British legal history that someone had thought to use the lifecycle of a maggot to determine how long a victim had been dead. It had proved revolutionary and the technique would soon be adopted in future police and forensic investigations and become standard practice. The Ruxton maggots would be preserved in their original test tube with Glaister's handwritten label, stating: 'Maggots from bodies of Ruxton's victims, 1935, Moffat', and kept for posterity at London's Natural History Museum.

Birkett asked Glaister about the cyclops eye: 'Was that not a very remarkable and startling discovery?'

'A most unusual find under the circumstances,' responded Glaister, confirming that it would have been the 'product of a monstrous birth'. The court was told that a cyclops eye occurred when a foetus, or child, was born not with two eyes but, 'by some irregular process of nature, one in the centre of the forehead, or at least two eyes very close together'.

Glaister said it was not possible to conduct a test that would have established whether the specimen were human or animal. Had it been the latter, it was most likely to be a grazing animal. 'A pig, very often,' he told the court.

Glaister's testimony had been long, tiring and graphic. There was more to come that afternoon as Dr Gilbert Millar, Professor James Couper Brash, dentist Dr Arthur Hutchinson and Professor Sydney Smith prepared to take the stand.

Millar confirmed Glaister's descriptions of the work they had done. He talked about the left foot recovered on 29 October that had the big toe cut away. Earlier in the trial, Isabella's chiropodist Enoch Edge had confirmed she had had a bunion on the joint of the big toe on her left foot. During cross-examination, Birkett led Millar to concede that bunions were very common, the implication being that this piece of evidence did not indicate the foot was Isabella's.

Brash took the stand. Mr Jackson began the questions for the Crown. He began with the matter of the cyclops eye.

'That, it has been suggested, is the eye of some monstrosity which, I understand it is suggested, was born to Mary Rogerson?' Jackson said, referring to Birkett's suggestion to that effect during the morning's proceedings.

Brash replied that he did not hold with the view that the eye was human. 'From the size of it, if it were human, it would have been the eye of a monstrous foetus,' he said, adding that he believed it was a pig's. It was never established where the cyclops eye had originated, but there were theories later that it had been a preserved specimen from Ruxton's surgery that had been dumped with the bodies by mistake.

Brash described the process of reassembling the bodies. He said the remains constituted two victims. 'I sorted them out to begin with in pairs of limbs, and formed an opinion about the number of bodies they probably represented. I found no evidence to show the presence of more than two bodies,' he said.

He explained that he was able to fit together perfectly the majority of 'Body No 2'. The remains that were left were the incomplete 'Body No 1'. There were around forty-three pieces of flesh that could not be assigned with any accuracy to either body. 'It was the parts containing bones I dealt with to reconstruct the skeletons,' he said.

Brash described taking casts of the feet and the attempts made to fit them into the shoes. He gave a demonstration to the court using a shoe belonging to Isabella and one belonging to Mary. The foot cast from 'Body No 1' fitted perfectly into Mary's shoe. It was like a morbid re-enactment of Cinderella.

It was time for Birkett to cross-examine Brash. He began with an attack on the evidence itself. He said that Brash's superimposed photographs of the victims' skulls and life portraits should not be allowed as evidence. 'It is constructed evidence which is so liable to error, in view of the admission of the photographer that it is impossible to get an exact life-size photograph; approximate is the best that can be done,' he said, urging Mr Justice Singleton to rule the evidence as inadmissible.

Singleton asked Brash, 'Have you done that sort of thing before?'

Brash replied, 'There is a great deal of literature on the subject which I have followed.'

'Do you think it may be useful to one side or the other in demonstrating one point or another in this case?' Singleton asked.

'I think they do demonstrate a certain point without any doubt,' Brash replied. 'The value of it is not for me to say.'

Singleton gave Birkett his decision: 'I do not feel able to exclude the evidence on that.'

Brash proceeded to explain to the court the work he had done with the heads, preparing them to be photographed, and the line tracings he made and then how he superimposed these over the life portraits of the two women.

He then presented his conclusions with regard to the portrait of Isabella: 'In my opinion these demonstrate conclusively, in the first place, that Skull No 1 could not possibly be the skull of Mrs Ruxton ... they also demonstrate, in my opinion, that Skull No 2 might be the skull of Mrs Ruxton.'

He continued: 'I formed the same opinion that they proved that Skull No 2 could not possibly be the skull of Miss Rogerson, but that Skull No 1 might be.'

The court heard next from Dr Hutchinson, Dean of the Edinburgh Dental Hospital, who confirmed the missing teeth from both heads, some that were clearly extractions done by dentists when the victims were alive; others had been the result of mutilation post-mortem. His evidence harmonised with that of Isabella's dentist, John Thistlethwaite, and Mary's Samuel Fawcett and James Priestley. Fawcett and Priestley recalled extracting some of Mary's teeth, while Thistlethwaite had fitted Isabella with a denture, which had been secured by means of a gold wire that fastened on to the adjacent teeth. Dr Hutchinson had observed the marks of this clasp on a tooth in the head of 'Body No 2'.

The final witness on day eight was Professor Sydney Smith. He began by telling the court:

> I have examined the remains in this case, have made a reconstruction of the bodies with Professor Brash, and have been in constant consultation with Professor Glaister and other medical witnesses. I agree with ... regard to the evidence they have given, and I agree with the height, ages, and sex of the two bodies.

In his cross-examination of Brash's evidence, Birkett had tried to elicit doubt that the two hands of 'Body No 1' were a pair, by pointing to an apparent ring mark on one hand. Mary Rogerson had not worn a ring; Birkett was seeking to introduce the possibility of a third body, which would undermine the scientific evidence suggesting identification as Isabella and Mary. Smith confirmed that he thought the hands were a pair. 'I have no doubt of this at all,' he said emphatically.

It had been another long day. It had been fascinating; the scientists had dazzled the court with their brilliance. Birkett had deployed all of his legal wiles to score points in Ruxton's favour. The press had notebooks full of juicy content for the next morning's papers.

The court was adjourned.

That evening, following his appearance in the witness box, Glaister received a telephone call in his hotel room in Manchester. He was surprised when the caller revealed himself: Norman Birkett, calling from his own suite. He was inviting Glaister to dinner. Glaister accepted and spent an enjoyable evening in the company of the land's most famous barrister, all courtroom hostilities put to one side. Afterwards, Glaister joined Birkett in his suite, where they continued talking until almost three in the morning. 'I tore myself away with the greatest reluctance,' Glaister later wrote.

The trial had also brought Glaister back in touch with an old acquaintance, Jack Buchanan, whom he had been friends with when both were members of a swimming club in Glasgow. Glaister had bumped into Buchanan in the foyer of the hotel shortly after arriving in Manchester. Buchanan was now a famous actor, singer and dancer, and a star of movies and theatre. Glaister was thrilled to see his tall, thin, handsome friend once more. Buchanan was staying in the same hotel and was fascinated to hear about Glaister's role in the infamous Ruxton case.

Glaister arranged for his celebrated friend to sit in the public gallery while he was giving evidence. Buchanan had never seen a trial in court before. Glaister later wrote that in the lunch recess he met his friend, who 'looked like a limp rag'.

Buchanan told him, 'John, I've never had an experience which has taken so much out of me. What a difference it was from acting a part to see the real thing in operation. It absolutely shook me.'

59

FINGERPRINTS

The ninth day of the trial, Wednesday, 11 March, began with Detective Lieutenant Bertie Hammond on the stand again. It was time to reveal the conclusions of his extensive and painstaking fingerprint work.

He described how he had gone into 2 Dalton Square on 13 October and removed many items belonging to Ruxton, including a table leaf, bottles, plates and dishes. These articles were exhibited in the court. As he spoke, he indicated which item he was referring to. All bore fingerprints or palm imprints. He explained how he compared these prints with those taken from the left hand of 'Body No 1'.

Maxwell-Fyfe, for the Crown, said to Hammond:

I want you to tell us from your study of this matter how many points of similarity you think are necessary to show that these fingerprints are of the body of which you are speaking and no other. What is the minimum number of points required before you are satisfied that the prints were made by the fingers of that body and of no other?

Hammond responded, 'In certain prints I would be satisfied with eight; in other prints I would be satisfied with less.'

Maxwell-Fyfe: 'We may take the number eight as being the minimum number which has satisfied you?'

Hammond: 'Yes.'

Maxwell-Fyfe: 'In these prints you have shown more than eight in every case?'

Hammond: 'Yes.'

Maxwell-Fyfe: 'Is the photograph on the left on page one of Exhibit 197 an enlargement of the palmar impression on the leaf of the table?'

Hammond: 'Yes.'

Maxwell-Fyfe: 'There you have marked twenty points of similarity?'

Hammond: 'Yes.'

It was a stunning moment. Hammond's work had been meticulous; he had been tenacious. When questioned by the judge, Hammond explained that he had spent some time working at Scotland Yard in London and that fingerprint officers there insisted upon the same threshold of eight points of similarity. His evidence showed that the left hand of 'Body No 1' had made the finger and palm prints on the Ruxton articles. That person was believed to be Mary Rogerson.

All the Crown witnesses had given their evidence. Now Norman Birkett had a decision to make: should he allow Ruxton to take the stand and give evidence in his own defence? It was the defendant's right to choose not to if he so wished. Birkett considered which course of action was most advantageous to Ruxton's case.

On Tuesday, 10 March, he had written down his thoughts in a memorandum, to be shared with Ruxton:

Re Evidence for the Defence
The moment has come in this Case where a decision must be taken as to the Evidence to be called for the Defence.
It falls into three divisions –
The Prisoner himself.
The evidence relating to the spotting of the suit by operatives.
The Medical Evidence.

Birkett disregarded Ruxton's claims that Isabella and Mary had been seen alive after 15 September as 'being so unreliable as to be fantastic and indeed ridiculous'. He wrote: 'The Prisoner can give evidence if he so desires, when, of course, he would be subjected to cross-examination.'

Birkett considered it 'of greater importance than anything else in this case' to have the final word before the judge's summing up. He wanted the jury to adjourn with his words fresh in their minds before considering their verdict. The only way to ensure this was to present Ruxton as the sole witness for the defence: after the Crown's cross-examination he would be able to re-examine Ruxton.

Birkett's legal brilliance was evident as he worked out the best strategy for countering the prosecution case. Any evidence of a medical nature that he might present 'to be of any avail' would have to disprove the medical evidence of the Crown that the recovered remains were those of Isabella and Mary. In terms that must have left Ruxton despondent, Birkett wrote, 'I am informed by the Medical Experts that this is impossible.'

In his closing paragraph, Birkett, who had won the acquittal of Toni Mancini twelve months earlier, wrote:

> In my clear and very strong view, if Dr Ruxton desires to give evidence we should confine our evidence to him, and exercise our right of the last word to the Jury.
>
> I particularly desire Dr Ruxton's assent to this course, which is the best possible course in his interest.
>
> Any other course, in my view, would be absolutely fatal.

After reading Birkett's note, Ruxton scribbled his response: 'I entirely agree with you. I wish to give evidence on my own behalf, and I also note that it is not in the interest of defence that further evidence should be called.'

And so the stage was set for the trial's final act: Dr Ruxton, the sole witness for the defence, giving his account of what happened to Isabella and Mary the previous September.

60

RUXTON ON THE STAND

Birkett stood and said, 'My lord, I call the prisoner.'

There was a stir when Ruxton rose and walked from the dock to the witness stand. It was the moment the public and press had been waiting for; the star turn in this macabre circus.

Ruxton was on oath and answered questions about his name, explaining that he was Buck Ruxton, formerly Gabriel Hakim and Buck Hakim. He talked about his medical qualifications. He had qualified as a doctor in 1922 but Lancaster had been his first practice. He became very emotional and started sobbing moments into his evidence when he spoke about his children and his life at 2 Dalton Square with Isabella.

'I can say honestly we were the kind of people who could not live with each other and could not live without each other,' he said, then uttered something in French, which was one of his native languages due to his French mother.

Birkett asked him to explain.

Ruxton replied, 'Forgive me the interruption, but I just used the French proverb, "Who loves most chastises most". My mentality thinks in French and I have to translate into English everything you are asking me.'

Birkett asked Ruxton to talk about his arguments and domestic disputes with Isabella and how long they lasted. 'Oh, hardly two hours or three hours,' the doctor replied, 'and every time a quarrel arose I paid dearly for it, and I can prove it.'

Birkett asked what his relations with Isabella would be like following such a quarrel. Ruxton said, 'Oh, more than intimate. If I may add, sir, in fact Mrs Ruxton many a time has come jokingly into my surgery with a smile on her lips and said, "I wonder how I could pick up a row with you".'

Birkett took Ruxton through many of the alleged incidents of his verbal and physical abuse of Isabella as described by his servants. Ruxton denied calling Isabella derogatory names such as 'dirty prostitute' and forcefully disputed saying he would kill her.

Birkett asked about a servant's claim to have seen Isabella with a bruised arm. Ruxton said he remembered the incident and that he may have caused the bruising as he had tried to snatch a photograph of a man from Isabella's hands as she was trying to hide it from him. He accepted he told the servant to prevent Isabella going off with the children. 'Yes, it is true,' Ruxton said, 'because my Belle was very erratic. She would just happen to do anything most silly, and I naturally would not like my children to be the victims of her temporary silliness or anything you like to call it.'

Ruxton denied many of the claims of his servants, including the remark that if she left him, he would bring Isabella back from a mortuary. He denied having a knife when a maid saw him with his hand around Isabella's neck. He put that incident down to 'love-making'.

Birkett questioned Ruxton about Bobby Edmondson. Ruxton burst into tears, unable to talk about his suspicions.

The questioning shifted to 14 September, the last day Isabella was seen alive. Ruxton confirmed she had left Lancaster at 6.30 p.m. to go to Blackpool to see her sisters. He said he was at home with Mary and the children. He said Mary was staying the night rather than going home to Morecambe because 'there was nobody for the children' as Isabella was out and he was on call. Mary went to bed at half past ten or eleven o'clock, he told the court.

Isabella returned from Blackpool 'pretty much after half past twelve', he said. 'I was waiting up, not actually in bed, when Isabella came for the bunch of keys that was with me and on which was the key of the garage … I gave her the keys and she went to put the car away and returned to the house. By that time I was in my bedroom.'

Birkett: 'Where did she sleep?'

Ruxton: 'On the top floor of 2 Dalton Square. There are three rooms on that floor; one is next to the Cinema, one adjoins the Brittanic Assurance Company, and there is one bedroom on the landing on that side, which is my Mary's room, exactly opposite my bedroom.' He added that the children were in Isabella's room.

Ruxton said he was not asleep in his room, but going through paperwork. 'When Belle passed my room on the top landing one could see the light burning through the crevices of the door although the door is shut, and she just called out 'Good-night' in the usual female tone and went to her bedroom, taking the bunch of keys with her.'

Birkett said to Ruxton, 'I want to put this question quite plainly and directly: it is suggested here by the Crown that on the morning of the Sunday after your wife had come back you killed her?'

Ruxton became emotional, angry: 'That is an absolute and deliberate and fantastic story; you might just as well say the sun was rising in the west and setting in the east.'

Birkett: 'It is suggested also by the Crown that upon that morning you killed Mary Rogerson?'

Ruxton: 'That is absolutely bunkum, with a capital B, if I may say it. Why should I kill my poor Mary?'

Birkett asked what Mary had done that Saturday. Ruxton said it had been well known by his servants and local people that he intended to have the house redecorated and that Mary had lifted the carpets on the hall stairs and landings.

He said that on the morning of Sunday the 15th Isabella went into his room, around 6.15, to discuss their customary trip out. He said it was Isabella's suggestion to tell Mrs Oxley not to call in for work that day.

It was a little later in the morning, Ruxton said, when Isabella decided to go to Edinburgh. He was irritated by this and told her she couldn't take his car. He said he was in the bathroom – 'just for a short call, if I may say' – when 'I actually heard them go, because I heard the vestibule door lock click'. He said Isabella did not explain how she and Mary might get to Edinburgh without his car.

He went in to see Elizabeth, Diana and Billy and he was angry that 'there had been no attempt made to wake up the children'. No breakfast had been prepared for them, and Diana said she was hungry. Ruxton said he went looking for food and found a tin of peaches. He then had a look for a tin opener 'because I did not know where the servants kept those things'. He found one downstairs. Ruxton demonstrated for the jury how he attempted to open the tin in the bedroom using the tin-opener, which he said was old and blunt. He said he had to bang the opener with the disused arm of a sofa that the children played with.

As he banged it, the sharp edge of the opener cut deeply and savagely into the fingers of his right hand, he claimed. A huge amount of blood poured from the wound and he wrapped it using a towel from his consulting room downstairs.

There were blood splashes up and down the staircase, he said.

Birkett asked Ruxton about his trip to Seatle on 17 September, the accident in Kendal and conversation with the traffic officer in Milnthorpe.

Birkett: 'Did you say anything to the constable as to where you had been?'

Ruxton: 'I told him that I had come along the Carlisle road, but I did not say that I had come from Carlisle. I could not have gone to Carlisle.'

Birkett: 'Let me ask you directly the plain question, had you been to Carlisle that day?'

Ruxton: 'No, I could not have done. It would have required Sir Malcolm Campbell to go there.'

Sir Malcolm Campbell was the famous world land speed record-holder.

Birkett said the Crown contended that Ruxton had not gone to Blackburn on Thursday, 19 September, to see a room he believed had been rented by Isabella, but in fact had driven north to Moffat.

Ruxton was emphatic: 'No, I had never been north. On the contrary, I was absolutely in Blackburn.'

Ruxton told the jury he had begun to compile the 'My Movements' document because he was feeling under pressure and wrongly suspected in relation to Mrs Smalley's death and the discovery of the bodies in the ravine at Moffat.

Birkett's questioning was long and covered every event between 14 September and Ruxton's arrest on 12 October, minutely picking over the evidence of the Crown witnesses. It was an emotionally draining ordeal for Ruxton. It was no doubt quite overwhelming for the jurors who listened intently, and the packed public gallery and press bench who hung on every titbit.

It was time for Birkett to bring his questions to a close. But first he had to leave the jurors with Ruxton's emotional and emphatic denials of the charges fresh in their minds.

Birkett: 'So far as Mrs Ruxton is concerned, did you do any violence of any kind to her on the morning of Sunday?'

Ruxton: 'Never, never, never, sir.'

Birkett: 'If she was strangled, had you any part or lot in it?'

Ruxton: 'Sir, I have never done it. It is a fact that Isabella did leave the house on Sunday morning.'

Birkett asked if he had killed Mary Rogerson.

Ruxton stood defiantly and denied that he had. 'Mary has always been a dear child to my heart. Never regarded as a servant – always one of the family. I always called her "My Mary".'

Ruxton finished by saying: 'I do not know anything about their disappearance apart from their going.'

That was the easy part. Now Ruxton had to face cross-examination by the Crown.

Joseph Cooksey Jackson stood and approached Ruxton on the stand. He said to the doctor, 'I understand Mary was very dear to your heart and you were always very good to her?'

Ruxton replied: 'Yes.'

Jackson: 'And was she a very loyal girl?'

Ruxton: 'Yes, I could stake my reputation on it.'

Jackson: 'One who would never allow any harm to come to her mistress?'

Ruxton: 'Well, of course Mary was not primarily meant for Bella, but only for my children.'

'Was she loyal to her mistress?'

'Yes, loyal to everybody. Mary was a good girl altogether, a 100-per-cent girl.'

'Was Mary a girl who would have stood by her mistress and defended if she was attacked?' Jackson asked.

'She would have stood by her master as well, or by the children or anybody,' replied Ruxton firmly.

'She would stand by you, would she?' pressed Jackson.

'Yes,' said Ruxton.

Jackson then said, 'Why is not she standing by you today if she is alive?'

Silence.

Ruxton remarked, 'I cannot fathom the inscrutable workings of Providence. I cannot answer that.'

Next Jackson turned to Ruxton's diaries. He asked the doctor, 'Were the diaries which have been produced in court yours?'

'Yes.'

'In your diaries you kept a careful note of your movements?'

'Practically, yes,' replied Ruxton.

Jackson asked Ruxton about the one diary that was missing. 'Do you realise how important it would be to have your diary for 1935 up to the time of the disappearance of your wife?' Jackson asked. Ruxton implied Isabella had disposed of the journal.

Jackson said, 'Let me ask you about something else that is missing. Why throw away a full tin of peaches?'

Ruxton: 'Because I could not open it.'

Jackson: 'But somebody else can open it at some other time?'

Ruxton: 'It was done in a thoughtless manner. I was an aimless man at that time.'

Jackson said, 'You threw away the tin-opener?'

'Because it was rather a dangerous thing,' responded Ruxton.

Jackson moved on.

'Are you a very emotional man and a man of very short temper?' he asked the doctor.

Ruxton replied, 'Not actually emotional in the sense you are suggesting – rather quick tempered.'

Jackson asked, 'Do you lose absolute control of yourself when you get in a temper?'

Ruxton: 'No, I would not say that, but, naturally, if somebody is trying to deceive me I can see through it much quicker than a man of ordinary intelligence.'

Jackson asked Ruxton about his suspicions of Isabella's infidelity.

'I did think that, yes, but it was not the first occasion, mind you. If you refer to my diaries it will be recorded even in 1932,' Ruxton said.

Jackson said that they could take it Ruxton had for some time believed Isabella to be unfaithful.

'Isabella has done some silly things which would not be done by a sensible woman – put it that way,' Ruxton responded.

Jackson asked Ruxton about evidence he had given to Birkett about his inability to drive to Moffat on account of his injured hand. 'You could take up the carpet with an injured hand?' Jackson said pointedly.

Ruxton retorted, 'My dear friend, taking up the carpet is something like taking this up –' and he picked up the Testament used for swearing an oath – 'and throwing it away.' Ruxton described how he had driven his car at the time of the injury: 'I had to go very slowly and drive with my left hand … I could go to the North Pole in a motor car, but it would take time and I would go slowly. That is my point, I was driving the car with my left hand which is not my usual way of driving.'

Ruxton became emotional, feeling slighted, at Jackson's suggestion he had acted unprofessionally in wearing his stained blue suit during operations as it would be 'a potential source of infection'. He interrupted Jackson's questioning, shouting, 'It is a disgrace; it is a reflection on my professional capabilities.'

When Jackson told him it would be better for him and for everyone in the court if he listened to the questions, Ruxton became contrite. He said, 'Forgive me; I am sorry. I humbly beg your pardon. Cannot you see how I am feeling? Everybody is cornering me, and trying to get me in a corner.'

Birkett reassured him: 'I am watching the case for you and I will deal with all these matters.'

Jackson suggested Ruxton had asked Mr and Mrs Hampshire to leave the light on in his house on the night they cleaned up because he wanted to present the impression that he was at home when in fact he had driven to Moffat to dispose of the bodies. Ruxton said he often left the light on when nobody was at home. Ruxton admitted he had given Mrs Hampshire his blue suit but denied ever having been to her house to inquire if she had cleaned it, and also demanding she burn the label with his name on it.

Jackson asked if Ruxton had been to Moffat and through the Devil's Beef Tub area.

Ruxton said it was a route he and the family had taken a number of times to Scotland, describing it as 'the most gorgeous snowclad scenery'. He denied knowing the bridge or the ravine where the remains were found. 'Whenever we go by motor car, we never study the road because my children were in the car and my Bella, and we make so much enjoyment in the car. We are so busy we have no time for all that,' he said.

At one point in Jackson's questioning, Ruxton took exception to Crown evidence that he had lit a fire in his yard. He accused the witness of lying. Mr Justice Singleton scolded Ruxton: 'You will find your learned counsel is quite able to argue for you!'

To which Ruxton replied, 'I have a brain of my own and I cannot help it. I am fighting for my life.'

It was the end of Ruxton's two days on the witness stand. He stepped down, exhausted, and returned to the dock.

It was time for the closing remarks. Birkett's strategy to present evidence from one witness only, Ruxton, was now about to pay off: Jackson for the Crown would speak first, then Birkett.

Jackson told the jury there should be no doubt these two, intermingled bodies were those of Isabella and Mary, who had gone missing at the same time. He said, 'If you come to that conclusion – and I submit you have irresistible evidence to make you come to that conclusion – then I suggest your task is simple, for who could have killed those two women?' The answer to that question, he suggested, was Dr Ruxton.

Now Norman Birkett stood to his feet to make the case for Ruxton in his closing speech. He picked over the main points in the Crown's case that were open to question: the newspapers the bodies were wrapped in were not necessarily from Ruxton's home, the blood on the stairs found by Glaister could easily have been from Ruxton's injured hand. He told the jury that if they were satisfied that these bodies were indeed those of Isabella and Mary – and he stressed that he was not satisfied they were – then that still did not prove that Ruxton had killed the two women. Had they left 2 Dalton Square on 15 September as Ruxton asserted, then they might have been killed and disposed of subsequently by another's hand, he suggested.

He told the jurors:

> The true verdict according to the evidence must always bear in mind the golden rule – the case must be proved beyond all reasonable doubt. The decision which you have to make, members of the jury, is a decision of the greatest solemnity and the greatest responsibility. It is irrevocable, and if you have doubt give utterance to it now … I submit to you … the Crown have failed to prove this case beyond all reasonable doubt, and … your verdict for Dr Ruxton must be a verdict of Not Guilty.

It was the end of the tenth day of the trial.

The court was adjourned. Ruxton was taken back to his cell at Strangeways.

The next day, Friday, 13 March, was the eleventh day of the trial. Friday the 13th. Did the date register with the superstitious Ruxton? There was a palpable, rising sense of tension and anticipation as people in the public gallery began to speculate on what the prisoner's fate might be.

It was time for the judge, Mr Justice Singleton, to give his summing up to the jury. This would be no quick and easy task, given the complexity and emotional nature of what had been heard in the previous days. Yet it was in 'quite unimpassioned tones', as newspapers would later describe it, that he delivered his remarks for an intense five-and-a-half hours, beginning at ten o'clock in the morning.

For the benefit of the jury, he painstakingly combed over the evidence that had been presented and examined in the courtroom, attempting to frame what had been heard. He paused to take some time to talk about Bobby Edmondson and Ruxton's jealousy of him, which the Crown had suggested was the cause of the crimes. He said, 'I have told you already it is not necessary that any motive should be proved; but I was interested,

I confess, to see that young man in the witness-box. You and I sitting on a matter of this sort are not here to judge a question of morals.' On that particular part of the evidence, Judge Singleton directed the jury thus: 'I leave the Edmondson part of the case, telling you this, that, so far as I can see, it has nothing to do with this case, apart from the fact that it may have been made a reason for jealousy on [Ruxton's] part.'

He told the jurors they should bear in mind that Isabella and Mary were missing at the same time that remains were found in the ravine in Scotland. He praised the work of Brash and Glaister in piecing together the gruesome jigsaw puzzle. He said:

> No one could sit in this court and listen to the evidence of Professor Glaister, either in examination-in-chief or in cross-examination, without feeling that there is a man who is not only master of his profession, but who is scrupulously fair, and most anxious that his opinion, however strongly he may hold it, shall not be put unduly against the person on his trial, and the same applies to the others.

The packed courtroom hung on every word. Outside the assize building, the streets were lined with large crowds, desperate to learn what was to become of the handsome, popular doctor whose alleged crimes they had been following intently in sensational newspaper reports.

'Members of the jury, I have finished,' Judge Singleton concluded.

> I have been a time, but I dare say you do not grudge me the time ... It is most important, as Mr Birkett has said to you, that no innocent man should suffer – most important ... Let me end as I began by saying, if there be any doubt in it, he must have the benefit of the doubt. If there be none, let your verdict be equally clear and let justice be carried out.

Then he asked the jury, 'Will you consider your verdict?'

It was two minutes to four when Mr Justice Singleton sent out the twelve jurors; Ruxton was taken back down to the cells.

Nobody could tell how long the jurors would take to reach their verdict. Nobody could tell how it would play out for Ruxton, who sat nervously below the court.

The tension in the courtroom was temporarily lifted; such an atmosphere cannot persist indefinitely without relief, and within moments of the jurors retiring, a buzz of excited chatter rose from the public gallery. The barristers talked among themselves, while the newspaper reporters traded opinions on whether Ruxton would get off or whether he would hang.

At two minutes after five o'clock, the chattering came abruptly to an end and the courtroom fell into the deepest silence when the jury filed back in and each took his seat. They had been in deliberation for just over an hour.

The silence was broken as the Clerk of the Assizes ordered Ruxton to be brought up to the dock. Moments later, led by four prison warders, Ruxton stepped into the huge dock, with its tall spiked railings. Reporters noted that the prisoner's face 'showed a pallor which was emphasised by his black wavy hair'. Drained and spent, Ruxton was outwardly calm as he stood awaiting his fate. One newspaper later noted he appeared to have a faint smile on his lips as he stepped into the dock.

There were two minutes of silence as the court waited for the judge. Ruxton licked his lips and nodded to Birkett. The prison doctor at Strangeways, Dr Shannon, who had inspected Ruxton's injured hand, sat in the dock near the prisoner.

The entire courtroom rose to their feet as Mr Justice Singleton returned, carrying a black cap, and took his seat. As he did so, Ruxton gave a deep, respectful bow, a gesture he had done without fail throughout the course of the trial.

There was fidgeting and coughing from the public gallery. The tension had returned to the room.

The Clerk of the Assize turned to face the jury and said, 'Members of the jury, are you all agreed upon your verdict?'

The foreman of the jury responded in a low tone, almost a whisper, but still clearly audible to the court: 'Yes.'

'Do you find Buck Ruxton guilty of murder, or not guilty?'

'Guilty.'

Ruxton, who was standing with his hands behind him, did not look at the foreman as he spoke; instead he gazed fixedly at the courtroom's high ceiling. On utterance of the word 'guilty', Ruxton flashed the foreman a look before glancing across at Birkett, to his left.

The Clerk asked, 'You find Buck Ruxton guilty of murder, and that is the verdict of you all?'

'Yes.'

Ruxton looked across to the judge.

'Dr Ruxton,' said the Clerk, 'you have been convicted of murder upon the verdict of the jury. Have you anything to say that sentence of death should not be passed according to law?'

Ruxton, his face betraying no emotion, a shadow of himself, then spoke. His voice was low, his words broken and largely incoherent to almost all in the courtroom save those nearest to him. He said:

> I am very sorry. Subject to the point that I be allowed to appeal – in the administration of justice. I submit that to your lordship and the jury. I want to thank everybody for the patience and fairness of my trial. I have never attempted to pass any special restrictions. I should like to hear whatever his lordship has to say about it.

The Clerk stepped up beside Mr Justice Singleton and gently laid a black cap on his head, and said, 'My lords the King's Justices do strongly charge and command all persons to keep silence whilst sentence of death is being passed upon the prisoner at the bar on pain of imprisonment.'

The judge began:

> Buck Ruxton, you have been convicted on evidence which can leave me no doubt in the mind of anyone. The law knows but one sentence for the terrible crime which you committed.
>
> The sentence of the court upon you is that you be taken from this place to a lawful prison, and that you there be hanged by the neck until you are dead, and that your body be afterwards buried within the precincts of the prison in which you shall have been last confined before your execution, and may the Lord have mercy on your soul.

Reporters noted that some of the women in the public gallery wept as the judge passed sentence.

Ruxton stared at the judge throughout.

The Chaplain of the court uttered, 'Amen.' A few other people in the court also whispered the word. Dr Shannon, seated in the dock, shook his head, and as Mr Justice Singleton passed sentence, he began to speak with the words 'My Lord' but fell silent when a prison warder placed a hand on his shoulder.

In a final gesture of respect, or perhaps it was one of acceptance at the mention of the Lord's name, Ruxton raised his right arm from the elbow in a salute.

One of the prison warders stepped forward and grasped Ruxton by the arm, but the doctor gently shook the grip away and walked towards the steps down to the cells. As he reached the top of the steps, he turned to face Mr Justice Singleton once more and raised his arm in a final act of respect. Then he turned and descended the steps with a warder either side of him and two behind.

Once the prisoner had been taken down, the emotional charge of the courtroom dissipated: Ruxton's fate was known, justice had been done for Isabella and Mary.

The eleven-day trial had been harrowing and Mr Justice Singleton was conscious of the toll it had taken, particularly on the members of the jury. Thanking each of them, he said, 'You have been serving the ends of justice, and I thank you. Beyond the time you have spent on the case, you have been faced with dreadful and gruesome detail.' He recommended they not be called upon as jurors in a trial again, if that was their wish.

He said one final thing: 'I thank you indeed.' Then he rose and left the courtroom.

Ruxton's legal team intended to lodge an application to appeal against the conviction. Immediately after the court was adjourned, Mr Justice Singleton agreed to see Norman Birkett. After hearing the barrister's words, he assented to the request. Birkett delivered the news to Ruxton in the assizes cells. Ruxton was then taken back to his cell at Strangeways next door.

The courtroom and public gallery emptied, emotionally drained members of the public spilling out into the weak evening sunlight. Under the direction of Captain Vann, police officers from Lancaster began the considerable task of packing the trial exhibits stored in two large rooms on the lower floor of the assize building. There were 213 items in total, ranging from personal effects such as photographs and sections of the staircase from 2 Dalton Square to Ruxton's bath. Officers hammered pieces of plywood around the bath and safely enclosed other bulky items in wooden frames. Personal effects, including the photographs, were sealed in tins.

All of the exhibits were then transported back to Lancaster police station in Dalton Square, a grim and macabre cargo that would be stored under lock and key until the final act of the case had played out: a successful appeal by the legal team or Ruxton's execution.

Traffic on the Manchester streets around the court building was brought to a halt by the large crowd awaiting the verdict. Once Ruxton's guilt was known, they remained, as if in a daze. Many remained to watch the departure of the witnesses and barristers, including Birkett and Maxwell-Fyfe, who had become celebrities over the course of the hearing. Reporters approached Ruxton's solicitor Edwin Slinger for a comment on the appeal, but he brushed the question aside, saying it was too early. 'The evidence and summing up will be carefully reviewed and a decision arrived at later,' he told newspapermen.

The newspapers were plastered with sensational headlines the following morning. 'Dr Buck Ruxton sentenced to death for the terrible Moffat ravine crime' was a typical example. Newspaper reporters, always looking to titillate their readers, noticed – or contrived might be a better word – the significance of the number thirteen in Ruxton's case.

The *News of the World*, like many papers the next day, carried the following:

RUXTON'S UNLUCKY THIRTEEN
The 'unlucky' number 13 has figured prominently in the Ruxton drama.
The doctor was
Arrested, Sunday, Oct. 13.
Sent for trial, Friday, Dec. 13.
Sentenced to death, Friday, March 13.
His prison number – 8410 – totalled 13, and his address, 2, Dalton-square, has 12 letters and one figure – 13 again.

Norman Rae and John Milligan's thorough background research and interviews with Ruxton now saw the light of day. The paper emblazoned its pages with such headlines as: 'The inside story of the Ruxton crime' and 'He killed his "Belle" because she knew his secret'. The latter was Rae and Milligan's own interpretation of what had triggered the explosion of violence on the night of 14 September. Their report began: 'Now at last it is possible to tell the real story of this Parsi doctor, bigamist, unscrupulous borrower and convicted murderer.' It continued:

Many guesses have been made at the real reason for the murder of Isabella Ruxton. It has been suggested from time to time that an intrigue with Mary Rogerson led to the double tragedy on that September day; and also that Ruxton, a notoriously jealous man, believed his 'wife' had a lover or lovers, and killed her rather than 'share' her. Neither of these suggestions is true.

The reporters tantalised their readers: 'Isabella Ruxton was murdered because she had found out that Ruxton was already married and that his real wife still lived in India.'

This was quite a remarkable claim because it did not reflect what had been said in court. It was based purely on supposition and the fevered imaginings of the reporters. Rae and Milligan's reporting prowess was nevertheless impressive. They had tracked down Ruxton's wife, Motibal Hakim, in Bombay and had seen correspondence between her and Ruxton. In one letter, Motibal told Ruxton, 'I have always believed, and still believe, that you married me not for the sake of my money but for myself.'

The newspaper suggested that Ruxton had not told Isabella about his wife and that when she discovered the truth she realised her children had been born illegitimately and this triggered her apparent disdain for Ruxton, her dalliances with other men and her suicide attempts. The reporters also gave credence to Ruxton's claims in his diary that Isabella had poisoned his coffee. Again, none of these details were supported by evidence in court. They did, however, make for a sensational piece of journalism that titillated the millions of *News of the World* readers.

'That Ruxton was the victim of a score of fears is true,' the reporters wrote. 'Devoted to his growing family, he knew his life was a living lie. Vain and ambitious, he dreaded the terrible crash which would follow the exposure of his Indian obligations and English debts.' In Rae and Milligan's view, this had been the reason for the murders: to silence Isabella. Mary had been in the wrong place at the wrong time.

Meanwhile, the *Daily Mirror* informed readers that Ruxton's children were still being cared for at Parkside in Lancaster. 'When they went to bed last evening they did not know that their father was under sentence of death,' the report ran. A spokesman at the children's home told the reporter, 'We don't know what will happen to them, but if the secret of their parents is kept from them in the future as closely as it has been up to now, then they will never know anything about the murder.'

Elizabeth, Diana and Billy believed their parents and Mary had gone on a long holiday.

Reflecting on the verdict and the success of the investigation, Professor Glaister wrote, 'In the Ruxton case I had realised for the first time what I had always envisaged – absolute teamwork towards a common objective, a collective effort in which both scientists and police worked side by side.' And in a veiled criticism of Sir Bernard Spilsbury, he added, 'It made a refreshing contrast with an older outlook, which sometimes left one man sitting on a case on his own, guarding it against all comers like a dog savouring a juicy bone.'

Captain Henry Vann, the man who had arrested Ruxton, later wrote:

Much of the success of the police work must be attributed to the excellent team spirit which prevailed throughout, for it was the aim of everyone concerned to bring to a satisfactory conclusion a most perplexing problem. The detail work was most exhaustive and it was only after many weeks of patient inquiry that the intricate 'jigsaw puzzle' was finally fitted together.

He praised the generous support his officers had received from the scientists at Edinburgh and Glasgow.

APPEAL

On Monday, 16 March, the *Daily Mirror* ran a piece that was headlined: 'Ruxton's aged mother thinks him innocent'. The newspaper's correspondent began the piece thus: 'An old Parsee woman, withered and bent with age, is praying every hour of her waking life in Bombay for her son, Dr Buck Ruxton, who is lying under sentence of death at Strangeways Prison, Manchester.'

Aimal Hakim, Ruxton's mother, collapsed when the reporter told her of her son's fate at her small basement flat in India. 'Oh, my baby,' the heartbroken woman wailed. 'I don't believe it. My son would never commit such a murder. All is gone.'

Mrs Hakim told the reporter that her son had been the quietest boy in school; he had been driven by ambition yet was 'full of affection for his relatives and friends'.

The reporter, having dropped the bombshell, left her then; she repeated the same phrase over and over: 'How could he do this?'

The reporter also tracked down and broke the news to Motibal Ghadiali, Ruxton's true wife. Her reaction was: 'Poor Bhukthiar.' His original, Indian name. Despite the way Ruxton had treated her, there was no animosity on her part. She believed Ruxton 'possessed a fortune' but he 'might have willed it all away'. She could not have known that all of Ruxton's money had long gone to pay for his defence.

There now began the long wait for the appeal. Ruxton spent his thirty-seventh birthday on Friday, 27 March a broken man in his cell at Strangeways. It was 167 days since he had seen his children, since he had slept in his own bed at Dalton Square, since he had been a free man. It was almost 200 days since Isabella and Mary had been seen alive.

On Easter Sunday, 12 April, Elizabeth, Diana and Billy Ruxton had two visitors at Parkside. They were excited to see their aunts, Jeanie Nelson and Eleen Madden. Isabella's sisters had travelled from Edinburgh and brought them chocolate Easter eggs. The sisters were relieved to see the children were settled in their new home. None of Ruxton's 'wee mites' asked about him or Isabella.

After their brief visit, Mrs Nelson and Mrs Madden went to Thornton Road in Morecambe to see Mary Rogerson's parents. It was the first time the grieving relatives of both victims had met.

The date for Ruxton's appeal was set for Monday, 27 April, at the Appeal Court in London. Ruxton was transferred from Strangeways to London the day before, Sunday, 26 April, and he spent the night at Pentonville prison. It was here that Oscar Wilde and Dr Hawley Harvey Crippen had once been prisoners. Ruxton spent the night in the cell Crippen had been held in a quarter of a century earlier: apparently he slept well.

With three warders at his side, Ruxton was brought into the dock from behind what the press later described as 'some plush curtains'. He looked noticeably older and wearier than at his trial.

The courtroom was packed. Ruxton saw Birkett and the presiding judges – the Lord Chief Justice Lord Hewart and Justices Du Parcq and Goddard. The press bench and public gallery were a sea of expectant faces staring back at him. The unspoken question in the air they all wanted answered was: would Ruxton hang?

The prisoner was ordered to stand and give his name to the court. This done, he stood with his head bent forward respectfully until he was told he could sit. And so began the lengthy, detailed appeal hearing. Norman Birkett, on whose shoulders rested Ruxton's fate, stood and began his deposition, which lasted for a full three hours. Throughout, Ruxton sat listening intently, his elbows resting on his knees; from time to time he smiled or nodded at a point he believed Birkett had made well.

Birkett outlined the main grounds for appeal against conviction. He said the guilty verdict had gone against the clear weight of the evidence heard at Manchester in March. That evidence, he believed, did not prove Ruxton was guilty. He also claimed Mr Justice Singleton had misdirected the jury in his summing up. Birkett said the Crown had presented a strong case for identifying the bodies as those of Isabella and Mary, but he questioned whether it had proved beyond all reasonable doubt that Ruxton was responsible. The Crown had relied heavily, Birkett said, on the evidence of Mrs Hampshire, who had found the doors to upstairs rooms at

Dalton Square locked. 'It is difficult to recall in this court the sinister effect that was produced by the reference to locked doors – stressed in dramatic and impressive language – and the terrible secrets it was suggested those locked doors concealed,' Birkett said. 'The suggestion of the Crown, plainly stated, was that, having dismembered the bodies, Ruxton had taken portions of them up to the bedrooms, concealed them there, and locked the doors.'

Mr Justice Du Parcq spoke to Birkett: 'There was a strong indication that the women had been killed in the house by somebody connected with the house, and from that point one is carried very far on the journey.'

Birkett responded:

Let me assume that the bodies have never been found, and that the women went out of the house and have never been seen or heard of since. Could anyone really have said then that the evidence with its conflict and complexity, showed that the prisoner was guilty of murder?

Undeterred by the questioning of the judge, Birkett fought on: 'It is extraordinary how much of that other evidence is mere surmise – and very dangerous surmise at that. It is sheer speculation that somebody was killed in that house.'

Birkett now told the judges he wished to make an application to call further evidence as part of the appeal hearing. 'I desire to call Professor McFall, of Liverpool University. I also desire to call Professor Fraser, Professor of Anatomy at St Mary's Hospital School, Paddington.'

Birkett sat down to hear the judges' comments. His performance had been impressive, thorough and persuasive. Ruxton might have been forgiven for believing his fortunes were about to change.

Lord Hewart and Justices Du Parcq and Goddard huddled together to discuss Birkett's application to call further evidence. Seconds later, Lord Hewart indicated for Ruxton to stand in the dock.

Ruxton stood, shoulders hunched, hands clasped loosely in front of him, straining to hear each word as Lord Hewart spoke. His eyes were fixed intently on Hewart in his red robe.

Hewart dismissed Birkett's application to call new witnesses. Of Mr Justice Singleton's summing up, he said, 'There is nothing in it that can be said even faintly to resemble misdirection. On the contrary, as one reads it, one is impressed by the care, thoroughness, patience and discernment which it shows.'

Ruxton's gaze dropped from the judge, moving to the packed court-room. Those who witnessed it saw a look of hopeless resignation in the doctor's face; a chilling realisation dawning on him.

Hewart continued, 'The judge at the trial has said that the appellant [Ruxton] was convicted on evidence which could leave no doubt in the mind of anyone. That was a perfectly correct statement.'

Ruxton looked dazed. His appeal had failed; the conviction for the murder of Isabella would stand. He would never see his children again. He would be hanged.

With the final words of Lord Hewart's judgement resounding in the courtroom, the three prison warders turned Ruxton around gently and led him down from the dock to the cells below.

ELEVENTH-HOUR REPRIEVE?

In the early hours of Saturday, 2 May, Isabella's mortal remains made the long, slow journey by motor hearse from Ancoats Hospital, in Manchester, to Edinburgh. In a sad, slightly macabre twist of fate, the vehicle bearing her coffin passed over the bridge at Gardenholme linn.

The hearse was met at six o'clock in the morning by a police officer and was directed to a funeral parlour in Edinburgh, where it remained while Isabella's sisters made arrangements for a funeral at Warriston Crematorium.

Meanwhile, on the same day, Mary's remains were laid to rest in an unmarked grave in the churchyard of St Helen's church, Overton, the small village near Morecambe where she was born. Mary's father James and stepmother Jessie led the small number of family mourners. The church was three-quarters full with grieving relatives and many women from the village, who sobbed during the singing of the hymns, 'Lead Kindly Light' and 'Abide With Me'.

Covered with a mass of flowers, Mary's plain oak coffin bore the inscription: 'Mary Jane Rogerson, died September, 1935, in the 20th year of her age.'

The service and burial were too much for Mary's distraught father; he had to be helped by his wife Jessie and the vicar of St Helen's, the Rev. W. J. Lancaster.

After the funeral, and back at their home in Morecambe, the Rogersons lifted the blinds in their window for the first time in six months.

The date was set for Ruxton's execution. He would be hanged at Strangeways on Tuesday, 12 May. The fight was not over, however. Ruxton's solicitor Fred Gardner believed enough goodwill towards Ruxton and public sympathy for Elizabeth, Diana and Billy existed to justify a petition seeking a reprieve. If Ruxton hanged, the children would be orphaned.

On Sunday, 4 May, Gardner set up the petition on a small table in the vestibule of Ruxton's home in Dalton Square and an invitation was issued to the public to sign it. Gardner's intention was to forward the document to the Home Secretary, Sir John Simon. There was a steady stream of people who wished to add their name. At times as many as thirty people were in line to show their support in writing. A policeman stood by to marshal the crowd. Most who signed were women. Many called at the house on their way home from church. *The Scotsman* newspaper reported that a large proportion of the signatories were Dr Ruxton's patients, moved by Gardner's appeal to sign 'for the sake of the children'. One woman was aged 89 and told reporters Ruxton was her doctor, while another had travelled from Glasgow by bus to add her support.

On the first night, Gardner told the press 900 had signed the petition; the following day, Tuesday, 5 May, the number had grown to 2,000. There was, he said, a strong swell of support for clemency for the doctor. He told reporters the celebrated anti-death penalty activist Mrs Violet Van Der Elst would organise fifty aeroplanes to fly over Manchester in protest if Ruxton's execution went ahead.

On Monday, 11 May, the petition stood at more than 6,000 signatures. The *Aberdeen Press and Journal* reported that support had come from patients, businessmen, magistrates and prosecution witnesses in Ruxton's case. 'Ruxton has been buoyed up with the hope that his life will be spared,' the paper said, but added: 'Unless clemency is shown in response to the reprieve petition, Buck Ruxton, the 37-year-old Urasian doctor, will be hanged in Strangeways Prison tomorrow morning for the Moffat ravine crime.' The decision of the Home Secretary in response to the petition would be delivered to Fred Gardner on the morning of Ruxton's scheduled execution.

If Ruxton were to be spared the hangman's noose, it would be at the eleventh hour.

Ruxton was in turmoil in his cell. *News of the World* reporter John Milligan wrote that he would be off-hand with the prison staff and refused to answer to his prison number, insisting they use his name. He was 'pacing his cell like a caged tiger and speaking with a snarl'. Capricious as ever, Ruxton would at other times be friendly and co-operative.

Meanwhile, he was corresponding with those on the outside. He wrote to Milligan, recalling their interview conducted in the library at Dalton Square: 'Pity! The library is no more. Only the bare walls of that spacious room remain to bear mute testimony of my choice of treasures.' He told Milligan he wished his daughters to go into the medical profession and for Billy to become either a solicitor or a doctor. In his final request to the reporter, Ruxton wrote, 'My solicitor has my Isabella's oil painting in life size. It is the talk of the art world. Could you help to get it sold for a fair price to raise an education fund for my children?'

He wrote to a friend, 'Please do speak me fair in death. Try to be good to my children. They are my own flesh and blood. Do something for them. I appeal to you to help my solicitor as much as you can for my children.' Underneath his signature he wrote: 'Crushed'.

The night before his execution, Ruxton wrote to Birkett. Resigned to his fate, he had a few last things to set straight. This is what he wrote:

Manchester Prison.
7.20 p.m., Monday, May 11,
1936

Dear Mr Birkett,

This letter will be forwarded to you by my solicitor and trustee Mr C. F. Gardner of 31, Sun Street, Lancaster.

Thanks awfully, old man, for all you have done.

Please accept a trivial token of gratitude I have left you in my will. I am sure your wife will be delighted with it. Mr C. F. Gardner will send it on to you in due course.

May I beg a favour of you? If there should be any litigation re my estate, will you kindly give your services as a favour to a dying man?

I am leaving three bonnie little mites behind.

If you can, please do be good to them. They are intelligent and good looking.

May you reach the highest pinnacle of the Legal Pedestal.

I'll bless you from above. Try your best to get in touch with Mr Gardner now and again and do your best for my children.

God bless you and yours,

Yours very sincerely,

BUCK RUXTON

The 'trivial token of gratitude' was a set of silver forks and fish knives with handles of mother-of-pearl. Birkett felt he could not accept them under the circumstances.

A few hours before the execution, Ruxton received a letter. It was postmarked Leicester. He tore it open and read the contents. The writer promised the doctor that a plan was under way to rescue him from Strangeways prison by twenty men with machine guns. The letter was clearly a hoax and it can only have served to torment Ruxton.

A huge crowd assembled outside Strangeways prison early on the morning of Tuesday, 12 May. The newspapers later put the figure at around 5,000 people. Ruxton was due to be hanged at nine o'clock. A barrier had been erected to keep the masses back. A single row of people was afforded seats in front of the barrier, mostly women; one nursed her baby, which she kept wrapped in the folds of her coat. Newspaper reporters and press photographers were out in force; the expectant crowd was good enough to smile for an Associated Newspapers photographer who captured the sea of faces, caps, oiled-back hair and warm coats.

At just after eight o'clock, the well-known anti-death penalty campaigner Mrs Van Der Elst arrived outside the gaol in her Rolls-Royce. She boasted a large personal fortune and poured her energies into fighting to overturn the death penalty in England. She had often run into trouble with the law during her well-publicised protests. She had made her way through the Manchester side streets to reach the prison, but had been forced by the crowd to stop at Carnarvon Street, directly opposite Strangeways' gates. She had paid for a van with a loudspeaker to park outside the prison. There were posters on the van bearing statements such as: 'HANGING IS MURDER. THE STATE COMMITS 40 MURDERS A YEAR.' and 'HEARKEN, SIR JOHN SIMON, THOU SHALT NOT KILL', the latter a reference to Sir John Simon, the Home Secretary in Prime Minister Stanley Baldwin's government.

When they saw Mrs Van Der Elst's car, the crowd ran forward, surrounding and swamping her. She was within 70yds of the prison. As the crowd grew ugly, the van reversed down the street. The police, fearing a riot, tried to push back her car, but it was useless.

Mrs Van Der Elst believed the crowd was there in support of Ruxton; she was wrong, their sympathies lay with his victims. She sat at the wheel of her motorcar for ten minutes, arguing with the crowd, but they were not listening. A loudspeaker on the top of her car was not working. She wanted to make a speech, to present her argument.

She was shouted down by a woman in the crowd, who scolded her, 'How would you like your daughter cut up?'

The mood of the crowd was darkening, turning further against Mrs Van Der Elst. A man shouted a suggestion about her Rolls-Royce: 'Pawn it and give it to the poor.'

She was not for being silenced. She retorted that she had done much for the poor, but this was shot down by the crowd, who drowned out her further attempts to engage them.

To many she was a diversion, a sideshow attraction. She was seen as an eccentric, a millionaire who indulged her odd beliefs in sensational public-ity stunts. Many in the crowd lifted their eyes to the sky. They were looking for the aeroplanes she had promised would loop over Strangeways prison in protest at Ruxton's execution. They looked in vain: the aircraft never materialised. The normally steely-grey Manchester skies were hazy that day; this was the reason later given by Mrs Van Der Elst for the no-show.

She climbed out of her limousine to speak to a police officer, one of a number controlling the mob. She was overheard saying, 'It is a terrible thing that civilisation –'. The rest of her sentence was lost under the crowd's roar of 'Aw. Get out!'

As nine o'clock neared, the hour of Dr Ruxton's execution, the crowd fell into an eerie silence; even those around Mrs Van Der Elst's car in the side street were quiet.

Fred Gardner received no word of a reprieve from Home Secretary Sir John Simon.

Ruxton was to be hanged by Thomas Pierrepoint and his assistant Robert Wilson. Pierrepoint and his brother Henry were famous executioners. His nephew Albert would continue the family business and would retire with the macabre honour of being England's last hangman.

The executioners arrived at Strangeways the day before to calculate the necessary drop required to execute Ruxton cleanly, based on his height and weight. Without the prisoner's knowledge, Pierrepoint and Wilson observed him discreetly, for a final assessment.

Ruxton spent the night in the condemned cell, which adjoined the execution chamber, eating his final meal and most likely playing cards, chess or dominoes with the two guards whose job it was to watch over the condemned prisoner. The execution chamber was a small room. Occupying a large area in the centre was the mechanism used to end the lives of countless criminals: a trapdoor comprising two hinged leaves that were released by a lever.

Pierrepoint and Wilson tested the equipment twice using a sack weighing approximately the same as Ruxton. The correct drop was calculated by consulting a special mathematical table, which factored in details of age and physical attributes. Above the trap hung a rope attached to a chain that ran over an overhead beam. The place where Ruxton would stand, one foot either side of the wooden leaves, was marked with chalk.

Just before nine o'clock on Tuesday, 12 May, it was time to call upon the prisoner.

Outside Ruxton's cell assembled the following: Pierrepoint, Wilson, Under-Sheriff Jeffrey Wright, Strangeways prison governor Lewis Ball, the prison's medical officer Dr Stanley Shannon and prison chaplain the Rev. D.E. Lloyd.

Under-Sheriff Wright gave the signal.

Pierrepoint and Wilson entered the cell.

Pierrepoint pinioned Ruxton's arms behind his back.

The guards led Ruxton to the execution chamber.

The guards positioned Ruxton on the chalk mark.

Wilson pinioned Ruxton's legs.

Pierrepoint slipped a white cap over Ruxton's head.

Pierrepoint fitted the noose around Ruxton's neck.

Pierrepoint tightened the knot under Ruxton's jaw.

Pierrepoint pulled the lever.

Ruxton dropped through the trap.

Pierrepoint went to the side of the scaffolding and stepped down into the pit beneath, where the prisoner's lifeless body was suspended. The hangman was followed by Dr Shannon. Pierrepoint undid Ruxton's shirt. Dr Shannon inserted his stethoscope to check the prisoner was dead. Prison governor Lewis Ball witnessed it all. With the doctor's confirmation, the party departed, leaving Ruxton's body in place.

Pierrepoint would have returned within the hour. In 1936, he was required to undertake a morbid task, compelled by a regulation that dated back to the days when prisoners' bodies were exposed for public inspection on the gibbet. The regulation would, many years later, be repealed. Pierrepoint placed a measuring tape on Ruxton's heels and unrolled it upwards to the level of the scaffold from which the prisoner had dropped. The distance was greater than that Pierrepoint had carefully allowed in order to kill Ruxton as swiftly and humanely as possible. The difference was due to the stretch in Ruxton's body caused by hanging.

Pierrepoint's role as executioner was complete. His next duties were conducted with the respect and dignity afforded by one man to a fellow human being. He prepared the prisoner for burial. With Ruxton still hanging, Pierrepoint carefully stripped the clothing from him, the hood still in place. Pierrepoint's nephew, Albert, described this process in his memoirs thus: 'It was not callous, but the best rough dignity [he] could give [the prisoner] as he swung to the touch … He yielded his garments without the resistance of limbs.'

Ruxton was left in his shirt, which would serve as a shroud, tied at the hips, before Pierrepoint and his assistant began the task of removing the body from the scaffold. The hangman passed a rope under Ruxton's armpits up to his assistant before the body was hauled upward. With Ruxton's body drooping, Pierrepoint removed the noose and the hood. He took the dead man's head in both hands, moved it from side to side to assure himself the break of the neck had been a clean one.

And then Pierrepoint took down the rope that had ended the life of Dr Buck Ruxton, late of 2 Dalton Square, Lancaster, Lancashire.

Ruxton's body would later be buried in an unmarked grave within the grounds of Strangeways.

Outside the prison the speakers on the top of Mrs Van Der Elst's van clicked into life at the moment of Ruxton's execution. A voice could be heard: 'Will gentlemen in the crowd please bare their heads?' Many women were weeping and dabbed their eyes with handkerchiefs. Few men removed their hats or caps. Then came the singing. Plaintive and moving, the words of 'Abide With Me'. Some in the crowd began to join in. Then a woman's voice was carried over the heads of the crowd towards the prison: 'Nearer My God To Thee'. These were the songs played by the band as the *Titanic* went down.

At 9.15 the great wooden doors of Strangeways creaked open. A prison warder, in peaked cap, emerged. He was carrying two documents.

He attached them to the wall. One was a certificate – 'judgement of death was executed on Buck Ruxton' signed by Mr Jeffrey L. Wright, the Under-Sheriff; Mr Herbert Entwistle, Mr L.C. Ball, governor of the prison; and the Rev. D.E. Lloyd, chaplain of Strangeways prison. The second document confirmed Ruxton was dead, certified by Dr S.S.H. Shannon, prison medical officer.

The crowd started to disperse, heading down Southall Street, where police were controlling traffic on the main road, to allow the hundreds of people to leave safely. Mrs Van Der Elst was not done. She got out of her car and tossed copies of a pamphlet entitled: 'Barbarism in the Twentieth Century'. It read:

> Dr Ruxton was without doubt the maddest of all insane people that have ever been executed. After all, it was only on circumstantial evidence that he was convicted but, even if he did commit the crime, then it was only because jealousy drove him mad, and how can a man be hung for something he did when he was not in his right mind.

Police officers told her to drive her car to the front of Strangeways. She told the officers, 'I would not fight the battle I am doing now if I were frightened of arrest.' Then she climbed into her Rolls-Royce and drove away from the prison at a walking pace, a swarming crowd trailing in her wake along Great Ducie Street. The crowd was so heavy around the vehicle that police had to form a human barrier by linking arms. At one point it looked as if the crowd might turn violent. Police drew their batons to push back the surging crowd. Fearing there might be injury, one officer got behind the wheel of her car and drove it to Albert Street police station nearby. One of the car's windows had been smashed.

Mrs Van Der Elst was later charged with 'behaving in a manner whereby a breach of the peace might have been occasioned, obstruction, and driving in a manner likely to endanger life'. She appeared at Manchester Police Court on 20 May and was fined £3 for refusing to stop her car when police asked her.

News of the World reporter Norman Rae had been in the thick of the crowd outside Strangeways, formulating the crisp, laconic sentences for his readers the following day. As he was jostled in the rolling sea of figures, he was approached by a man, collar turned up and hat brim shading his eyes. The man thrust something into Rae's hand: it was an envelope. Inside, the man said, was a letter from Dr Ruxton, who had instructed him to deliver it after his death. Rae looked at the envelope: it was addressed to the editor of the *News of the World*.

63

THE LETTER

The letter was opened hours later in the *News of the World* offices on Bouverie Street when Rae returned to London. There was little expectation among the journalists: the letter was likely to be a final, desperate plea of innocence written by a condemned man, a final act of defiance, the last stage direction in the tragic drama of the Lancaster doctor. After all, Ruxton had protested his innocence from the very start.

But the letter was not what they expected. It read:

Lancaster
14.10.35
    I killed Mrs Ruxton in a fit of temper because I thought she had been with a man. I was Mad at the time. Mary Rogerson was present at the time. I had to kill her.
    B. Ruxton

It had been written on 14 October, the day after his arrest by Vann. Apparently, Ruxton had given it to a friend who visited him in the police cells in the bowels of Lancaster Town Hall with strict instructions to keep it in a secure place.

During his trial at Manchester, Ruxton had asked his friend if he still had the letter secured away. Ruxton had been convinced he would be acquitted, but had nevertheless instructed his friend: 'In the impossible event of a verdict of guilty and if – God forbid – I am to die, I want you to hand the envelope unopened to the editor of the *News of the World*. But remember – it has not to be opened until I am dead.'

The *News of the World* wasted no time in publishing the confession. They featured advertisements in the regional press to maximise sales of that Sunday's edition. Huge banner adverts proclaimed: 'NEWS OF THE WORLD. RUXTON'S WRITTEN CONFESSION. (EXCLUSIVE)'.

At one time it had been common practice at the inquest of an executed criminal for the prison governor to reveal any last-minute confession. Huge numbers of newspapers were sold on the back of this practice. The Home Office put an end to it, much to the chagrin of newspaper editors.

So the Ruxton confession was a sensation. It was later thought Ruxton's entrusted friend struck a deal with Norman Rae after Ruxton's execution for payment of £3,000 for the written confession. As Birkett's fee came to £2,000, there was talk that Ruxton, realising he was heading for the gallows, wrote the confession as a way of ensuring his children would be well provided for.

Efforts were made by the Home Office to identify Ruxton's entrusted friend and there was talk that each person who visited him in prison should be interviewed, but nothing came of it. There was speculation it had been his close friend, Herbert Anderson. Nearing retirement, Anderson was not keeping good health following the death of his daughter Beatrice early in the summer of 1935 and the turmoil of the Ruxton case. In November 1936, just six months after Ruxton was hanged, Anderson put his head in the oven at his home on Balmoral Road in Morecambe. Because of his links to Ruxton, Anderson's death warranted a few paragraphs in the newspapers, which said a photograph of his daughter had been found next to him.

Ruxton's estate was valued at £1,765 7s 10d. On 19 June, newspapers published details of the codicil, or addition, to his will, which he had written four days before he was hanged. In it he offered tokens of appreciation to those who had shown him kindness and compassion.

He left his plated tray and tea and coffee service to Mr and Mrs Tomlinson, the master and matron at the Parkside children's home, for 'their great kindness in looking after my three children during the last few months'.

His solicitor, Fred Gardner, was to receive his leopard-skin rug and polar-skin rug 'as a humble token of gratitude'.

His canteen of silver forks and fish-knives with handles inlaid with mother of pearl were left to Norman Birkett, the items he had alluded to in his letter to his defence barrister, while Edwin Slinger, his solicitor from Accrington, was to receive yet another canteen of fish-knives and 'forks of metal'.

In an emotionally charged document, Ruxton wrote:

> Unfortunately I am not allowed to leave any tokens of gratitude to any of
> the staff of the prison on account of the rules. To all concerned in my case
> I leave behind my warmest wishes for their courtesy and consideration.
>
> I fail to find suitable words to express my gratitude fully to
> Mr Patterson, the prison commissioner, and the Rev. D.E.G. Lloyd, who
> have been arranging for the well-being of my three dear children, and my
> trustee, Mr C. Fred Gardner.
>
> I wish to invoke my prayers of blessings on all those who have been,
> who are still and who will continue from time to time to be kind to my
> three dear children and who will see that they are brought up as worthy
> citizens in respectable callings – my daughters as qualified medical
> graduates and my son as a solicitor or medical man, whichever he may
> wish to become.

In the shadow of the hangman's noose, Ruxton's concerns with
respectability had transferred from his own shoulders to those of his
children. In the codicil, Ruxton stipulated that the residue of his estate
should be held by his trustees for twenty years to care for and educate his
three children. In the meantime, Fred Gardner set up a fund for Elizabeth,
Diana and Billy. On 24 June, he told reporters that he had received a pledge
for £1,000 – an astronomical sum – but was unable to disclose who the
generous benefactor was. He also revealed he had received a shilling from
a Birmingham woman who suggested the formation of a 'shilling fund'.

The children's long-term future was under discussion. They were still
being cared for at the Parkside children's home in Lancaster. Reports varied
over what they had been told. On 18 May, the *Aberdeen Press and Journal*
reported: 'As orphans they have now been led to believe that their parents
were killed in a motoring accident.' This contradicted early reports that
they had been told their parents were holidaying, but perhaps it was a ploy
to deter future awkward questions.

One thing was certain, the authorities in Lancashire were keen that
Elizabeth, Diana and Billy be shielded. On 28 May, *The Scotsman* reported,
'The greatest secrecy is to be observed in deciding the future of the three
Ruxton children … Everything possible is to be done to hide their identity,
and to ensure that the tragedy of their parents is not disclosed to them.'

Mr G.O. Holloway, the Public Assistance Officer to the Lancaster
County Council, told reporters: 'If these poor tragic children are to have

a chance of remaining in ignorance of their history and parentage, it is absolutely essential that steps should be taken to secure that they cannot in future be connected with the past.' He added that if the public wished to show kindness to the children, they should 'cease interesting themselves in them'. He would not confirm if their names would be changed or when they would leave Parkside.

'You can take it for granted,' he told the press, 'that everything that can be thought of that will be to their present and future advantage will be done.'

On 3 July, the *Western Gazette* reported in a single paragraph: 'That the three children of Dr Buck Ruxton should be adopted by Lancashire County Council was resolved on Monday by the Lancashire Public Assistance Committee at Preston.'

And so a protective cloak of anonymity was wrapped around Elizabeth, Diana and William Ruxton, the three children of Dr Buck Ruxton and Isabella Kerr of 2 Dalton Square, Lancaster. The secret of what became of them is locked away in archives in Preston until 2035.

EPILOGUE

The Ruxton case was a landmark in British legal history because of the incredible pioneering achievements of the police officers and forensic scientists. Their ground-breaking work in the fields of anatomy, photographic reconstruction, entomology and fingerprinting cast a long shadow and their new techniques were adopted and championed in the coming decades. Much of it is still being used today.

Glaister wrote many years later in his memoirs, *Final Diagnosis*:

> When it was over, like many of my colleagues, I was showered with invitations to lecture and speak at a variety of gatherings. Many were requests from the police in various areas, and lecturing on the medico-legal aspects of the Ruxton case took me in a matter of months to Scotland Yard, the Midlands, the South West and many other places.

Glaister maintained that the key to their success had been teamwork, and interdisciplinary co-operation between the scientists and the police. It signalled the end of the days of the untouchable lone-wolf pathologist. In the years that followed, Sir Bernard Spilsbury's career began a slow decline. In 1947, with failing health and crumbling finances, Spilsbury took his own life in his laboratory.

Glaister and Couper Brash wrote a technical book about the startling investigative work done on the case. It was called *Medico-Legal Aspects of the Ruxton Case* and was published in 1937. It was filled with minute forensic detail about the bodies and the gruesome work required to solve the jigsaw murders. Its pages were filled with the most stomach-churning images imaginable that only future students would find useful. It won the international Swiney Prize, a prestigious accolade awarded once each decade for the most outstanding book on forensic medicine.

Unsurprisingly, it was not a bestseller.

In the 1960s Glaister was among a team of scientists asked to test a hair belonging to Napoleon Bonaparte to see if the emperor had died of arsenic poisoning. The tests were inconclusive.

Professor Sydney Smith, who was later knighted, dedicated a whole chapter to the Ruxton case in his memoirs, *Mostly Murder*. Unlike the Glaister and Brash book, Smith's was aimed at a popular audience and it became a huge success, especially when reprinted as a mass-market paperback. It would still be in print a quarter of a century later.

Detective Lieutenant Bertie Hammond's brilliant and dedicated work in the field of fingerprinting had been revolutionary. In the days after Ruxton's conviction, the *News of the World* stated that Hammond's achievements would 'go down in police records as among the most remarkable ever achieved by a fingerprint man'.

J. Edgar Hoover, head of the FBI, hailed Hammond's use of Mary Rogerson's 'chance' fingerprints as 'unique'; previously police had consulted existing fingerprints on police records or else did not consult any at all. Hammond's work was praised in a 1957 academic paper, *The Ruxton Trial Revelations* by George W. Wilton.

A decade after Ruxton's execution, Norman Birkett was a judge at the Nazi War Trials at Nuremberg. Coincidentally, two of the Crown prosecutors he had jousted with at Manchester Assizes also participated in the trial of Hermann Göring, Martin Bormann and Rudolf Hess. Hartley Shawcross was by then the United Kingdom's Attorney General and David Maxwell-Fyfe his deputy. Maxwell-Fyfe's cross-examination of Göring is still regarded as one of the most noted in legal history.

Birkett fulfilled Ruxton's request to help Elizabeth, Diana and Billy where he could in the years after the case, though it was done discreetly to protect the children. He was made Baron Birkett of Ulverston in 1958 and died in 1962. He might have turned in his grave when the *News of the World* published an article in 1976 with the headline 'I've Got Away With Murder'. In it, Toni Mancini confessed to killing Violette Kaye.

Bobby Edmondson, the young man alleged by Ruxton to be Isabella's lover, lived a long life. He married aged 31 in 1941 and had a son, Piers. He died in 2008 at the age of 98.

The Ruxton case had made legal and forensic history. The name of Dr Buck Ruxton entered British folklore in the form of a schoolyard rhyme, sung to the tune of *Red Sails in the Sunset*, with the following lines:

Red stains on the carpet,
Red stains on the knife;
Oh, Dr Buck Ruxton,
You murdered your wife.
Then Mary she saw you;
You thought she would tell;
So, Dr Buck Ruxton,
You killed her as well.

In time, the Devil's Beef Tub area in the Scottish Borders became known locally as 'Ruxton's Dump'. The *New York Times* of 27 March 1937, a year after his execution, reported that Ruxton's waxwork had joined the likes of movie actress Mae West, British Foreign Secretary Anthony Eden, Princess Elizabeth (later Queen Elizabeth II) and Adolf Hitler (this was two years before the start of the Second World War) at Madame Tussaud's in London. Newspapers are always eager to attach a catchy name to notorious murderers and Ruxton became known as the 'Savage Surgeon', while his crimes would be best remembered as the 'Jigsaw Murders'.

For many years, the bath in which Ruxton chopped up Isabella's and Mary's bodies was used as a water trough for the horses at Lancashire Police headquarters near Preston. It is now the centrepiece of a Ruxton exhibition at Lancaster Castle.

Nobody would ever live at 2 Dalton Square again. Like so many buildings associated with murder, the Georgian property took on a spooky reputation in the local community. Stories abound to this day of children daring each other to enter the yard and peer in through the windows. The house remained empty until the 1980s when Lancaster City Council decided to turn it into offices, combining it with the old County Cinema next door to form Palatine Hall.

Today, Dalton Square is a peaceful, comely place in the centre of Lancaster. The ghosts of the past, perhaps, have finally been laid to rest.

ACKNOWLEDGEMENTS

I was haunted by the Ruxton case from an early age. I grew up in the Lake District in the 1970s and whenever we visited Lancaster, my dad would point to 2 Dalton Square and tell me and my brother the story of Dr Ruxton. To two young boys it was a very creepy tale that left an indelible mark. I always tried to imagine what had happened behind that front door. My family's links with Lancaster went back even further. My grandparents arrived there with three young sons in 1935, the year of the murders, and my dad was born two months after Ruxton's execution in 1936.

My fascination continued when I was a student in the city and after university when I became a newspaper reporter, often covering Lancaster's magistrates' and crown courts. Again, my thoughts would be brought back to Dalton Square and the spectre of Buck Ruxton. I remember the controversy when a pub off Dalton Square was insensitively renamed Ruxton's. My knowledge of the case, however, was limited to what my dad had told me and the basic facts trotted out in crime magazines and compendium true crime books. It seemed like nothing new had been said about the case in decades.

I was certain there was much more to the story and the people involved. I felt Isabella and Mary in particular had been poorly served by previous accounts. When I decided to write about the case, I wasn't prepared for the wealth of untapped information waiting to be brought back into the light.

From the start I was determined to go inside 2 Dalton Square, to see first-hand the scene of the murders. I am indebted to Mark McTigue, Lancaster City Council's marketing and tourism team leader, who very kindly gave me a tour of the property on a very wet day in February 2020. I had naively expected the house to be as it was when Ruxton and Isabella lived there. It is now home to the council's planning offices and betrays none of its notorious past in appearance or atmosphere. I tried to picture Ruxton in his Oriental room or sitting in the lounge listening to the Derby at Epsom on his wireless. The former bathroom where the dismemberment took place is now a bright staff kitchen area.

Mark also showed me the former police station and cells underneath the Town Hall on the opposite side of Dalton Square. This is where Ruxton was arrested by Captain Vann, gave his account of 'My Movements', and was held immediately afterwards. The cells are completely unchanged, typically Edwardian in appearance with their white tiles and metal bars. Mark led me from the cells up winding steps into the dock of the former police court where Ruxton's remand hearings were heard in the winter of 1935. The court is quiet now, but it's not hard to imagine Ruxton's emotional outbursts shattering the silence. It too is unchanged, with the original dock handrail that Ruxton gripped, and the heavy door that police officers closed when Ruxton complained of a draught. It is possible to take an organised tour of the courtroom if one so desires. Council staff have helpfully placed old newspaper and magazine articles about the case in plastic wallets on the clerk's desk.

I also visited Lancaster City Museum where site supervisor Naomi Parsons showed me the Ruxton archive. It isn't extensive; it includes photocopies of a letter written by Mary Rogerson, a *Police Journal* article by Captain Vann, a number of photographs and a doctor's note signed by Ruxton.

The item of primary interest, however, is Ruxton's pocket diary for 1934. It was a strange, unsettling feeling to hold the journal, a physical connection with Ruxton himself. The entries, while brief, are revealing. These have been woven into the fabric of *The Jigsaw Murders*. Its journey into the archives is unclear; despite checks, Naomi was unable to ascertain when or how it was deposited there.

Interestingly, Naomi has links to the Ruxton case. Her late grandfather was a patient of Ruxton's. Jim Stewart was born at Castle Hill, and always told the story of how his life was saved by the doctor when he was treated for a childhood illness. He wouldn't hear a bad word said about him.

So many people have helped me during my research. The kindness and generosity of the following are greatly appreciated.

Hannah Priest, author and – what a small world – fellow lecturer at Manchester Metropolitan University, very kindly showed me research she and her parents have done into Isabella Ruxton's life and family. Their link was Isabella's brother John, who married into Hannah's family. She told me of the Kerr family's displeasure at wayward Isabella's choice in men.

Emma Yan, Claire Daniel and Moira Rankin, archivists at the Archives and Special Collections of the University of Glasgow, were patient and obliging in fulfilling my requests during the challenges of the Covid-19 pandemic when a visit in person was out of the question. They also allowed me to use many of the images from the Ruxton archive there.

Likewise, archivist David Tilsley and conservation technician Liam McLaughlin at Lancashire Archives at Lancashire County Council in Preston were extremely helpful.

Ana Paun of JPI Media granted me permission to reproduce photographs of Glaister, Brash and Smith from the *Leeds Mercury*.

Helen Churchill kindly told me the story of the young girl whose sight was restored by Dr Ruxton. In the 1970s, Helen taught the girl – by then a middle-aged woman – at an adult education class in Lancaster.

I found the lively discussion about the Ruxton case on the Lancaster Past and Present Facebook group fascinating. So many people in Lancaster have family stories about Ruxton, Isabella, Mary and other related figures. I would like to thank the following for corresponding with me: Andrew Reilly, Jean Nelson, Bruce Phillips, Peter Akister, Martin Lewis, Bernard Cruikshank, Jan Cook and Eileen Lucas.

I am deeply indebted to the number of people who contacted me as a result of early publicity about the book. Each had an untold story and their inclusion has, I believe, resulted in a much richer narrative.

Sandy Crosthwaite told me the story of his stepfather, Richard Dugdale, a nightmarish scenario straight out of a Hitchcock film. Mr Crosthwaite, who is 87, is originally from Warton, near Carnforth, but now lives in Scotland. He says Mr Dugdale mentioned the Ruxton case only once, prompted by an item about it on television. 'I was arrested for those murders,' Mr Dugdale had said, almost in passing, adding: 'I had a devil of a time getting out of it.'

Joanna Clark very kindly spoke to me about her grandfather, Dr Leonard Mather, and shared the letters he wrote to her in the 1980s, in which he described his memories of Ruxton and the case. These documents are invaluable artifacts of social history, and have not previously been published. Thanks to Joanna's mum, Katie, for scanning them for me.

Bernard Drumm told me about his brother who worked with Professor Glaister in his lab at Glasgow University. Mr Drumm actually met Glaister in the 1960s when he visited his brother at work. Thanks to Mr Drumm for telling me about Glaister's involvement with Napoleon's hair. *Scottish Mail on Sunday* reporter Katherine Sutherland, who interviewed me for an early article about *The Jigsaw Murders*, kindly introduced me to Mr Drumm, who is coincidentally her neighbour.

Richard Wilson introduced me to his mother, Marilyn Wilson, who spoke at length and with great pride about her grandfather, Detective Inspector William Thompson, one of the key Lancaster officers who worked on the case. The Wilson family very kindly allowed me to reproduce the wonderful – and to my knowledge unpublished – photograph of Thompson and Chief Constable Henry Vann standing on Ruxton's doorstep during police investigations in October 1935.

Donal Lowry kindly shared details about his great-uncle Jeremiah Lynch, of Scotland Yard, and his involvement in the Ruxton case.

Jo Porter loaned me a fascinating scrapbook of old newspaper cuttings (all mostly macabre and strange) that included insightful ones about Ruxton. Jo's grandparents, Horace and Irene Potter, were patients of Ruxton's and shook his hand as they queued outside the County Cinema the week before his arrest.

There was one story I was unable to corroborate and so sadly could not include. Nevertheless, I would like to thank Andrew Smith for contacting me. His 90-year-old mother, Janet Smith, believes Dr Ruxton called at her family home for a glass of water on the road to Moffat on his way to dispose of the bodies in the ravine in September 1935. She was aged 5 at the time and her mother later reported the incident when police appealed for witnesses.

Late in the writing of *The Jigsaw Murders*, the book was optioned for television by Elaine Collins of Tod Productions and STV Productions. I was absolutely thrilled. I would like to thank Elaine, script editor Clare Batty and screenwriter Thomas Eccleshare for their encouraging Zoom calls. Thanks also to Elaine's husband, Peter Capaldi, who graciously sent my children a letter at the height of the Covid-19 lockdown. That meant a lot.

My literary agent Joanna Swainson of Hardman and Swainson showed great faith in this project and me as a writer. Without her encouragement I would not have been able to do this. I hope this is the 'gritty northern story' she was expecting. Marc Simonsson of SoloSon Media was spectacular in finding the perfect TV producer to option my work. The deal gave me extra buoyancy as I completed the manuscript.

I am indebted to Mark Beynon and everyone at The History Press for all their support. It's very much appreciated.

For their encouragement, I would like to thank the many newspaper colleagues with whom I have talked about writing over the years. Among them are Adrian Mullen, Steve Barber, Andrew Thomas, Colin Shelbourn, Andrea Ashworth, Anne Rothwell, Mick Middles, Chris Wood, Mike Critchley and Robbie McDonald.

To my teaching colleagues in the Multimedia Journalism department at Manchester Metropolitan University, I thank you for your support and for being such a pleasure to work with: Nathalie Griffith, Dave Porter, Pete Murray, Andy Dickinson, Dawn Bryan, Eleanor Shember-Critchley, Deborah Linton, Vince Hunt, Liz Hannaford, Jenna Sloan, Paul Clark, Lawrence Brannon, Carmel Thomason, Lara Williams, Fiona Ennys, Gerry Sammon and Simon Webb.

Thanks to the following friends who listened to updates on my writing progress, usually at the Parr Arms pub quiz in Grappenhall: Will Johnston, Ivor Stevenson, John Norman, Phil Savage, Marc Littlemore and Dave Williams. Thanks also to my Lancaster friends Kerry, Andrew, Edward and Olivia Higgs for their love and support.

Much love to my brother and sister-in-law, Justin and Jackie Craddock, who have followed and supported my writing career from a distance in San Diego. The road trip to the Grand Canyon and Las Vegas in 2017, when I was first thinking of this book, will always be special.

My biggest regret is that my parents are not able to see this book published. My mum, Gerry Craddock, died in 2016, a few months before I began work on *The Jigsaw Murders*, and as strange as it sounds, I felt her spirit guiding me. She was fascinated by true crime and I have vivid memories of her reading seminal books such as *Helter Skelter, Beyond Belief* and *Somebody's Husband, Somebody's Son.* I owe a huge debt to my dad, Geoff Craddock, in first telling me the Ruxton story and then showing me the house in Dalton Square in the 1970s. Sadly, Dad died a few weeks before this book was published. Looking back, I think I was destined to write this story.

I would like to express my love and thanks to my wonderful in-laws, Allan and Freda Wilde, who have been such a huge support to me over the years. As with my parents, it is a great source of regret that Allan is not here to see this moment. Happily, Freda is.

My 91-year-old uncle, Gordon Craddock, was a small boy at the time of the Ruxton killings. He has faint memories of the furore in Lancaster when Ruxton was accused of the murders. He and my auntie, Ann Craddock, have always encouraged my love of books and writing. The book tokens they sent for my birthdays and at Christmas sustained and nourished me over the years. I will never forget their support.

Finally, I could not have achieved any of this without the love and patience of my wonderful children, Emily and Matthew, and my beautiful wife and soulmate, Louise, who sustained me with craft beer and giant Cadbury's Buttons.

NOTES ON SOURCES

For the sake of brevity, I have used the following abbreviations for the core sources that underpin *The Jigsaw Murders*. All other sources are provided in full. It is worth noting that this book is non-fiction. Nothing is made up; every last detail is derived from a documented account or an interview.

Source abbreviations:

150 Years	*150 Years of True Crime: Stories from the News of the World*
FD	*Final Diagnosis*
MLA	*Medico-Legal Aspects of the Ruxton Case*
MM	*Mostly Murder*
NB	*Norman Birkett: The Definitive Biography of the Legendary Barrister*
TBR	*The Trial of Buck Ruxton*

Archive abbreviation:

UoG	University of Glasgow Forensic Medicine Archives Project

Prologue

Details are drawn from various sources: *TBR*, *The Butchers* and *150 Years*. The history of the Devil's Beef Tub and John Hunter is taken from the excellent blogs, *Jardine's Book of Martyrs* and *Scottish Covenanter Memorials Association*. Details of Sloan's resilience were uncovered in *The Scotsman*, Thursday, 10 October 1935.

There is a discrepancy in the spelling of Gardenholme. In all the contemporary newspaper accounts I consulted it was spelt with the final 'e', which was repeated in many true crime magazines and memoirs. However, maps of the area show the hamlet spelt without the 'e'. I have retained the original press spelling for consistency. I have also chosen to spell 'linn' with a lowercase 'l'. In the same vein, I have aimed for consistency in using 'Isabella' rather than 'Isobel' (Ruxton's spelling) or 'Isabelle' as it occasionally appears in press accounts. The Ruxtons' second daughter's name is sometimes given as 'Diana', at other times as 'Diane'. I have chosen to refer to her as 'Diana' because that is how it is recorded in the register of her birth in January 1931. I settled on 'Billy-Boy' for the Ruxtons' son William, rather than 'Billie-Boy', which is used in some accounts, again for consistency's sake.

Details of Professor John Glaister's initial involvement are taken from his memoirs, *FD*.

The newspaper report of the 'Scottish ravine mystery' is taken from the *Portsmouth Evening News*, 4 October 1935. 'Do you see, Mrs Oxley...' Ruxton's reaction to the *Daily Express* report of the ravine discovery is from *The Butchers* and *TBR*.

PART ONE: EDINBURGH

Chapter 1
Details of Ruxton and Isabella in Edinburgh are from *TBR*, *The Butchers*, *150 Years*, *The Mammoth Book of CSI* and *News of the World* reports from March and May 1936. The history of Burke and Hare and the act of body snatching is very well documented; a particularly useful online source is Edinburgh-history.co.uk.

Chapter 2
Ruxton's birth, childhood and pre-Edinburgh life are constructed using details from UoG. The letter of recommendation is item GUA FM/2A/25/10. Further details are taken from *TBR*, *FD*, *MM* and *The Butchers*.

Chapter 3
Smith, Littlejohn and Joseph Bell: *MM*.

Chapter 4
Details of Isabella's birth and early life are sketchy. I found reports in the *Lancashire Daily Post* of 28 November 1935 and the *Western Mail* of 29 May 1936 particularly helpful. Evidence given by Isabella's sisters at Ruxton's trial, transcribed in *TBR*, also shed light on this period of her life, as did information on West Lothian Museum's Local History page on Facebook. Information about Isabella's marriage to Van Ess are from

the aforementioned *Daily Post* cutting and information supplied to me by Isabella's distant relative, Hannah Priest, which included the couple's marriage certificate. Hannah told me of the Kerr family's displeasure at Isabella's impulsive marriage to Van Ess, and later relationship with Ruxton.

The early part of Ruxton and Isabella's relationship, their first argument and Ruxton's early diary entries are drawn from a number of invaluable newspaper clippings: *Daily Mail*, 14 March 1936, and the *News of the World*, 8 and 15 March, and 3 May 1936.

MLA outlines Ruxton's keeping of diaries. On Wednesday, 4 February 1931, Ruxton wrote that he and Isabella had driven to Edinburgh, passing through Moffat and over the bridge at Gardenholme linn.

Chapter 5

Glaister's early life is based on *FD*. Contextual details about the Glaisters and their impact on forensic medicine was provided by the excellent *On Soul and Conscience: The Medical Expert and Crime.* The description of Glaister's marriage to Muff is based on wedding footage by British Moving Picture News, and accessed at the Moving Image website of the National Library of Scotland. It is a quite remarkable piece of archive material, a time capsule from another age.

Chapter 6

Coverage of the case in the *News of the World* on 8 March 1936 provided the source material for descriptions of Ruxton leaving Edinburgh for London in 1927. The same paper's edition of 3 May 1936 outlines Ruxton's telegram to his first wife's family requesting money and the testimony of Motibal Ghadiali. *Killers, Crooks and Cons: Scotland's Crimes of the Century* was consulted on Ruxton's Parsi background forbidding his divorce. Excerpts from Ruxton's diary from this period are drawn from the *News of the World*, 15 March 1936. Information about Motibal Ghadiali's family and the repair of the clock at Bombay University is from *Before Memory Fades*. Further details of Ruxton's early life, education, first marriage and Isabella's divorce are taken from *Antecedents of Dr Ruxton* at UoG, item GUA FM/2A/25/11.

Chapter 7

Glaister in Cairo and call back to Glasgow: *FD*. Details of the deaths of Professor and Mrs Glaister to influenza are taken from the obituary of Glaister senior found at SemanticScholar.org.

Chapter 8
The harrowing details from Ruxton's letter are taken from the *News of the World* of 8 March 1936.

PART TWO: BRILLIANT MINDS

Chapter 9
The life and career of Spilsbury was created using *Bernard Spilsbury: His Life and Cases*, and Bentley Purchase's arresting comment is also taken from here. To add extra depth to my descriptions of his influence and reputation, I turned also to *MM* and *FD*. Dr Crippen's remark upon being apprehended – 'Thank God it's all over' – is taken from the *Reading Evening Post*, 4 September 1975.

Chapter 10
Isabella's letter was made public in a *News of the World* article from 15 March 1936.

Chapter 11
The description of Spilsbury at work is taken from *Bernard Spilsbury: His Life and Cases*.

Chapter 12
The details of the Ruxtons in London and the birth of Elizabeth Ruxton is from *News of the World* accounts from March 1936.

Chapter 13
The story of Sidney Fox and Smith's meeting with Spilsbury is derived from *MM*. Also helpful was the *Western Daily Mail* of 7 December 1929. The description of the Metropole Hotel in Margate is based on information taken from a historic tourist pamphlet from 1903, which I found online at MargateLocalHistory.co.uk.

Details about Alfred Waterhouse, architect of University College Hospital, were taken from *Alfred Waterhouse 1830–1905: Biography of a Practice*. The *Daily Telegraph* of 1 August 2017 revealed the fact about George Orwell's death at the hospital. For details about the Queen of Crime, I consulted the Londonist.com website's wonderful page on Agatha Christie's London.

The pen portrait of Dr Robert Brontë was done using his obituary from the *Belfast News Letter*, 23 March 1932, an Associated Newspapers photograph of 7 April 1925, owned by Shutterstock, and *Bernard Spilsbury: His Life and Cases.*

Chapter 14
The Fox trial is recreated using *MM* and *Bernard Spilsbury: His Life and Cases.*

Chapter 15
Migrant Architects of the NHS is a fascinating account of the many doctors and medics from South Asia who came to Britain in the 1920s and 1930s. It was extremely useful in bringing context to Ruxton's story.

Details of Ruxton's purchase of the practice in Dalton Square from Dr Gonsalves is taken from *Antecedents of Dr Ruxton* at UoG. History of Dalton Square is from the Localhistories.org website and includes fascinating facts about John Dalton (not the scientist) who built it and many of the surrounding streets, bearing names of members of his family, such as Robert Street, Edward Street, Alfred Street and Lucy Street.

Isabella's time working at the Woolworth's cafeteria is from *150 Years.*

PART THREE: HYDE

Chapter 16
Descriptions of the Ruxtons in Dalton Square and their furnishings are pieced together from various sources. These include *The Mammoth Book of CSI*, the evidence of Jeanie Nelson and Ruxton himself from *TBR*, *MLA*, the *Daily Mail* of 14 March 1936, the sales catalogue of Ruxton's possessions in 1936, and Ruxton's 1934 diary, both of which are held in Lancaster City Museum. Ruxton's income rising to £3,500 is from the *News of the World*, 15 March 1936. The Bank of England's inflation calculator revealed the startling fact that this would today equal around £250,000. 'You know some of the police.' *Daily Mail*, 14 March 1936.

Details of Isabella's portrait come from the 15 November 1935 edition of the *Morecambe Guardian* and the aforementioned edition of the *News of the World*.

Information about James Williamson, the lino king, is derived from *The Buildings of England, Lancashire: North* and the VisitLancashire.com website. I am indebted to Andrew Gough's excellent blog about Golgotha village. Cinematreasures.org provided information about Dalton Square's cinemas. The tragic story of the Storeys' factory chimney collapse is from the *Morecambe Visitor*, February 2016.

Chapter 17

Stories of Ruxton's kindness and compassion to patients are well known. The following sources have been used: *Daily Mail*, 14 March 1936; Naomi Parsons, of Lancaster City Museum, told me about Ruxton's treatment of her grandfather, Jim Stewart; my interview with Helen Churchill revealed the story about the girl whose sight was restored by Ruxton; Ruxton's interest in ophthalmology was revealed in *MLA*. The story of PC Wilson's broken nose is from his son Tom's account on the excellent ITV documentary, *Nightwatch Mysteries*, from 2008. Information about the Ruxtons' domestic help was drawn from the *Hull Daily Mail* of 6 March 1936 and from *TBR*. A press photograph of Elizabeth Curwen from 3 December 1935 owned by Shutterstock assisted in describing her.

TBR was used for information about the Jeffersons and the Andersons, while further detail about Herbert Anderson is derived from Ancestry.com and Ruxton's 'My Movements' reproduced in *TBR*.

Ruxton's relationship with Dr Leonard Mather is taken from personal and unpublished letters he wrote to his granddaughter, Joanna Clark, in the 1980s, while Dr Mather's history is taken from the 1939 England and Wales census, sourced at Ancestry.com.

Chapter 18

TBR was used to describe the toxic atmosphere at Dalton Square and the damaging effects of the Ruxtons' relationship. Details of Isabella's acts of penance performed at Ruxton's instigation are taken from Henry Vann's article 'Rex v Ruxton' in the *Police Journal*. The account of Isabella's suicide attempt is based on the testimony of Jeanie Nelson found in *TBR*.

Chapter 19

Details of the stillbirth are taken from *TBR*, the testimonies of nurse-maid Jane Grierson and Jeanie Nelson, as well as the personal account of Dr Leonard Mather in his private letters. Dr Mather's granddaughter Joanna Clark told me that the family later got rid of the table Ruxton had given her grandfather, not wanting to have it in their possession. *News of the World* stories from 15 March 1936 provided the shocking details of Isabella's further suicide attempts and her arguments with Ruxton.

Information about the Ruxtons' money problems, Ruxton's 'particularities' and his taste for primary colours is taken from *TBR* and Ruxton's evidence at the trial reported in the *News of the World* of 15 March 1935. Mrs Nelson's comment on Isabella's shabby clothes is from the *Lancashire Daily Post* of 28 November 1935.

Chapter 20

Stories persist to this day among Lancaster people about Isabella Ruxton's friendships with other men behind Ruxton's back. I found many, many comments on a Lancaster Facebook group posted by people repeating stories their parents and grandparents had passed down. While these people found Ruxton's crimes sickening, there was nevertheless still a level of sympathy towards the doctor because of the provocation they felt Isabella had caused. The only documentary evidence I have found of these apparent dalliances of Isabella is in Ruxton's diaries and his testimony at his trial. In other words, they are not wholly to be trusted.

Ruxton's outburst, 'You know some of the police …' is from the *Daily Mail* of 14 March 1936.

The accounts of Ruxton's domestic abuse of Isabella are taken from *The Trial of Buck Ruxton*. The *Hull Daily Mail* of 3 December 1935 provided details of the Ruxtons' drive out following a row.

Excerpts from Ruxton's diary and details of their rows are from the *News of the World* of March 1935. The *Lancashire Daily Post* of 28 November 1935 provided details of Isabella's break in Edinburgh. Billy-boy's birth is from *The Antecedents of Buck Ruxton*, UoG.

Chapter 21

Details about Mary, the children's parties and the Jackson children are taken from *TBR*. Bernard Cruickshank shared his memories of his mother, Isabel Fryers, with me.

Ruxton's diary extracts and Isabella chloroforming herself are from the *News of the World* editions of March and May 1936.

Chapter 22

How the Edmondsons became friends with the Ruxtons is drawn from *TBR*. A range of sources was used for Isabella's complaint of attempted assault: Ruxton's 1934 diary, the *News of the World*, 8 March 1936 and Detective Inspector Walter Stainton's evidence at the trial in *TBR*.

Agatha Christie was fascinated by the Ruxton case and mentioned it in *One, Two, Buckle My Shoe* in 1940. Details of her disappearance are taken from Giles Milton's excellent article in the BBC's *HistoryExtra* magazine.

Chapter 23
Toni Mancini's arrest and initial court appearance are pieced together from *NB, Bernard Spilsbury*, the *Daily Mirror* of 16 July 1934 and the *Hampshire Telegraph and Post* of 20 July 1934.

Chapter 24
Extracts from Ruxton's 1934 diary, held at Lancaster City Museum, provided most of the details. Information about Rajpipla are from the *Staffordshire Sentinel* of 26 July 1934. Reports of the Derby in *The Age* of 8 June 1934 and the *Londonderry Sentinel* of 7 June 1934 were invaluable.

Chapter 25
Fascinating information about the assize circuit system was drawn from the National Archives at Kew's website, detailing criminal trials 1559–1971. The account of Birkett's assignment to the Mancini case is derived from *NB*.

Chapter 26
Birkett's remarkable performance at the Mancini trial is reconstructed from *NB* and *Bernard Spilsbury: His Life and Cases*.

Chapter 27
Mr Justice Branson's summing up in the Mancini case is taken from the *Sunderland Echo and Shipping Gazette*, 14 December 1934. The reaction to the verdict and immediate aftermath is from *NB* and *The Butchers*. Toni Mancini's marriage and new-found celebrity are recounted in the *Daily Independent* of 28 December 1934.

Chapter 28
Ruxton's rising paranoia, the suspicions of poison in his coffee, and his bended-knee appeal to Isabella in Edinburgh are all taken from his 1934 diary at Lancaster City Museum, as are the entries relating to Christmas.

PART FOUR: MURDER

Chapter 29
The account of New Year's Eve 1934 at the Elms Hotel is drawn from Ruxton's 1934 diary. Details of the Elms are from a historic promotional leaflet sourced at Flickr.

Chapter 30
Cecil Thomas, the portrait photographer, gave his account of Isabella's visit to his studio at the trial, recounted in *TBR*, and it features also in *MLA*. There is also reference to it in Henry Vann's report in the *Police Journal* of 1937. Further details about Thomas are from CompanyCheck.co.uk and Ancestry.com.

PC Wilson's pocketbook is held at Lancashire Archives in Preston. It contains his notes following the domestic disturbance at the Ruxton home on 27 May 1935. A scan of Wilson's page can be viewed on the LancashireHistory.files.wordpress.com site.

Information about the two-week holiday at Seatle is derived from Mrs Edith Holme's and Mr Jefferson's evidence at Ruxton's trial in *TBR*, while Mary Rogerson's unpublished letter is held at Lancaster City Museum.

Chapter 31
TBR and the *Nottingham Journal* of 5 December 1935 provided background for the trip made by Isabella and the Edmondsons to Edinburgh … and Ruxton's trip following them.

Chapter 32
The account of the room arrangements at the Adelphi Hotel and Ruxton's snooping is derived from evidence of witnesses recorded in *TBR*.

PART FIVE: THE DEVIL'S PATHOLOGY

Chapter 33
The events leading up to the murder are based on *TBR*, the *Lancashire Daily Post* of 28 November 1935, Audrey Mossom's obituary in *The Independent* of 1 October 2009 and 'The railway queen who met Stalin' from RailwayMuseum.org.uk.

Ruxton, the only surviving witness to the events, never provided an account of what happened when Isabella arrived back in Dalton Square on the night of 14 September 1935, and I have not tried to speculate. Instead, I leave the reader with the tantalising line: 'Isabella went inside to die.' The later supposition of the police and scientists is shocking enough when it comes at the trial, I believe, without any leap of imagination required from me.

Chapter 34
Ruxton's actions immediately after the murder were reconstructed using trial evidence from *TBR* and *MLA*. The death certificate of William Waite, sourced at Ancestry.com, was helpful in researching the Waite family. Interestingly, William Waite's nephew is John Waite, the singer-songwriter who had a worldwide hit with *Missing You* in 1984.

Chapter 35
The events of Monday, 16 September were drawn from *TBR*. Information about Tymns café was found in the *Lancaster Guardian* of 25 June 1937.

The private letters of Dr Mather revealed that Ruxton intended asking him to act as guarantor and also Billy's statement about 'Daddy's garden'.

Chapter 36
Evidence of witnesses from *TBR*.

Chapter 37
Details about the sad and distressing story of Florence Smalley are pieced together from a number of sources: the *Lancashire Evening Post* of 20 September 1935 and 25 October 1935, and the *Daily Independent* of 26 September 1935. Mrs Smalley's taste for alcohol is taken from the Morecambeology website's page about Ruxton.

TBR was used for the descriptions of Ruxton's fires, Mr Hall's work on the new lighting, Ruxton's request to Thomas Harrison, Mary's brother Peter's concern, and Ruxton's visit to the County Cinema.

Chapter 38
The *Lancashire Daily Post* of 25 October 1935 provided information about Detective Inspector Moffat's inquiries into Mrs Smalley's death and the subsequent police announcement about her cause of death. The trial evidence of John Cook and James Jefferson was helpful.

Chapter 39
Details of Ruxton's trip to Gretna Green are taken from *TBR*.

Chapter 40
Neil Root's excellent *The Murder Gang* provided context for the newspaper coverage of the discovery near Moffat. Finer detail is sifted from *TBR*, while *MLA* provided information about the scene in Moffat mortuary. Some information about Chief Constable Black's statement to the press is from *The Scotsman* of 2 October 1935.

Information about Willie Ewing and his work on the scraps of newspaper is drawn from the *Daily Record* of 23 July 1963 and from the excellent Dutch family website, Ewing.nl. Bertie Hammond's rise to become head of Glasgow's Fingerprint Department is taken from Policemuseum.org. uk. Details of the newsmen who covered the discovery are sourced from *150 Years* and *Frenzy! Heath, Haigh and Christie* by Neil Root.

The Rogersons' visit to see Ruxton is taken from their evidence in *TBR*.

Chapter 41
Details are from *MLA*, *TBR*, and *150 Years*. Glaister's description of the cyclops eye is from *FD*. Norman Rae's advertising 'autobiography' is from the *Coventry Evening Telegraph* of 9 April 1960.

Chapter 42
MLA was used to reconstruct Glaister and Millar's examination of the bodies.

Chapter 43
Details of Ruxton's visit to the Edmondsons' and Thomas Harrison are from *TBR*, while the Edmondsons' family tree at Ancestry.com was consulted.

Chapter 44
Details about Brash are from his In Memoriam piece in the *Journal of Anatomy*, Vol. 92, Part 4. Brash's reconstruction is from *MLA* and *FD*.

Chapter 45
TBR and *MLA* were the main sources. Information about Jeremiah Lynch was supplied by Donal Lowry and Lynch's obituary in *The Times* of 5 July 1953. My interview with Sandy Crosthwaite provided details about his stepfather Richard Dugdale.

Chapter 46
Ruxton's repeated visits to the police station and the arrival of the Scottish officers are from *TBR*. Also consulted were Vann's account in the *Police Journal* and Dr Mather's unpublished letters.

Chapter 47
TBR. Henry Vann's life is reconstructed using the *Western Mail* of 23 March 1937 and the record of his birth sourced at Ancestry.com.

The description of Ruxton's arrest is based on *MLA*, *TBR*, *150 Years*, Vann's *Police Journal* account, Ruxton's document, 'My Movements' and Dr Mather's letters.

Chapter 48
Vann's *Police Journal* article; Dr Mather's letters, 'My Movements', *TBR* and *MLA*.

PART SIX: SEEK

Chapter 49
The *Morecambe Guardian* of 18 October 1935 was packed full of fine-grain detail about the events immediately after Ruxton's arrest and his first court appearance. The *Hull Daily Mail* of 19 June 1936 provided details of Fred Gardner, as did births, marriages and death records sourced at Ancestry. com, and Ruxton's creditors' announcement in the *London Gazette*. Also useful was Alan Hayhurst's *Lancashire Murders*.

TBR and *MLA* were used for the police search of the house, including Hammond's fingerprinting work. Description of the police cells at Lancaster Town Hall is based on my visit in February 2020. Testament to the grey in Ruxton's hair is from the *News of the World* of 15 March 1936. His request for morphine is from the *Aberdeen Press and Journal* of 18 May 1936. Ruxton's letter entrusted to a friend is taken from *150 Years*, *The Daily Herald*, 15 May 1936, and the *Aberdeen Press and Journal*, 18 May 1936.

Chapter 50
Glaister's account is from *FD*. Mrs Anderson's comments about the children are from the *Morecambe Guardian* of 18 October 1935. This was also used for details of the ongoing police appeals and investigation. *TBR* also

consulted. The *Northern Whig* of 16 October 1935 gives an account of the
police appeal for witnesses to the Austin car.

Chapter 51

MLA, Fingerprints and the Ruxton Murders, and *Fingerprints: Scotland Yard
Ruxton Trial Revelations* were used for Hammond's work, Glaister's work
on blood and the shoes; *TBR* for Green and Ewing's road trips.

Chapter 52

The Scotsman of 6 November 1935 and the *Morecambe Guardian* of
15 November 1935 provided details of Ruxton's fourth and fifth court
appearances, and Ruxton's serviette message. Details about Lancaster
mayor William Simpson are from the historic list of holders of the post on
Lancaster.gov.uk. The first occasion Ruxton was charged with murdering
Isabella is from *TBR*. The story of PC Wilson stopping the police van for
Ruxton's fish and chips is from ITV's *Nightwatch Mysteries*.

Chapter 53

Smith's return and the shark case are from *MM*, the *Yorkshire Evening Post*
of 13 June 1935 and *TBR*. The revolutionary photographic work and
Hammond's fingerprint breakthrough are from *MLA, FD* and *MM* and the
News of the World of 3 May 1936. Percy Sillitoe's comment is also taken from
FD. G. W. Wilton's *Fingerprints Scotland Yard: Ruxton Trial Revelations* helped
with the section about FBI involvement, as well as Bertie Hammond's own
paper on the Ruxton fingerprints. Stobie's need to step outside for fresh
air during the photographing of the bodies is taken from the *News of the
World* of 3 May 1936.

The description of Dr Hutchinson's dental investigation is based
on *MLA*.

Chapter 54

The *Lancashire Daily Post* of 28 November 1935 provided details of the
court hearings of late November and early December. Dr Mather's account
is from his unpublished letters. The planned auction details are from the
Morecambe Guardian of 20 November 1935 and Procter and Birkbeck's sales
catalogue, kept at Lancaster City Museum. The catalogue has Mrs Parish's
notes. Details about her were sourced from her 1933 marriage registration,
which revealed that Edith Lynch married Charles Parish in 1933. She visited 2 Dalton Square on 2 December 1935 for the sale. The description of

the queues outside the house and the boy in the pillbox hat is taken from a news photo of the day, owned by Shutterstock. The day of the auction was described using a press photo owned by Shutterstock. Adverts for Procter and Birkbeck auctions in the *Lancaster Guardian* and *Morecambe Visitor* from 1935 were helpful. The *Aberdeen Press and Journal* of 10 December 1935 provided details of the arrival of 'the Big Six'. Newspapers that provided the weather details and an account of the hearing were the *Lincolnshire Echo* of 11 December 1935, the *Leeds Mercury* of 12 December 1935 and the *Daily Independent* of 12 December 1935. Details of the Ruxton children and Parkside are from Dr Mather's letters, the *Daily Mirror* of 2 March 1936, Workhouse.org.uk and the National Archives at Kew.

PART SEVEN: TRIAL

Chapter 55
Announcements of Birkett's and Spilsbury's involvement with Ruxton are from the *Aberdeen Press and Journal* and the *Sheffield Daily Independent* of 8 February 1936 and also *Bernard Spilsbury: His Life and Cases*. Also helpful was the *Gloucestershire Echo* 'late news' column of 3 February 1936. Birkett's ethics on defending a guilty man are taken from *NB*.

Descriptions of the arriving witnesses are derived from the Associated Press photographs owned by Shutterstock. Details of the intense public interest and demand for a place in the public gallery are from the *Hartlepool Northern Daily Mail* of 2 March 1936.

TBR was used for the legal teams. Two sources were used for the Lancaster links of Singleton, Jackson and Birkett's mother: the *Oxford Dictionary of National Biography* and *A Cambridge Alumni Database (University of Cambridge)*, and *NB*. The *Daily Mirror* of 2 March 1936 included the report about the Ruxton children. *NB* explained the single murder charge Ruxton faced.

The description of Ruxton leaning forward is from *150 Years*, while the *Dundee Courier* of 3 March 1936 details Ruxton's appearance. The *Othello* quote is from the *Hartlepool Northern Daily Mail* of 2 March 1936 and the *Dundee Courier* of 3 March 1936.

Chapter 56
TBR.

Chapter 57
TBR and Dr Mather's letters.

Chapter 58
TBR for all the trial scenes. For the maggots evidence, the following sources were used: *FD, MLA*, the *Coventry Evening Telegraph* of 10 March 1936, *A Fly for the Prosecution*, the *New Scientist* of 30 May 1985, *The Ruxton Maggots and the Case of the Jigsaw Murders* from TheCultureTrip.com, and NHM.ac.uk for its article on the case.

The story about Jack Buchanan is from *FD*, and *NB* was used for Birkett's decision about Ruxton and his memorandum.

Chapter 59
TBR.

Chapter 60
TBR, the *Nottingham Journal* of 14 March 1936, *The Scotsman* of 12 March 1936 and the *Dundee Courier* of 14 March 1935. Norman Rae and John Milligan's contentious report is from the *News of the World*, 3 May 1936. The *Daily Mirror* of 14 March 1935 included the report about the children. Glaister's comment about teamwork is from *FD*, while Vann's is from 'Rex v Ruxton' in the *Police Journal*.

Chapter 61
Daily Mirror, 16 March 1935: interviews with Ruxton's mother and wife.

The aunts visiting the Ruxton children is from the *Daily Mirror* of 13 April 1936. The report of Ruxton's appeal: *Hull Daily Mail*, 27 April 1936 and *TBR*.

Crippen's cell: *The Deadly Doctor Ruxton*.

Chapter 62
The victims' funerals: *The Scotsman*, 4 May 1936 and *News of the World*, 3 May 1936.

The petition: *The Scotsman*, 4 May 1936, and *Leeds Mercury*, 5 May 1936.

Letters from Strangeways: *150 Years* and *NB*. The hoax letter to Ruxton: *Daily Mirror*, 15 May 1936.

The description of the crowd at Strangeways: Shutterstock photograph and Associated Newspapers photograph of 12 May 1936. Mrs Van der Elst and the planes: *The Incredible Mrs Van Der Elst* and the *Weekly Telegraph* of 16 May 1936.

No record exists of Ruxton's hanging. There may have been one at Lancashire Archives at one time, but it is no longer available. This scene is based on the description of a typical hanging provided by Thomas Pierrepoint's nephew, Albert, in his memoir *Pierrepoint: Executioner*, and *Pierrepoint: A Family of Executioners*. Background to Lewis Ball is from LostMedalAustralia.blogspot.

The *Weekly Telegraph* of 16 May 1936 provided details of the aftermath of the execution outside the gaol, while the Norman Rae scene is from *150 Years*.

Ruxton's unmarked grave: Murderpedia.

Chapter 63

Ruxton confession: *150 Years* and *The Murder Gang*; NB was used for the confession practice at inquests. Anderson death: the *Western Daily Press* of 18 November 1936, the *Yorkshire Evening Post* of 17 November 1936 and the *Dundee Courier* of 19 November 1936.

Ruxton's estate: *Hull Daily Mail*, 19 June 1936. Ruxton children: *Birmingham Daily Gazette*, 24 June 1936, *The Scotsman* of 28 May 1936, the *Western Gazette* of 3 July 1936, and the Lancashire Archives catalogue.

Epilogue

Mancini's confession to the *News of the World*: *The Butchers*.

FD was used for Glaister's celebrity after the trial, while for the story of Napoleon's hair, my interview with Bernard Drumm and *On Soul and Conscience* were used. Smith: *MM*. Bobby Edmondson: 1911 census and his family tree on Ancestry.com. Praise of Hammond's achievements is from the *News of the World* of 3 May 1936.

Waxwork: *New York Times*, 27 March 1937.

ARCHIVES AND BIBLIOGRAPHY

Primary Sources

Archives

Edinburgh University Library Special Collection: GB 237 Coll-704
University of Glasgow: Forensic Medicine Archives Project
Lancashire Archives, Preston
Lancaster City Museum
Lancaster City Council Palatine Hall (including 2 Dalton Square)
Lancaster Town Hall (former police court and police cells)
National Archives, Kew
Private and unpublished letters of Dr Leonard Mather (courtesy of Joanna Clark)

Books

Blundell, R.H., and Haswell Wilson, G., eds. *The Trial of Buck Ruxton*. London: Hodge & Co., 1937.
Glaister, John. *Final Diagnosis*. London: Hutchinson, 1964.
Glaister, John, and Couper Brash, James. *The Medico-Legal Aspects of the Ruxton Case*. London: W. Wood & Co., 1937.
Hammond, Bertie James. 'Fingerprints and the Ruxton Murders'. *Journal of Criminal Law and Criminology*, 1953.
Smith, Sydney. *Mostly Murder*, London: Harrap, 1959.
Vann, H. J., 'Rex v. Ruxton'. *The Police Journal*, 1937.

Newspapers and Journals

Aberdeen Press and Journal
Birmingham Daily Gazette
Coventry Evening Telegraph
Daily Express
Daily Herald
Daily Independent
Daily Mail
Daily Mirror
Daily Record
Dundee Courier
Gloucestershire Echo
Hampshire Telegraph and Post
Hartlepool Northern Daily Mail
The Herald
Hull Daily Mail
The Independent
Lancashire Daily Post
Lancashire Evening Post
Lancaster Guardian
Leeds Mercury
Lincolnshire Echo
Londonderry Sentinel

Morecambe Guardian
Morecambe Visitor
New York Times
News of the World
The Northern Whig
Nottingham Journal
Police Journal
Portsmouth Evening News
Reading Evening Post

The Scotsman
Sheffield Daily Independent
Staffordshire Sentinel
Sunderland Echo and Shipping Gazette
Weekly Telegraph
Western Gazette
Western Mail
Yorkshire Evening Post

Secondary Sources

Interviews
Helen Churchill, 2020
Joanna Clark, 2020
Sandy Crosthwaite, 2020
Bernard Drumm, 2020
Jo Porter, 2020

Books and Articles
Baggoley, Martin. *Strangeways: A Century of Hangings in Manchester*. Barnsley: Wharncliffe Books, 2005.
Browne, Douglas G., and Tullett, E.V. *Bernard Spilsbury: His Life and Cases*. London: White Lion Publishers, 1976.
Crowther, M. Anne, and White, Brenda. *On Soul and Conscience: The Medical Expert and Crime*. Aberdeen: Aberdeen University Press, 1988.
Cunningham, Colin, and Waterhouse, Prudence. *Alfred Waterhouse 1830–1905: Biography of a Practice*. Oxford: Oxford University Press, 1992.
D'Cruze, Shani. 'Intimacy, Professionalism and Domestic Homicide in Interwar Britain: The Case of Buck Ruxton'. *Women's History Review*, 16(5), 2007.
Erzinclioglu, Zak. 'Few Flies on Forensic Entomologists'. *New Scientist*, 30 May 1985.
Evans, C. *The Father of Forensics: The Groundbreaking Cases of Sir Bernard Spilsbury, and the Beginnings of Modern CSI*. New York: Berkley Books, 2006.
Fielding, Steve. *Hanged at Manchester*. Stroud: The History Press, 2008.
Fielding, Steve. *Pierrepoint: A Family of Executioners*. London: John Blake Publishing, 2006.
Gattey, Charles Neilson. *The Incredible Mrs Van Der Elst*. London: Leslie Frewin, 1972.
Gibson, Kenneth. *Killer Doctors*. Castle Douglas: Neil Wilson Publishing, 2012.
G.J.R., R.W. 'In Memoriam: James Couper Brash'. *Journal of Anatomy*, 92(4), 1958.
Goff, M. Lee. *A Fly for the Prosecution: How Insect Evidence Helps Solve Crimes*. Cambridge, MA: Harvard University Press, 2001.
Goodman, Jonathan. *Bloody Versicles: The Rhymes of Crime*. Kent, OH: The Kent State University Press, 1993.
Griffin, Brendon, and Munro, Keith. *Pocket Rough Guide Edinburgh*. London: Rough Guides, 2018.
Hardwick, M. *Doctors on Trial*, London: H. Jenkins, 1961.
Hartwell, Clare, and Pevsner, Nikolaus. *The Buildings of England, Lancashire: North*. New Haven, CT: Yale University Press, 2009.

Hawthorne, Nathaniel. *Our Old Home: A Series of English Sketches*. Auckland: The Floating Press.

Hayhurst, Alan. *Lancashire Murders*. Cheltenham: The History Press, 2012.

Hodge, James H., ed. *Famous Trials 3*. Harmondsworth: Penguin, 1994.

Howorth, Billy F. K. *Secret Lancaster*. Stroud: Amberley Publishing, 2019.

Hyde, H. Montgomery. *Norman Birkett: The Definitive Biography of the Legendary Barrister*. London: Hamish Hamilton, 1964.

Hyde, H. Montgomery. *Sir Patrick Hastings, His Life and Cases*. London: Heinemann, 1960.

Lane, Brian. *The Butchers: A Casebook of Macabre Crimes and Forensic Detection*. London: BCA, 1991.

McKay, Reg. *Killers, Crooks and Cons: Scotland's Crimes of the Century*. Edinburgh: Black and White Publishing, 2007.

Milton, Giles. *The Mysterious Disappearance of Agatha Christie*. HistoryExtra.com, 2014.

Morris, Jim. *The Who's Who of British Crime in the Twentieth Century*. Stroud: Amberley Publishing, 2017.

Nariman, Fali S. *Before Memory Fades: An Autobiography*. New Delhi: Hay House, 2012.

Neilson Gatty, Charles. *The Incredible Mrs Van Der Elst*. London: Leslie Frewin, 1972.

Odell, Robin. *Medical Detectives: The Lives and Cases of Britain's Forensic Five*. Stroud: The History Press, 2013.

Pierrepoint, Albert. *Executioner, Pierrepoint*. London: Harrap, 1974.

Potter, T.F. *The Deadly Dr Ruxton*. Preston: Carnegie, 1984.

Robins, Jane. *The Magnificent Spilsbury and the Case of the Brides in the Bath*. London: John Murray, 2010.

Root, Neil. *The Murder Gang: Fleet Street's Elite Group of Crime Reporters in the Golden Age of Tabloid Crime*. Stroud: The History Press, 2018.

Rowland, David. *The Brighton Trunk Murders*. Peacehaven: Finsbury Publishing, 2008.

Roy, Kenneth. *The Invisible Spirit: A Life of Post-War Scotland 1945–75*. Edinburgh: ICS Books, 2013.

St Clair, Muriel. *Doctors of Murder*, London: J. Long, 1962.

Seal, Lizzie. *Capital Punishment in Twentieth-Century Britain: Audience, Justice, Memory*. Abingdon: Routledge, 2014.

Simpson, Julian. *Migrant Architects of the NHS: South Asian Doctors and the Reinvention of British General Practice (1940s–1980s)*. Manchester: Manchester University Press, 2020.

Spark, Muriel. *The Prime of Miss Jean Brodie*. London: Macmillan, 1961.

Sparks, Jon. *Lancaster History Tour*. Stroud: Amberley Publishing, 2015.

Stevenson, Robert Louis. *The Body Snatcher*. London: Pall Mall Gazette, 1884.

Stevenson, Robert Louis. *The Strange Case of Dr Jekyll and Mr Hyde*, London: Longmans, 1886.

Wilkes, Roger, ed. *The Mammoth Book of CSI: Over 30 Real-Life Crime Scene Investigations Solved by Forensics*. London: Robinson, 2007.

Wilton, G.W. *Fingerprints: Scotland Yard: Ruxton Trial Revelations*. London: Tantallon Press, 1957.

Wynn, Douglas. *On Trial for Murder*. London: Pan, 2003.

Online Resources

Ancestry.co.uk
AndrewGough.co.uk
Blog.railwaymuseum.org.uk
Cinematreasures.org
Ewing.nl/files/police
Jardine's Book of Martyrs
Leamingtonhistory.co.uk

Localhistories.org/lancaster
Murderpedia.org
Scottish Covenanter Memorials
    Association
SemanticScholar.org
Workhouses.org.uk/lancaster

Television Documentaries

ITV: *Nightwatch Mysteries: Buck Ruxton*, 2008.

Photo Credits

1. University of Glasgow Archives & Special Collections, Department of Forensic Medicine & Science collection, GB248 GUAFM_2A_25_35_2of2.
2. University of Glasgow Archives & Special Collections, Department of Forensic Medicine & Science collection, GB248 GUAFM_2A_25_43i.
3. University of Glasgow Archives & Special Collections, Department of Forensic Medicine & Science collection, GB248 GUAFM_2A_25_148.
4. Copyright holder unknown. Public domain.
5. University of Glasgow Archives & Special Collections, Department of Forensic Medicine & Science collection, GB248 GUAFM_2A_25_266.
6. Author's photograph.
7. Author's photograph.
8. University of Glasgow Archives & Special Collections, Department of Forensic Medicine & Science collection, GB248 GUAFM_2A_25_109.
9. Courtesy of Marilyn Wilson.
10. Courtesy of JPI Media.
11. Shutterstock.
12. University of Glasgow Archives & Special Collections, Department of Forensic Medicine & Science collection, GB248 GUAFM_2A_25_267.
13. University of Glasgow Archives & Special Collections, Department of Forensic Medicine & Science collection, GB248 GUAFM_2A_25_141.
14. University of Glasgow Archives & Special Collections, Department of Forensic Medicine & Science collection, GB248 GUAFM_2A_25_81.
15. University of Glasgow Archives & Special Collections, Department of Forensic Medicine & Science collection, GB248 GUAFM_2A_25_249.
16. University of Glasgow Archives & Special Collections, Department of Forensic Medicine & Science collection, GB248 GUAFM_2A_25_293.
17. University of Glasgow Archives & Special Collections, Department of Forensic Medicine & Science collection, GB248 GUAFM_2A_25_27a.
18. Shutterstock.
19. University of Glasgow Archives & Special Collections, Department of Forensic Medicine & Science collection, GB248 GUAFM_2A_25_297_dr_ruxtons_execution.
20. Author's photograph.

INDEX

Note: illustrations are indicated by *italicised* page references.

The History Press
The destination for history
www.thehistorypress.co.uk